POPE PIUS X
3 2528 01271 0192
Y0-EFZ-179

EUROPEAN DRAMATISTS

EUROPEAN DRAMATISTS

3/6
02

BY

ARCHIBALD HENDERSON, PH.D., D.C.L., LL.D.

Of the University of North Carolina

AUTHOR OF

"GEORGE BERNARD SHAW: HIS LIFE AND WORKS,"
"THE CHANGING DRAMA," "MARK TWAIN,"
"INTERPRETERS OF LIFE," ETC.

D. APPLETON & CO.

NEW YORK: LONDON: MCMXXVI

Copyright, 1913, 1926, by
D. APPLETON & CO.

Printed in the United States of America

Copyright by E. O. Hoppé

BERNARD SHAW AND HIS
BIOGRAPHER, ARCHIBALD HENDERSON

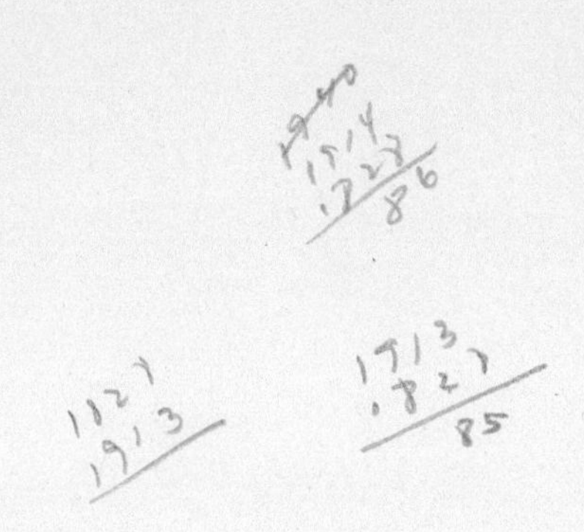

TO

V. E. A.

MIRACLE AND DREAM

PREFATORY NOTE

The last essay in the present volume has not hitherto appeared in print. The essay on Schnitzler, which in the last edition of this book dealt only with his one-act plays, is extended to include his entire dramatic work. The remaining essays, appearing in former editions of this book, have in all possible cases been brought to date. The essay on Granville Barker appeared originally in the *Forum* (New York) and the *Mercure de France* (Paris). For permission to reproduce fragments of essays formerly published I am indebted to the editors of the *Deutsche Revue* (Stuttgart and Berlin), *Mercure de France* (Paris), *La Société Nouvelle* (Ghent and Paris), *Finsk Tidskrift* (Helsingfors), *Illustreret Tidende* (Stockholm), *Atlantic Monthly* (Boston), *North American Review* (New York), *Bookman* (New York), *Sewanee Review* (Sewanee and New York).

ARCHIBALD HENDERSON.

Fordell.
Chapel Hill, N. C.

CONTENTS

ILLUSTRATIONS

AUGUST STRINDBERG

" May we then secure a theater where we may be horrified over the horrible, laugh over the laughable, play with the playful; where we can see everything and not be offended, when we see what lies concealed behind theological and esthetic veils, even if the old conventional laws must be broken; may we secure a free theater, where we shall have freedom for all things save to have no talent and to be a hypocrite or a fool."

— August Strindberg: *The One-Act Play.*

AUGUST STRINDBERG

I

The supreme goal of the great literature of our era has been and remains the expression, in some form of final artistic denotement, of the struggle of the ego at self-realization. This recurrent note in the eternal symphony of life rings out again and again in the authentic, harmonic intuitions of the supermen of contemporary thought, philosophy and art. This dionysian searching after the divine in the human, this headlong struggle for the exaltation of the individual soul to the heights of superhuman conquest and super-moral ethics, is the sign-manual of the dæmonic dissonance and spiritual chaos of to-day. That free and daring individualist, philosophic progenitor of Nietzsche and contemporary anarchism, Max Stirner, repudiated the claims of the species in behalf of the ideal of Man, the individual. The realization of man as the generally human was abandoned for the sake of the realization of man as the anarchic unit of life. "I am my own species, without law, without model"— such is the clamant individualism of Stirner.

From Stirner and his ultimate philosophy of the

autonomous will, stem the clamant and revolutionary forms of contemporary egoism, individualism and spiritual anarchism. With Nietzsche entered into modern consciousness the sense of a superhuman ideal for man, springing phoenix-like from the ashes of universal illusionism, the relativity of the concepts of good and evil, the fundamental amoralism of Nature. In Halvard Solness, Ibsen presents the disquieting figure of the superman in embryo, vainly seeking that freedom which Nietzsche defined as the will to be responsible for one's self. The happiest of the optimists, Maeterlinck, who suavely wrests consolation from the very thought of dissolution, has succumbed to the pressure of the new ideal in the words: "There is more active charity in the egoism of a strenuous, far-seeing soul than in all the devotion of a soul that is helpless and blind." Bernard Shaw, the Socialist, with his inherent sense of the inter-dependence of all the units of society, nevertheless is driven to the ideal of the human temperament, guided by passion and operating instinctively. From the Life Force of Shaw, the *élan vital* of Bergson, emerges the identical concept of creative evolution — the individual soul, continually creating beyond himself, "rising above himself to himself," in the struggle to attain the supreme, ineluctable purposes of Life.

From the study of the work of August Strindberg, the spiritual autobiography of the greatest subjectivist of modern times, there emerges the inevitable conviction that here is, in a spiritual sense, a tentative incarnation of the superhuman ideals of contemporary thought and sensibility. Above all the dissonances of that inharmonious and jangled existence sounds the clear strain of persistently lofty idealism. This figure of strenuous mental vitality, of transcendent spiritual energy, thrilled with the towering ambition of the individual will, tumultuous, passionate, unstable. And yet the alluring contours of his art-work are chiseled with the cold, merciless steel of the sculptor-analyst. In conjunction with this towering ambition is discernible the supersensitiveness of the shy, wild, primitive creature, cowering beneath "all the weary weight of this unintelligible world." In inexplicable union are found the arrogant individualist, shyly naïve even to very charlatanry, and the intuitive subjectivist, ruthlessly exposing to view the tragedies of humanity and the antinomies of his own soul. Strindberg is the congenital dualist of our epoch — a dualist in every faintest manifestation of his nature. In him the spirit eternally warred against the flesh, the flesh against the spirit. The incarnation of that pure energy, dionysian in origin, which Blake described as eternal delight, Strindberg shrinkingly sought refuge from the storms of life in the haven of mysticism and occultism. As artist, the paradox of his dualism is no less astounding; for the integrity of his intellect, in achieving the realism of fact, is equalled only by the intuitive power of his artistry, in sensing the illusory and the romantic. His whole life was a passionately defiant assertion of the individual will; and yet he eternally bore the burden of the disillusioned idealist, sardonically delineating the dreadful, inescapable obligations of contemporary civilization. With high, tragic mien he walked the painful path to the scene of his own self-crucifixion, searching for God if haply he might find Him; and yet this relentless searcher for the good had his gaze eternally fixed upon evil and the source of evil. Like another Dante, he haunted the shades of a modern Inferno; but, unlike Dante, in searching for God he found the devil. In his sympathetic contemplation of the tragedy of human destiny, is felt the strange, sweet pathos of one who is somehow strong and good; yet evil, the knowledge of evil, so obsessed his consciousness that he stands forth today as that artist of modern times whose power of painting the evil genius of humanity, of turning up the seamy side of the garment of life for our horrified yet fascinated contemplation, is unique and incomparable. In his lifetime, he sought to annex the entire domain of the human spirit; and yet this search for cosmopolitan culture, for the highest, deepest reaches of the artistic consciousness, left him as it found him, a plebeian of the soul. It is scarcely an exaggeration to affirm that Strindberg is the diarist, one had almost said, the journalist of personal consciousness. A great artist with all the allure of genius — tainted with the dross of charlatanry and arrogance. Like another Knute, he bade the waves of life to recede; but for all his categorical imperative, life in the event still obdurately refused to do his imperious bidding. He was like a brilliant comet out of the North, flaming across the contemporary consciousness with radiant coruscations, leaving behind, in its extinguishment, a deeper, more chaotic gloom.

II

This country has for long paid the penalty for the popular, insistent demand that, in analyzing the great contemporary writers who have given rise to the intellectual and spiritual ferment of modern Europe, our native critics must carefully skirt the deeper sources and causes of the peculiar manifestations, *indicia,* hallucinations, *stigmata,* of genius. Accompanying this pressure of public opinion is the equally insistent convention that European figures must be presented to us solely as leaders in tendency, specialists in morbidity, heralds and promulgators of aberrant and distorted theories of conduct and philosophies of life. In consequence, the meaning and significance of so important a spiritual manifestation as was August Strindberg is totally evaded and missed, in particular by those who seek to pan-der to popular standards by emasculating him of the barbaric, virile qualities which constitute his most persistent temperamental fascination. In the dry, hard silhouette, projected for American inspection, there has been no adequate perspective, no subtle delineation, no rendition of the composite and multiple shades of his nature, character, and spiritual physiognomy. From time to time one has heard faint rumors of a Swedish madman who was married thrice in proof of his hatred of women; a gruesome naturalist who was so obsessed with the mania of sex aversion that he achieved European notoriety by depicting all women as beasts of prey; an hallucinated mystic who found his intellectual level in the *fumisteries* of Sar Péladan; an egoist who was so self-assertive, so dogmatic in his assertions, so ineffably vain that he devoted his life to heaping scorn and ridicule upon all the rest of the world, pouring out upon them the vials of his vulgar wrath and contempt. At last, the moment is arriving when the first promise of adequate interpretation and appreciation of Strindberg is coming to fulfil itself. Plays revealing various sides of his multiplex genius, the burning intensity, the marvellous realism, sublimated by the inspiration of a hidden mystic feeling, the ruthless naïveté irradiated with powerfully vibrant temperament, are now accessible to American readers, through the painstaking labor of devoted translators.[1] Less rarely now are given, under semi-professional or even experimental, popular conditions, productions of the plays least foreign to the taste presumed to be characteristically American, notably *The Father, Miss Julia, The Stronger,* and *Pariah.* The promise of translations of the most significant and self-revelatory of the novels and short stories, now being realized, may go far towards giving form and color to the figure of Strindberg, and enabling us to arrest and fix the alternations of light and shade, the fluctuations and play of motives, the spiritual chiaroscuro of his intimately confessed, tragic, morbid life. It may then dawn upon the consciousness of the English-speaking world that this red specter, Strindberg, the bogy of feminist hysteria, was a soul "wind-beaten, but as-

[1] The pioneering work of Mr. Edwin Björkman, the Swedish-American critic, both as interpreter and translator, is deserving of high praise. He has achieved terse, clear-cut translations, at times deficient in the flexibility of conversational English, at times too colloquial in tone. As an interpreter, he is lucid and sympathetic; yet toward the grave shortcomings of his fellow countryman, Strindberg, whom he seems to regard as an Olympian "tendency" phenomenon, he is too insistently apologetic. A debt of gratitude we owe to Mrs. Velma Swanston Howard for her important service in accentuating the bright, cheerful side of Strindberg in the selection for translation of *Lucky Pehr, Easter* and some of the more charming sketches; her translations are singularly free and graceful. There are other translators of Strindberg's plays; their contributions, by no means negligible, are in the main quite lacking in literary distinction.

cending"; a creative thinker essentially strong in character if not always delicate in tone; an investigator with a scientific equipment of no mean order; a seeker, a delver in the mysteries of both matter and soul; critic, historian, philosophic experimentalist, a titan in imagination. This titanic figure, embodying a life of truly protean productivity, roughly expressed in the fifty odd volumes of his works now publishing, has entered into the world-consciousness of modern Europe, bequeathing to this and subsequent generations the herculean task of elucidating countless unsolved problems, hazards, dubieties, hypotheses, riddles, and enigmas.

III

The life of August Strindberg is so predominantly chaotic, the lines of his career run in such amazing zig-zag, his personality is so rich, his temperament so volcanic, that it seems to defy analysis, or even adequate comprehension. The dualism of his nature is so persistently assertive that it is hazardous to attribute to Strindberg some trait or quality, solely upon the evidence of any single work of his, however authentic or artistically final. It is only after the whole amazing drama of his variegated life and disparate achievements lies before us in its entirety that we are enabled to gather up the far-flung and scattered threads, to weave them into some sort of credible pattern which may serve as the design of his life. For his was a life compact of struggle and resignation, conflict and reconciliation. Only through the most precise, sympathetic and unprejudiced contemplation can we chart the shifting vital currents of his psychic evolution by the moored buoys of his written works.

The will of those who are no more, Anatole France has said, is imposed upon those who still are. It is the dead who live. They are to be found in the habits, in the lives of us all. Our destiny sleeps with us in our cradles. We are not straining credulity in attributing Strindberg's profound ethical and moral sense to that ancestor of his who preached to the peasants of Strinne, whence was formed the family name; nor in finding cause for his barbaric, headlong martial spirit in that ancestor who was a captain, descendant of one of that splendid band of victorious fighters who served under Gustavus Adolphus, and received knighthood at his hands.[1] The mingled strains of his ancestry warrant the assertion that he was the incarnation of the Pan-Germanic spirit. In the portrait of his grandfather, Zacharias Strindberg (1758-1829), a dramatist of considerable talent, we may trace the lines of virile intellectuality and artistic sensibility. It is however to his mother, a creature of sentimentality, tender and passionate, that he owes more immediately the vibrant sensitivity and innate subjectivism

[1] "Die Familie Strindberg": *Das Neue Magazine;* 75, 16.

of his nature. For her he felt the tenderest attachment, which reveals itself in his later confession; but the blight of his origin, he being born two months after the marriage of his mother, cast a lasting gloom over his soul.[1]

Oskar Strindberg, a steamship agent, had entered into a free union with Eleonora Ulrike Norling, a poor girl of the servant class by whom he had three children before August was born. Early in life, August came to feel the most devitalizing and depressing influences which can come into the life of a child. The family were in very straitened circumstances, and the father flung himself unstintedly into the struggle to raise his family to the position which his own forbears had held in life; and in consequence the children were neglected by the father — when they were not beaten. The sense of shame in his parentage, it is scarcely to be doubted, bred in August a shyness, a supersensitiveness, already inherent in his nature. The conditions of the family life were little elevated above the squalid. As Strindberg put it, there was "a surplusage of population, baptisms and funerals. There were not two christenings without a funeral in between." His first gloomy impressions of existence were received in such an atmosphere of joylessness and unsanitary overcrowding — eleven persons in three rooms.

Under happier surroundings with real parental

[1] August Strindberg was born in Stockholm, January 22, 1849.

oversight — impossible in such conditions — August might have blossomed out and expanded normally. But he was repressed, left undeveloped, rendered morbid and shy by the treatment he received.

"My rearing consisted in cuffings, scoldings and being made to obey. The child had no rights; only duties. Everyone's wishes but his own were heeded: his were stifled. He could touch nothing without being at fault, stand nowhere without being in the way, utter no word without making himself a nuisance. His highest duty, his highest virtue, was — to sit on a chair and keep still."

It was no wonder that Strindberg came to regard the family envisaged in his youthful consciousness as the home of all the social faults. To this dark experience of home as "the hell of all children" we may doubtless attribute the repellent qualities of the developed individual — intractability, rebelliousness, violence and habitual reaction against the influence or domination of others. This was a wonderfully precocious child who brooded again and again, in later life, over the bitter humiliation of his childhood in having his word doubted and then being goaded into making a false confession of his guilt. At the age of eight he even contemplated suicide, driven to the thought by his feeling of love for a young girl he was afraid to address; and the thought and intent of suicide reverted to him at intervals throughout his life.

There is nothing new in the spectacle of incipient genius repressed and retarded in an unsympathetic and harsh environment. It was fortunate in a sense that this timid child, with nerves stretched almost to the breaking point, felt the violent normal symptoms of reaction; for otherwise such discipline might well have resulted in arrested ethical development. The crassly pietestic tendencies of his mother, crossed with excessive sentimentality, seems in some measure to explain the self-torturing religious tendencies of the later Strindberg. If religion on the one hand gave him some consolation for the harshness of his conditions, on the other his rebellion against such a dicipline awoke in him the note of social revolt — revolt against that type of education railed at by Huxley, the senseless drilling and regimenting of individuals into mere dummies, mechanically playing their part in a mechanistic civilization. The man who could declare of his youth that " life, a terrible depressing burden weighed down upon me every day "— that man was but expressing a state of mind which was so deeply impressed upon his nature that he carried it with him his life long. As a child, as a youth, as an old man — it was always the same: he never ceased to " go about with a guilty conscience.

In his studies of Nature — flower and tree, animal and stone — he found keen intellectual satisfaction. Such consolation was very necessary for one who was left to mourn his mother at the age of thirteen; and when, nearly a year later, his father married the former housekeeper, his cup was full, since his efforts to establish sympathetic relations with her went all for naught. Again, more hopelessly than before, the spontaneous wells of instinctive love and longing were dammed back; and he was left to brood solitary over his loneliness. His early experiences at school were unfortunate; and even before he left school the lines of character had already set their mark upon his impressionable nature. When in May, 1867, he took his examination preparatory to matriculation at the University of Upsala, he had only a tiny sum which he himself had earned by tutoring; his father curtly packed him off with a "pocketful of cigars and the injunction to look out for himself."

Strindberg afterwards used to maintain that the one solid residuum of his first university course was a smart tailored coat, which bespoke cultured social experience. As a tutor in the family of a wealthy Jewish physician, he came to take interest in and even to study medicine; but the society with which he mingled there — artists, singers, people of social distinction — soon turned his thoughts in another direction, the direction of the stage. The glamour of the footlights obsessed him; and he vigorously devoted his energies to the one purpose of becoming an actor. He made his debut at the

Dramatiska Theatre in 1869 in Björnson's *Mary Stuart,* playing the part of a lord who has but one line to speak. After two months, desperation seizes him; he demands and receives a hearing. The rehearsal is disastrous, and Strindberg is sternly commended to the care of a teacher in expression — a result which drove him to attempted suicide. As chance would have it, the attempt did not prove fatal. He was in despair over his failure as an actor, for he felt the irresistible urge towards the artistic life without the ability to gratify it. Again and again he seemed to feel the stirring of the creative impulse; but — there was no creation, the muse was mute. But one day, to his vast astonishment, as he was lying upon the sofa, his stereoscopic fancy began to function; the scenes played themselves out upon the stage of his brain; and by a spurt of creative productivity, he wrote out in two hours the scenario for two acts of a comedy. Four days more — and we see the completion of Strindberg's first creative effort. It is the beginning of his life, if not of his career. Although not produced, it won commendation — and Strindberg knew at last that he had " saved his soul alive."

Now he yields to the hectic spell of his new-found talent; and within two months he has finished two comedies, and a tragedy in verse, *Hermione,* showing a marked advance in talent,— a play which was afterwards produced. His great promise as a dramatist led him to return to the University, in the effort to secure the degree deemed so desirable for anyone purposing to become a man of letters. During this year (1870) he wrote a one-act play, *In Rome,* based upon an incident in the life of Thorwaldsen, which was anonymously produced in August at the Dramatiska Theatre, Stockholm. His next play, written under the influence of Björnson, entitled *The Outlaw,* upon its production won him the favor of King Carl XV, who generously granted him a stipend of eight hundred riksdaler a year from his private purse.

The second period of university study, though it did not lead to his securing the coveted degree, is a period of distinct acquisition. In the atmosphere of knowledge, Strindberg, the genius in embryo, comes to some definite realizations of the obligations of scholarship, artistic creation and culture. There dawns upon him the realization of his epoch, of the streams of consciousness in art. He prefigured himself in imagination as the transitional link between two epochs of art. The influences of his studies and wide reading were ineffaceable and so determinative of the course of his future development. The scientific precision of Darwin tempered the strain of sentiment and naïve feeling due to his Swedish origin; the high ethical postulates of Kirkegaard, whose *Either-Or* affected him powerfully, stirred in him the larger humanistic concern so predominant in certain of his greatest works, and effectively gave them the note of the art work of the future — art for life's sake. The rationalistic clarity of Henry Thomas Buckle, his insistence upon the superior claims of the intelligence, his Nietzschean faith in the relativity of truth, his Marxian doctrine of the materialistic conception of history, as set forth in his *History of Civilization in England* — all these conceptions came to abide with Strindberg and are refracted, prismatically, from the mirror of his works. Most profound of all these influences was Eduard Von Hartmann's *Philosophy of the Unconscious,* with its doctrine of constitutional pessimism, the seeing in life an immitigable complex of woes, which must be borne even though we fail to fathom the meaning of such a freak of fate. In a letter to Tolstoi, Bernard Shaw once hazarded the irreverent suggestion that the universe might be " only one of God's jokes." It was some such mad conception as this which obsessed Strindberg during his life, but he always seemed to feel that God, like the Englishman, jested sadly. Never did so young a man show himself so pervasively impressionable to the influences of his studies and his reading. At the same time, it must be sharply stressed that Strindberg absorbed and made these ideas thus deeply imbibed an integral part of his own conception and interpretation of life. If he became ethical in tone, the mystic remained always the realist, the artist in temperament. If he became a pessimist, his was a pessimism not of disillusionment but of contemplation. If he became a rationalist, his was the rationalism of passion and of sentiment. If he can be called a philosophic spirit at all, it is only in the very special sense that he remained always a persistent and relentless seeker after truth, the ultimate truth, recking not of consequences either to himself or to others.

IV

The attempt to base an interpretation of Strindberg's character upon the unique basis of Strindberg's dramas of contemporary life proceeds from a basic failure to comprehend the true meaning of his life. These plays, in many instances, reveal either transitional phases of his own temperamental and cultural evolution, or else embody his efforts to arrive at some philosophical generalization upon the problems of human existence and human destiny. Strindberg is the arch-subjectivist of our era. In his novels and his short stories, and in particular the works confessedly autobiographical, shall we rather discover the inner workings of this tortured soul, seeking some ultimate forms of self-realization through self-expression and intimate confession. For Strindberg declaimed fiercely against the conventional approbation of the static character, the personality forever fixed and unalterable, rotating endlessly within the circle of his own limitation. Progress with Strindberg was synonymous with flux — with perpetual alteration and transition from one phase of psychical experience to another. To Strindberg, the soul of man was rich and wonderful in proportion to its potentiality for change, for transition, for elemental evolutionary cataclysms. The entire life of this strenuous, dynamic creature is marked by just such a series of volcanic cataclysms.

Little heed has been paid to Strindberg's early dreams for social betterment, as embodied in his *Swiss Tales*. They form a cardinally suggestive link in the chain of his spiritual evolution; for after this one flight into the blue of social idealism, Strindberg reverts to the passionate individualism which signalizes his greatest work throughout his career. Yet, it is something added to our conception of Strindberg, this knowledge that Strindberg fiercely protested against the human servitude imposed by the material conditions of modern life. Civilization has been paid for too dearly — thus early Strindberg speaks in resonant tones. As a social reformer, Strindberg showed himself to be pure communist. Abolish private ownership, and require of every man all that in reason and in conscience he can bring himself to contribute. The European dynasties must go, in the interest of the future of the average man; militancy must yield to the visionary ideal of world-peace. This strange anomaly of the Berserker-like Strindberg pre-visaging the tranquil communist state of the far future has a certain piquant charm — the charm of naïve inconsistency. The optimistic spirit of the utopist expires in the bosom of the temperamental pessimist. The later Strindberg sinks to the mean level of crass actuality and of individual strife, bafflement and trial.

There is no other striking or revolutionary event in the period from 1872 to 1877 which furnishes indicative prophecy of the later Strindberg. Perhaps some suggestions of later tendencies and dispositions are found here and there. Strindberg is essentially a pathological phenomenon; as subjectivist, his instinct for self-revelation arises from the felt need to express his own development as it is affected by the personalities of others, or by new social and religious influences. Those are prophetic words which he speaks at the farewell banquet on leaving the University, words foreshadowing the philosophy of acquisitiveness associated with Strindberg: "A personality does not develop from itself, but out of each soul it comes in contact with it sucks a drop, just as the bee gathers its honey from a million flowers, giving it forth eventually as its own."

It is customary to speak of *Master Olof*, written in 1872, as Strindberg's first great drama; but its distinction was and is, not international, but local. It marked an epochal development in the literature of Sweden, as we can easily recognize to-day; but at the time, criticism was scathingly derogatory. Once more, the creative impulse in Strindberg seemed to be stifled, throttled for a time by the powerful hand of hostile criticism. After failures one after another to win success in journalistic hack-writing, Strindberg finally secured a post as assistant at the Royal Library. This position, of modest but assured income, enabled him to devote his leisure hours to research — notably among Chinese parchments as yet uncatalogued. The restless energy of the man is betrayed in his study of the Chinese language, and the monographs which he wrote dealing with the relations between China and Sweden in the eighteenth century — which won him recognition from scientific bodies, such as the French Institute and the Russian Geographical Society.

Now supervenes one of those crucial events which affects a revolution in the life of a man, so deeply personal in his art and feeling as was Strindberg. This was the acquaintanceship formed by Strindberg with the wife of Baron Wrangel. The attachment instantaneously formed became more intimate; and finally the divorce of the Baroness enabled Strindberg to exchange the role of lover for that of husband, the marriage taking place December 30, 1877, when Strindberg was twenty-eight years old. When, in the following year, *Master Olof* was at last accepted for publication, Strindberg gave free vent to his suppressed resentment over the long delayed recognition of his genius, in the tremendous satire *The Red Room*. This was a "work of conflict," a satirical protest against cultural conditions in the Sweden of that day. Surcharged with the sardonic spirit of the scorner, it is a great pang of reaction against a world driven by the force of "vital lies." Its ruthless exposure of contemporary social strata vitiates it as a work of art. Yet we are left with the startled consciousness that here is a great personality, shooting up out of the sea of mediocrity, and aiming terrible blows at modern degeneracy in character, motive, and impulse. Its trenchant motto, after Voltaire, in view of Strindberg's threatened neglect, was astutely chosen: *Rien n'est si désagreable que s'être pendu obscurément.*

The first years of Strindberg's married life were undoubtedly happy — certainly in the passional sense, if not in the restful consciousness of hallowed union. There is a naïve admission of the character of the union in his description of himself as being in a "happy erotic state." If the cloud on the domestic horizon was no bigger than a man's hand, there were fierce storms of controversy about his head which finally decided him to leave Sweden in 1883. He lived for a time in France, later removing to Switzerland, where he wrote the two remarkable collections of stories published under the title of *Marriage*.

At this period, Strindberg was moved to conscious revolt against the extravagant idealization of woman which was sweeping over Europe in the wake of Ibsen's *A Doll's House.* His own marital relations — for Strindberg was always essentially *personnel* — were likewise a stimulant cause for his choice of subject. As he looked about him, he saw women everywhere living parasitical lives — taking no real part in the work of civilization. Under normal conditions, the social growth of woman was dependent upon their acquisition of the suffrage — this he frankly realized and advocated. His real attack was directed against the type of women lauded by those who were everywhere advancing the " equality madness "— women who in their unreasoning struggle for liberty were forsaking the privileges and the obligations of their sex. Strindberg made his first intimate studies of women and marriage, inspired by no hatred for the sex, but urged by a sort of innate reverence for woman as the mother of the race, the creative and regenerative force of civilization. He saw a generation making a religion of the woman-cult; and his own words adequately describe his point of view: " God was the remotest source; when He failed they grasped at the next, the Mother. But then they should at least choose the real mother, the real woman, before whom, no matter how strong his spirit, man will always bow when she appears with her life-giving attributes. But the younger generation had pronounced contempt for the mother, and in her place had set up the loathsome, degenerate Amazon — the blue-stocking!" In his almost old-fashioned veneration for woman as the creative force of life, he totally lost sight of the cruel inequality imposed upon woman by a man-made civilization. That is a secret shape of reaction which pretends to see in woman, under contemporary conditions, a free agent, the co-equal of man in the struggle for existence. Woman to-day is not only the creature which man, through his innate greed, vanity and selfishness persisted in for all the centuries, has made of her: she is, in no small measure, the creature which she has allowed herself to be made into by man. Woman, in Meredithian phrase, is the last creature that will be civilized by man — since he will fight bitterly with all his weapons against that "civilization."

The criminal proceedings started against the publisher of this book, actually for its excessive frankness in dealing with sexual relations, ostensibly for sacrilegious treatment of the established religion, eventuated in a verdict of "not guilty," after the case had been strenuously fought by Strindberg himself. The result was to give Strindberg a pre-eminent position in Sweden as a man of letters. Yet his satisfaction over the result of the case was sadly marred by the consciousness that his purpose in writing *Marriage,* essentially a worthy one, had been so grossly misunderstood.

The condemnation of Strindberg as a rank pessimist and thorough-paced misogynist aroused in him a spirit of violent, volcanic opposition. In the first volume of *Marriage,* he had left many things unsaid which he felt needed to be said about the relation of the sexes. Moreover, he felt a growing sense of disillusionment in his own marital venture. These two motives, as well as his revolt against the feminist movement in Scandinavia set in motion by Ibsen and Björnson, influenced him to publish a second volume of stories, also entitled *Marriage,* which appears at first sight to be nothing short of virulent in its animus against woman. It is with the publication of this book in 1886, that Strindberg began to be obsessed with the monomania of animadversion against the female sex. The emancipation he posits for woman is only a partial one — since he regards man and woman as fundamentally disparate. It is not equality with man which woman needs — social and economic equality; but a limited freedom to realize herself within a circle defined by the obligation of motherhood. He holds it rank heresy to advocate for woman complete equality with man, with its inevitable corollaries of the right to hold property and the right to work at any trade for which she fits herself by training. Strindberg is the powerful leader of a whole world of reactionary conservatives, who vehemently maintain that woman should " devote her entire interest to the family which man works to maintain."

This second volume of stories, entitled *Marriage*, was the intermediary between those two remarkable characters, so like in many respects, yet in the course of their development so remote — each touched with the blight of dementia — Strindberg and Nietzsche. In a letter to Peter Gast, Nietzsche remarked: " Strindberg has written to me, and for the first time I sense an answering note of universality." It was at this period that Strindberg conceived the idea of composing a chain of autobiographical confessions which might serve as the laying bare of a modern soul. His assertion that great art must be fundamentally autobiographical — a remarkable assertion which finds support in the confessions of Ibsen and the latest researches in regard to Shakspere — lay at the back of his conception of such a series of novels. *The Bondwoman's Son* is an unforgettable picture of the evolution of personal consciousness in an individual — Strindberg — through a minutely detailed succession of sordid and squalid happenings. If it is an " evangel of the lower classes," certainly it portrays in all their dark intimacy the devitalizing and repressive influences emanating from the class in which he was born — the atmospheric and actual productive causes of certain dominant traits and qualities in his own nature. The one clear note sounding above the discordant clash of harsh memories is the proclamation by Strindberg of conscious superiority to the conditions out of which he rose. Strindberg's realization, with certain of the leading spirits of the age, of the possibilities of a higher type of being, of the superman, found its origin less in Nietzsche than in Strindberg's own clear consciousness of differentiation in himself — the great man shooting up above the mean level, the illegitimate genius born of the bondwoman.

There was much attraction for Strindberg, with his strenuous individualism, in the conception of the far-sighted, self-contained, tolerant type, free with the freedom which Nietzsche has defined as the will to be responsible for oneself. In his own career we seem at times to discern his effort to rise above the plane of slave-morality and the herd-man, driven by primitive impulses and ruled by chaotic passions. Strindberg's ablest artistic formulation of the philosophy of the superman is his novel *At the Edge of the Sea,* published in 1890, which Hans Land has pronounced to be the only work of art, in the domain of Nietzschean morals, yet written which is destined to endure. True to his instincts, Strindberg has expressed in the person of Borg his own most intense convictions and ideals. Animated with an exalted sense of his own superiority, Borg

AUGUSTE STRINDBERG

revels in lording it over the world of beings made of commoner clay. In Nietzsche's conception of the Superman, there is something at once lyrical and fantastic — the product of decadent romanticism. Strindberg's incarnation in Borg is more valid and comprehensible as a human figure — reminding us of the Superman shadowed by Bernard Shaw, not "beyond man," but Superman in the making, the "moral aristocrat" in transition. Strindberg leaves us oppressed with a grim sense of the desperate nature of this new quest — to rise superior, under present conditions, to the sheer materialism of the "damned compact majority." Borg is not the laughing philosopher, but the presumptuous egoist — a magnificent, tragic moral "high-brow," toppled over by the arrant madness of his own individualism. Strindberg, the sincere artist, here proves his weakness as a social philosopher; his system falls to pieces of its own unbalanced weight. Here, as elsewhere, Strindberg reveals himself the disillusioned idealist, acknowledging the tragedy of social necessity, and unshrinkingly delineating the hideous, yet inevitable, penalties of contemporary civilization. Antipodal to the reflective and anemic mollycoddle, Strindberg glorifies the red corpuscle in art, and dares take the consequence of inconsequence.

The next great spirtual crisis through which Strindberg passed is revealed in that marvellous, yet glaringly personal, revelation, *A Fool's Confession* (1888). As his animus against the female sex, fortified by the attacks upon him by the advocates of the woman's rights movement in Scandinavia, became settled into an *idée fixe,* the relations between him and his wife became strained to the breaking point. He fretted against the matrimonial bond, seeking again and again to break away. The struggle was a titanic one — for deep seated within him, preserved intact from childhood, was his love for his mother which gave rise to his veneration for the conception of motherhood. The indestructible link which binds man to woman — the children — held him constant for a time; but at last the breaking point was reached. The dreadfully astute analysis of the torturing conflicts in that harassed household is the content of *A Fool's Confession.*

The unblushing frankness of this confession can only shock, with its basic indiscretion, the American reader, nurtured upon ideals of chivalry towards woman and shielded by Anglo-Saxon convention from the indiscretions of artistic autobiography. Even Strindberg himself felt the need of disclaiming responsibility for what he described as a "terrible book"; for he avers, correctly it is believed, that it was published in Swedish without his consent, and even without his knowledge. Nevertheless, it is the most significant exemplification which Strindberg has left of his esthetic doctrine that art is a vast arena for experimentation with self. Indeed, it may fairly be said that he used all experiences as esthetic material for self-justification. It was the fatal weakness of his temperament, as well as of his esthetic creed, to generalize from personal data, to identify the individual with the universe. It is the fundamental weakness of all thesis-literature: to put the part for the whole. Like a camera held too close to the object, Strindberg throws into ghastly disproportion that which is nearest to him. No artist of modern times has been so pre-eminently successful in the shattering of perspective. This confession of a fool is not misnamed — its mood is splenetic, atrabiliar, repulsive. Even the wonderful psychological skill in recreating experiences, the diabolic accuracy of the portrayal, cannot atone for its lack of refinement, its essential coarseness. If there can be any justification for this exposure of the life of a woman, his wife for thirteen years, the mother of his children, it is neither moral nor social. It is an esthetic plea for realistic freedom in art. But even an artist's sincere effort to depict the struggles of a highly intellectual person to emancipate himself from the obsession of sex does not excuse the grossest violation of the sanctities of personality.

The divorce from his wife in 1892 — a step undertaken only after many struggles and great stress of feeling, was momentous in a permanent sense. It is the preliminary to the supreme crisis in Strindberg's life. Strindberg was thrice married — the second time, to Frida Uhl, a young Austrian writer, in 1893, with whom he lived only a few years; and the third time to Harriet Bosse, the Norwegian actress, in 1901, from whom he was divorced three years later. These two unions appear to have been episodes in Strindberg's life — stages in the course of his spiritual development. For we must realize this truth about Strindberg — that life with him was a form of excuse for art. An investigator, a research-worker in the laboratory of the soul, he was willing to pay the price of the intensest emotional experiences for the sake of their value as art-stuff.

Inescapable is the conviction that in Strindberg is presented the dour tragedy of one surrendered to self-torture in behalf of art. His life continually lay shattered in pieces about him because of his passionate convictions. Strindberg makes many an arresting gesture of singularly alluring grace in his marvellous writings — but how dearly bought, how bitterly expiated these rapt ecstasies, these alluring gestures of fitful passion and melancholic despair! If he was ever witty, we feel that Strindberg — to employ a phrase of Benedetto Croce — was but laughingly snatching a nail from a gaping coffin.

The stress and dissonance of Strindberg's second marriage and subsequent divorce was the ultimate, the immediate signal for the crisis of the "great climacteric" in his life. If we glance for a moment, also, at the contemporary spirit with which Strindberg was vitalized, we shall attain to an intuitive comprehension of the subsequent confusion, groping and ultimate reconciliation of his spirit. From childhood, feeling reaction against his environment, conscious of his vast superiority to those about him, he feverishly struggled to elevate himself to the heights. Along with this titanic ambition went the hectic dream of idealism — the fanatical search for happiness. Guided by titanic ambition, he cast off the shackles of provinciality for the freedom of cosmopolitanism — seeking to realize himself as a great modern master, now in Switzerland, now in Germany, now in France. When Germany finally hailed him as one of the pre-eminent figures of the era, it was a Germany chaotically revolutionary in art, in a state of confused transition between headlong repudiation of the old, uncertain grasping after the unrealized new. The old beauties were no longer beautiful, the new truths no longer true. With the fierce zeal of the creator, the pioneer in art, Strindberg produced works which enraptured Germany and Europe, not less for their highly-colored tendency than for their artistic depth and validity as creations of enduring art. Without stressing the features of the change, it is indubitable that Strindberg finally reached the stage of disillusionment. Of life, he demanded happiness, the happiness of the marital state, with wife and children; but he forfeited the happiness that might perhaps have been his because he was never able to accept things as they are, never willing to surrender himself to life's immitigable conditions. For him, it was an impossibility, in Nietzsche's phrase, to say Aye to the Universe. One only hazards the surmise that, had Strindberg been capable of such self-abnegation, he might have developed into a great, strong, sweet soul, profoundly sympathetic with his fellow-beings, vibrant with comprehension of, commiseration for, human foibles and frailties. There were depths, profundities in Strindberg's nature, both as man and artist, which called to answering depths, profundities in human consciousness. His recognition of the ultimate futility of his marital experiences was no less pronounced in his career than his recognition of the instability of naturalism in art as a formula. At last he came to the full realization of the discrepancy between what life and the era had to offer him, a realization of the profoundest potentialities of his own nature and genius.

It was in this spirit — the spirit of one who flees to sanctuary — that Strindberg sought Paris in 1894. His old absorption in chemistry, the desire to surprise the mystery of atom, molecule and element, once more came over him. Along with it came the stirrings of the equally imperious impulse

— to surprise the mystery of faith, conscience and religion, and to merge himself in that spiritual world-consciousness which William Blake many years before had foreshadowed with the power and imagination of the seer. It was only another phase of Strindberg's life of disillusion that Paris had not to give him that which he sought. With this period of his career, it is virtually impossible to speak with critical authority, for there is no tracing, accurately, the thin line demarking the sound, the sane, from the obsessed, the hallucinated. There is abundant evidence of his lack of balance in his feverish wanderings in the mazes of the cruder forms of occultism. A Strindberg caught fast in the meshes of a weird complex of French mysticism and American theosophy!

To follow Strindberg through the Slough of Despond of his Paris days and after, one should read those strange, harassing books, *Inferno*, *Legends*, and *Alone*. Wonderful as are these works, viewed as the autobiographic confessions of a great creative artist, they chiefly serve as records of mental and spiritual obsession. Surely, here was madness to genius close allied. For it was not legitimate research in which Strindberg was absorbed, but pseudo-scientific superstition; not chemistry, but alchemy. His concentration upon the problem of the transmutability of elements, however, is just now beginning to appear in a more rational light, in view of the interpretation, by Sir William Ramsay, of some of his own discoveries. Strindberg's fascinated concentration upon the problem of religion, salvation and the future life is of a piece with his studies in alchemy — both are pathological symptoms. Shaken to the very centre of his spiritual existence by a close study of Swedenborg, Strindberg groped vainly about for spiritual consolation and the poetic certitudes of faith. His was a religion of tortured searching after spiritual faith. As he sought scientific truth in alchemy, so now he seeks spiritual truth in the obscurities of a hazy occultism. Surely at this time Strindberg's intellectual and psychical centres must have been in very unstable equilibrium. It was not the eternal verities of religion which drew him after them, but its transitory delusions, the speculations of mysticism — psychic states, second sight, telephatic communications, obsessions. There could be no permanent consolation in the problematical phenomena of spiritualism; and in the end Strindberg emerged triumphant from the Slough of Despond. In answer to his deep spiritual need, his profoundly felt longing for certitude, there finally came to him a gently consolatory faith — that faith which he pathetically describes in *Alone* as "a condition of the soul and not of the mind." With a consciousness fundamentally conscientious, a spirit innately religious, Strindberg may be said to have spent his life vainly listening for life's harmonies, vainly endeavoring to discover some latent, internal interdependence between the spiritual forces of the universe. That inner harmony discovered by Maeterlinck, the gentle optimist, was forever barred from the vision of Strindberg, the passionate pessimist.

V

In Strindberg's works of fiction, polemic, social, autobiographical, one seems to follow the errant pilgrimages of a soul distraught with the obsession of existence. It is the ancient cry from the depths: "Oh! that this too, too solid flesh would melt!" In Strindberg, the dramatist, one encounters the titanic struggles of an almost superhuman intellect, fretting vainly against the bars of life's mysteries. With every concession made to the fatal lack of balance, the futurist distortion of perspective, it must be granted that Strindberg was singularly original in genius and at the same time singularly consistent in his interpretation of the riddle of life. There is no error so crass as that of presuming, with hasty generalization, that Strindberg was essentially eccentric — dementedly swinging off from the central realities of life. This inner meaning of Strindberg's temperament lies at the very heart of his nature, which pulsed violently in the midst of the most fantastic realities. Never did artist so persistently cleave to the centre of his own being in his effort to project for the world's inspection the inner significance of contemporary existence. Strindberg is the most ego-centric dramatist who has ever lived. If Shakspere was actually, as Mr. Frank Harris vehemently implies, the Strindberg of the Elizabethan era, by the same token is Strindberg the Shakspere of the Nietzschean age — a supremely dæmonic bohemian of the soul.

It was Strindberg who embodied in his own personality the affirmative answer to Nietzsche's sinister query: "Why should not life be intolerable?" In him was a spirit of divine discontent, of volcanic denial — raging fiercely against the evils revealed to his searching gaze and giving no quarter to his adversaries. One of the most conclusive proofs of his greatness is the fact that no one has yet succeeded in taking the measure of his stature. He is that miracle in the hierarchy of genius — an incommensurable force in the intellectual and spiritual economy of the universe. Strindberg has been called the only dramatist of genuinely Shaksperean order in modern times — assuredly true in the dramatic sense that in the consciousness of no other contemporary dramatist do conflicts, antitheses, crises, emanate such trenchant, virile reality. The secret of his marvellous appeal is his headlong participation in the destinies of his dramatic characters. It is because he threw himself so vehemently into the arena of dramatic struggle and dramatized his own tremendous struggle that his art works seethe with such vital force and energy.

The primitive force of Strindberg starts into eager life in the early play, *The Outlaw* (1872) and foreshadows the leonine genius. The delicate beauty of womanhood, the enduring strength of loyalty, the tenacious rectitude of rude, primitive force — all are rendered with trenchant economy of means in this " dramatic experiment." Thus early Strindberg foresaw the virtue of intensive concentration of treatment — fusing an incohesive, scattered play of five acts into a single, organic play of a single act. Thorfinn, the heroic Norseman, adamantine in his barbaric strength, is shattered against the passive, supreme invincibility of the Christian ideal, the dawning ideal of the age. Says Orne to Thorfinn: " It is the age you have warred against, and that has slain you — it is the lord of the age, it is God who has crushed you." There is tragic majesty in the death of Thorfinn, who lacks the superhuman strength " never to regret anything one does "; and in dying, expiates and atones with a blessing upon his daughter, Gunlöd, a convert to Christianity, and her lover, Thorfinn's enemy. In yielding to the strength of supreme emotion, he yields in symbol his heart's blood — realizing at the last the divine force of woman's love. For " woman thinks, not with her head, but with her heart. That's why she has a smaller head, but a bigger breast than man."

Upon one occasion, I was conducted by Mrs. Ibsen into her husband's study at the apartment on the Victoria Terrace, in Kristiania; and there, above the mantel, was hanging a magnificent oil painting of August Strindberg. As presiding genius of the place, this impressive figure with noble head and tragic, haunting eyes seemed to dominate the room. Asked why he gave the place of supreme honor in that laboratory of the dramatic spirit to the titanic Swede, Ibsen — I was told by the querist — replied: "The man has a fascination for me — because he is so subtly, so delicately mad." There was something far deeper than this which caused the electric interaction between these two geniuses — so antipodal in temperament, yet so cognate in the faculties of intuitive perception and searching introspectiveness. Ibsen, Björnson, Strindberg — the three Scandinavian geniuses — each felt the mental pressure of the others, and responded to it. There yet remains to be written the history of that period in Scandinavian literature which shall reveal the influences these three exerted, the one upon the other. Certainly *The Outlaw,* if nothing else of Strindberg's, was suggested by Björnson's *Between the Battles.*

During the period from 1872 to 1884, the strongest indications appear of the influences Strindberg and Ibsen, more or less consciously, exerted upon each other. In *The Pretenders* (1862), Ibsen projects the conflict between two strong temperaments — Hakon, the incarnation of innate confidence, and Skule, the introspective and brooding Hamlet type; and the latter, after appropriating the former's intuitional conception and winning temporary success, ultimately goes down in tragic defeat, wrecked through his lack of faith in himself and his consciousness of guilt. This play must have exerted a powerfully suggestive influence upon Strindberg in the composition of *Master Olof,* originally entitled, more adequately, *The Renegade.* In Ibsen's play there is something schematic and artificial in the psychological basis of the action; Strindberg outstrips Ibsen in portraying a central figure more closely attuned to the temper of modern social feeling. The hero of Strindberg's play is a renegade because, like Peer Gynt, he yields to the blandishments of compromise, and in order to prepare the way for the ultimate realization of his larger purpose, strikes the banner of his ideal to sheer necessity. The philosophy of expediency oftentimes yields more tangible, more practically productive results; yet the seer, in whom we discern the spiritual lineaments of Strindberg, holds a renegade he who sacrifices to transient and temporal success the magic, affective force of the ideal. The prototype of the modern woman, of the Nora of *A Doll's House,* is found full-fledged in this same play — a remarkable evidence of the prophetic modernity of Strindberg's social vision. Strindberg's anticipation of Ibsen, which in this case takes the form of a single type, is more conclusively evidenced in *The Secret of the Guild* (1880), written twelve years before the appearance of *The Master-Builder.* Ibsen's early poem, *Architectural Plans,* must have been far less germinative for *The Master-Builder* than Strindberg's utilization in *The Secret of the Guild* of the building of the tower as a creative symbol in dramatic technique. Imperfectly employed by Strindberg, this suggestive symbol was utilized by the more experienced craftsman with magicianly mastery and far-reaching suggestiveness. Austin Harrison goes so far as to assert: "Through Solness Ibsen spoke directly at Strindberg. The much-debated line of *The Master-Builder,* 'It is youth that I fear,' was aimed across the border at the young Swede, in whom Ibsen saw already a peer and a highly dangerous rival." Compliment seldom takes so subtle a form as the bold utilization of an idea, and the expressed dread of the coming supremacy of its originator. Ibsen owed his debt to this young Norwegian rival who fascinated him with his not wholly deranged creative originality! In *Lady Margit,* with its torrential onslaught upon what he regarded as the essential defeminization of woman in *A Doll's House,* Strindberg takes his revenge — a polemic in dramatic form against the coming reign of the matriarch.

The most radiant proof of the happy, naïve side of Strindberg's nature, the grace of his fantasy and the delicacy of his imagination, is found in *Lucky Pehr* (1883), an allegorical play in five acts. It assuredly influenced Maeterlinck in the writing of *The Blue Bird* — each depicting, in allegorical guise, the spiritual progress of youth in the search for happiness. In the play of the lively fancy of the author, we see the young Pehr, endowed with the ring which will gratify all his wishes and under the protective care of the gentle, wisely maternal Lisa, start forth upon his aimless wanderings. In fastastic scenes, irradiated with shrewd philosophy and kindly humor, young Pehr, callow, innocently selfish, passes alternately from disillusion to disillusion — thinking naught of others, vainly seeking the self-gratification which ever eludes him. His friendship is sought for his gold, he is betrayed by a temptress; he learns the vanity of society, the shallowness of convention. The lawyer, with light cynicism, assures him: "When one through riches has risen to the community's heights, one belongs to the whole"— a satirical hit at the modern ideal of social service. Pehr sees no deeper than to wish to be a great reformer — that he may be "honored and idolized by the people, and have his name on everyone's lips"! He tries to carry out his reforms — but finds every man's hand against him. Even the cobbler objects to having flagstones instead of cobblestones, because, forsooth, it will "hurt business"— a familiar cry. The pillory is Pehr's final refuge as a reformer. His gratified wish to be great and powerful ends in like disaster — for in order to become ruler he finds that he must sacrifice all his ideals for political considerations. There is no real liberty, only Constitutional Despotism; no religious freedom, only the Established Church; no personal liberty, only Court Etiquette; no freedom to marry, only Considerations of State. Finally he faces Death — and pleads for life that he may search further for happiness among his own kind. Death warns him: "You should not seek human beings, for they cannot help you." When he learns that he who loves only himself can never love another, he is on the brink of discovery. Like Peer Gynt, he learns to slay the craving to make himself the centre around which all others revolve — and in the discovery of unselfishness comes safely to the glad haven of happiness with the tenderly faithful Lisa. *The Shadow* tolerantly voices Strindberg's view: "Life is not such as you saw it in your youthful dreams. It is a desert, that is true; but a desert which has its flowers; it is a stormy sea, but one that has its havens by verdant isles."

VI

Strindberg's headlong plunge into naturalism, marked by the appearance of the powerful drama, *The Father,* in 1887, registers a double turning-point in his life as artist and man. The monographic method of Maupassant and the de Goncourts in fiction awoke him to the possibilities of the naturalistic drama; and Zola's dramatized novel, *Thérèse Raquin,* produced by Antoine at his Théâtre Libre in Paris in 1887, furnished the clue for the new departure. Strindberg, ever the innovator, the *Bahnbrecher,* not only realized the dearth of creative genius and the sterility of invention in the drama, but even stood in fear of the threatened abandonment of the drama as a decaying form, in our time "when the rudimentary, incomplete thought processes operating through our fancy seem to be developing into reflection, research and analysis." Like Zola, he was ripe for rebellion against the prevailing artificial comedy, "with its Brussels carpets, its patent-leather shoes and patent-leather themes, and its dialogue reminding one of the questions and answers of the catechism."

Strindberg's revolt was experimental in the deepest sense — in the same sense in which Zola speaks of the experimental novel. The dramatist of the era seemed to have become a mere absorptive spirit, who vulgarized his art for the sake of rendering it intelligible to and effective with the masses. This reduction of electric genius to so many candle power, in order to penetrate the consciousness of intellectual mediocrity, revolted Strindberg. His own ideal was the precise reverse — to express his originality with pristine clarity and to achieve the most intensive, concentrated effect through bringing his complex and multiplex ideas to a burning, focal point.

About him he saw everywhere the predominance of the stereotyped in character-drawing, the prevalence of the static character — artificial automata, dummies labelled with a tag, incapable of change, development, growth. The hope for the drama — the drama which Ibsen and Björnson at this time were so triumphantly creating in new, mobile forms —lay in the enlargement of the conception of character, the objectification upon the stage of the dynamically evolutionary modern soul, such as Strindberg felt himself personally to be. Like Nietzsche before him, like Bergson to-day, Strindberg intuitively felt the pressure of the concept of creative evolution — seeing in the modern human temperament a vast complex of thought currents, emotive impulses — often self-contradictory, inconsequent, atavistic and yet instinctively vital, fervent, intense. Instead of regarding character as fixed, and the age as stationary, he determined to show both in flux. His characters may justly be described, in a German phrase, as the *Uebergangsmenschen einer Uebergangszeit* — transitional beings in a transitional era.

It is characteristic of Strindberg that, in his effort to portray the most vital, most intense form of conflict, he should instinctively find his dramatic theme in the torturing conflicts of his own family life.

Between Strindberg and his first wife, two highly individualized, fundamentally antipathetic characters, vital differences presented themselves — on the subject of feminism, woman's right to unbridled freedom, the direction and control of children, the relative measure of the sexes. In *Lady Margit,* with the sub-title *Sir Bengt's Wife,* a historical play of the Reformation period, Strindberg had already revealed, in pitiless, glacial analysis of a woman's soul, his intolerant attitude towards the modern type of the denaturized feminine. And yet, with all its implacability, it does not prepare us for the shocking figure of Laura in *The Father.* Here is revealed the fundamental weakness of the thesis-drama; for we cannot accept as representatively human a character reproduced with diabolic exactitude from a real person, who was almost certainly degenerate, and whom Strindberg hated as the incarnation of all that woman, the ideal woman, should not be.

The Father is a drama of the most powerfully intensive struggle, on the plane of mental suggestion — the supreme drama of its kind. These characters live with feverish and intense vitality — a vitality transfused into them from Strindberg's own powerfully vibrant being. Cut them, and they will palpably bleed — the blood of martyrs and impenitents. We achieve immortality through the transmission of personality and faith to our posterity

— the greatest mission, in Strindberg's eyes, is the mission of paternity. Hence the tragic conflict — between the father, fixed in his determination to direct and control the future of the child, and the mother, endowed with indomitable will, infinitely unscrupulous, diabolically cunning. By subtly poisonous suggestion, the woman implants in the mind of the distraught man the deranging doubt as to whether he is the father of his child — a doubt which grows into the *idée fixe* of mania. This tremendous drama can only be fully understood in its symbolic guise. It is the terrible plea of the elemental male for the rights of fatherhood, the patriarchal functions of man as the ruler of the family, holding within his hand the directive control of the future of his posterity. In this drama Strindberg gives free play to his essentially barbaric feelings, and arraigns woman with a ferocity little short of hideous.

We shall, assuredly, do Strindberg a gross injustice if we label him, inconsiderately, a misogynist. Laura is a symbolic figure; not the modern conception of Everywoman, but a super-real personification of the final possibilities of wickedness in woman. Laura is not that "female of the species," more deadly than the male, of which Kipling speaks, but the incorporation of the Principle of Evil as expressed in the attributes of the specific female. "Not long ago," says Strindberg in his remarkable

Preface to *Miss Julia,* "they reproached *The Father* with being too sad,—just as if they wanted merry tragedies. Everybody is clamoring arrogantly for 'the joy of life,' and all theatrical managers are giving orders for farces, as if the joy of life consisted in being silly and picturing all human beings as so many sufferers from St. Vitus' dance or idiocy. I find the joy of life in its violent and cruel struggles, and my pleasure lies in knowing something and learning something. And for this reason I have selected an unusual but instructive case—an exception, in a word—but a great exception, proving the rule, which, of course, will provoke all lovers of the commonplace."

Strindberg's attacks upon woman, so-called, are repellant and repulsive in an abnormal degree. It is no matter for surprise that he has been classified as the arch misogynist, the most radical woman-hater in the post-Schopenhauer era. He struck out ferociously against the woman-ideal of Ibsen's *Nora,* the "silly, romantic provincialism of Ibsen's epicene squaw." In his revolt against the position of Ibsen, he unhesitatingly said: "My superior intelligence revolts against the gyneolatry which is the latest superstition of the free-thinkers."

He could not regard with patience the movement for woman's emancipation, seeing in it an effort to dethrone Man in favor of Woman. The brute male in him revolted at the thought of seeing man, the "generator of great thoughts," the creator of modern civilization, displaced by woman whose intellect, as yet undeveloped, still belonged to the bronze age. He regarded the male as superior in intellect to the female, but weaker as an antagonist, owing to the imperfect and undeveloped moral sensibility of the female.

Comrades, arresting, brutal, is the cheapest thing that Strindberg has done. Again it is an arraignment of woman — a lightly sardonic resumption of the idea that woman is inferior to man, incapable of final rectitude, lacking that delicacy of conscience, that "moral elegance," which man wears like a plume! These are admirably drawn, burningly living, yet repulsively ignoble figures — it would be nothing short of farcical to see in each a typical specimen of their respective sexes — man, honorable, sympathetic, self-sacrificing; woman, treacherous, deceptive, feline. It is the philosophy of the cave man done over in modern terms; and the primitive woman actually likes it here when the cave man uses the club! The Strindberg woman is captivated, won by man-handling — *she would be;* but imagine the result of brute force tried on a gentlewoman!

It is, however, the gravest error to confuse Strindberg's attitude towards woman, carried to abnormal extremes of polemic in his fierce reaction against the "new woman" propaganda of Scandinavia, with his own personal attitude towards woman of the ideal type present in his own consciousness. That abnormal sexuality which Laura Marholm attributes to Strindberg, resulting in fundamental sex-aversion, was probably only an apparent, and not an actual, abnormality of nature. Like the youthful Tolstoi, Strindberg as a young man indulged in orgiastic sexual excesses, with the inevitable result of brushing off forever the bloom from the surface of erotic life. The whole course of Strindberg's works shows him essentially clean, if subtly plebeian, in his feelings about sex.

Miss Julia is one of the most startling, most shocking plays of our era; but its ugly theme is its chief reason for existence. In his notable Preface, Strindberg — who really seems to have influenced Bernard Shaw in several striking respects — gives the most elaborate explications of the purpose, meaning, and significance of the tragedy. And yet, after all, the preface is a tricky means of eking out the deficiencies of the play. It may well be imagined that Julia would never have yielded had it not been for her condition; yet never a hint of it is found in the play itself. Then there is the artificial conflict suggested by the two strata of society — artificial because whilst Julia falls, even to death, a victim of progressive inbreeding of diseased stocks, Jean climbs not at all, instinctly servile, cringing at the sound of the master's bell. This " half-woman," as Strindberg calls her, is a vanishing type, perishing eventually "either from discord with real life, or from the irresistible revolt of her suppressed instincts, or from foiled hopes of possessing the man." Miss Julia is no stranger to America, often piqued to forbidden curiosity by the spectacle of the woman of society eloping with her chauffeur.

It was the tragedy of Strindberg's life never to rise above the sex-disillusionment which came from early excess. This was the penalty paid in full measure by one thrice married and thrice divorced. He was never able to awake in another a passion as intense as his own. In becoming the supreme specialist in modern eroticism he sacrificed the possibility of making the great discovery — of simple, enduring human love. There is no more tragic figure in modern times than this Knight of the Sorrowful Countenance, with pallid lips and stricken gaze, "dementedly wandering from Venusburg to Venusburg."

In his own consciousness, woman was worthy of all veneration — a veneration instinctive in him from his earliest childhood. Life itself cruelly persisted in the effort to shatter that illusion of his youth. The artist, the idealist in Strindberg romantically endowed woman with the supreme virtues — loyalty, faith, devotion, rectitude, moral integrity — and painted her as man's equal in intelligence, his superior in nobility. When life betrayed his faith, and the age threatened to enthrone above man this creature Strindberg had discovered to be so full of weakness and frailty, he burst forth in passionate protest, which was only a secret form of vindication of his own ideal of woman. His attitude towards woman — towards the type to-day expressed in the term militant suffragette — was not only ungallant, unchivalric: it was splenetic, atrabiliar. In his view of the sexes, woman is man's inferior in the life-scale — as yet undeveloped in intellect, artistic perception, and moral power; but he considers this biological inferiority counterbalanced by other specific *indicia* of the female — fixity of purpose, endless endurance, subtle calculation. Strindberg pays woman the high honor of holding her to be a foeman worthy of the sharpest steel of man. He holds woman fully worthy of man as an antagonist in the duel of sex. In his plays, woman fights for her own hand with unlimited will-power and intellectual skill.

Strindberg can only be properly understood if we realize that the duel of sex is not always a contest for sex supremacy. It is a contest, as Strindberg so diabolically shows in *Creditors,* of the woman for the right to illicit gratification of her own instincts — regardless of honor, fidelity, or modesty. Or it may be, as in *The Link,* a mortal struggle for the possession of the child. There was never a more realistic fragment of concentrated life than *The Link* — a virtual replica of Strindberg's own suit for divorce from his first wife. One by one, the curtains are drawn aside; and these two human souls, fighting like animals for the child that binds them together, stand at last in utter nakedness — separated by an abyss like a yawning hell. In the words of the pilgrim to his former wife, in *Damascus:* "We love. Yes, and we hate. We hate each other, because we love one another; we hate each other because we are linked together; we hate the link, we hate love; we hate what is most lovable because it is also the most bitter, we hate the very best which gives us this life." In the haunting words of Oscar Wilde:

> "Some kill their love when they are young,
> And some when they are old;
> Some strangle with the hands of Lust,
> Some with the hands of Gold:
> The kindest use a knife, because
> The dead so soon grow cold."

It is almost incredible that Strindberg never set his ideal woman before us on the stage. Previsions of this feminine ideal are found in certain of the early plays — in such a character, for example, as *Gunlöd* in *The Outlaw.* And yet this ideal of Strindberg's may definitely be disengaged, after a study of his works. For Strindberg has the antique, patriarchial conception of the family, with its veneration for the woman as wife and mother. Surpassing man in tenderness, in temperamental cleverness, with greater breadth of horizon, wider humanitarian concern, woman must nevertheless remain, in Strindberg's view, within the boundary of her own "sphere." Woman is a tremendously powerful original source of human energy, to which man must ever recur to escape annihilation — the intermediary between man and the child, upon which the world's future depends.

Having, then, this genuine ideal of womanhood, this old-fashioned conception of woman as mother and mate, Strindberg seems strangely illogical in giving us a gallery of hideous female types — incarnations of beasts of prey, deadly monsters, the hyena woman, the blue-stocking cocotte. The reason is not far to seek — inexplicable and damning as is the evidence to the contrary. With an imperfectly developed historic sense, so far certainly as concerned the subject of woman's economic and spiritual evolution, Strindberg was too arrant a worshipper of man as the creator of all that civilization has wrung from barbarism, ever to see that woman, as she is to-day, is in large measure the handiwork, the creature of this same admirable myth — the perfect man. If Strindberg's women are characteristic and representative figures of our era — which God forbid! — man cannot shirk the responsibility for these damning symptoms of man-made civilization. Strindberg's women are not typical of the female species, symbolic representations of Everywoman. They are specific, isolated, yet none the less actual, existent, types of feminine degeneration, fatally symptomatic of our own era in world-civilization. They are the most eloquent briefs in behalf of militant suffragism. Woman rightly seeks to shatter man's control over the processes of civilization, and to share it with him — to obviate the recurrence of the types of women which Strindberg has projected into the focus of modern consciousness.

VII

The historian of the contemporary drama of the past quarter of a century must recognize in August Strindberg a creative and original genius, of many-hued, radiant brilliance. In particular, his achievement in the field of the one-act drama on the stage of an intimate theatre has been nothing less than epoch-making. His method of focal concentration, of magnification of interest through intensiveness of treatment, imparts to even his briefest efforts the most complete illusion of reality. In his esthetic creed, the dramatist must be a magician, a hypnotist, weaving about the spectator a spell of atmospheric illusion which holds his attention with the utmost fixity. By the elimination of all superfluity in the stage sets and the scenery, the dramatic figures appear as integral, organic parts of their surroundings. These one-act plays of Strindberg's are essentially psychological, even psychical, or fantastic in tone; they may present an allegory or a realistic glimpse of life at a crucial point. The "stage-business" of the mechanical order is virtually eliminated; the play of emotion, the movements in the depths of character, are portrayed less by outcries or by violent gestures, than by the play of facial expression, indicative through mobility.

Strindberg's one-act plays have a strong cast of Maeterlinck about them — they are soul-interiors thrown for a brief space into glaring illumination. *The Stronger,* in which only two female characters appear, one remaining silent throughout reading a newspaper, is a remarkable dramatic monologue — the thoughts passing through the mind of the silent one mirrored as it were in the words of the speaker. The one actress in a flash of intuition, realizes the price she has paid for her husband — who is the lover of the other actress. All her tender little acts of solicitude for her husband — hideous mockery! — were indirectly suggested by the taste of the "other woman"— even to the tulips embroidered on his slippers. But she will never break with her husband — because the other woman seeks and desires it. This it is to be the stronger.

There is the fascination of psychological detection of crime in *Pariah,* a dialogue between two men,

Mr. X and Mr. Y,— which in a few brief exchanges of ideas gives a complete presentment of two well-defined characters — one, the man of courage and essential integrity, who has killed another and feels no pangs of conscience because he realizes its accidental character; the other, the coward and contemptible blackmailer, who has forged a note and cannot find within himself the saving grace of self-exculpation. There is the kindly, yet sharp, accent of satire in *Debit and Credit* — the man who has reached the pinnacle of fame in his profession suddenly finding all the obligations of his past rising with accusing hands before him — his brother demands the payment of the loan which he has long evaded; his fiancée is proven faithless; his former mistress appears to add the last drop of bitterness to his cup. A still darker theme — the germ idea of Shaw's *Mrs. Warren's Profession* — is presented in *Mother-Love*. By degrees, half accident, half design, the young girl's faith in her mother is destroyed, by overheard gossip and by the confession of her girl-chum, the legitimate daughter of her own father. Lacking the businesslike hardness of Vivie Warren, this young girl feels life turn black before her in the face of the hideous discovery — that she has no "father," not because he was faithless to her mother, but because her mother, even as his mistress, was faithless to him. In all these plays, life rises up for one dread instant and speaks its dread lesson — in

The Burned Lot, that sardonic picture of the shattering of youthful ideals in the discovery of their essential falsity, based on lies and fostered by deceit; *Simoon,* sinister pæan of revenge, pitched on a key of religious fanaticism; *The Spook Sonata,* with its morbidly fascinating concept of the room where falsity reigns and life's ugly shams are pitilessly revealed; *The Storm,* with its autobiographical ring — no more women, no more taking of mates who prove faithless — only peace and the drowning of memories. There is wide versatility of talent, a fingering of many themes, in these little intimate plays, this dramatic form which Strindberg created as distinctively as Maupassant and Poe created the form of the short-story — masters who exerted a powerful influence upon Strindberg.

To me it has seemed most singular that so gentle and beautiful a work of the imagination as *Easter* should have found among American critics no interpreter. Indeed, among English-speaking critics this unique art work has found no one to grasp its purport or to disengage its meaning. Yet this is the play which gives the clue to the unilluded, balanced Strindberg, instinct with the Christian spirit of tolerance, teaching a lesson of life which, had he been able to be his own pupil, would have saved him from unspeakable anguish. Strindberg's "Plays of the Seasons"— *Easter, Midsummer, Christmas* — are significantly representative of the three-fold nature of his temperament, as well as of his genius. *Easter* in its modernity of view-point — a sort of Swedish anticipation of the Emmanuel Movement — reveals Strindberg teaching the advanced lesson of psychic suggestion — the imaginary character of so many of our woes, the efficacy of certain desired, induced mental states. It is vastly superior to *Christmas,* suggestive of the influence of Maeterlinck, dour in tone, unrelieved by beauty, sweetness and light; or to the almost frivolous comedy of *Midsummer* — in which the bubble of youthful folly is pricked to the accompaniment of a peal of not unkindly laughter.

With a sadness not unlightened by subtly humorous perception, we are shown in *Easter* a family living under the shadow of disgrace, from the embezzlement of the funds of children and widows which have been entrusted to the father of the family. With restrained art of the most unobtrusive simplicity, the characters stand forth in chiselled distinctness — rich in homely virtues, patient, conscientious, energetic, but all narrowed by the cheap ideas of familiar convention, seeing heroes and heroines in each other and regarding their critics and creditors as the conventional demons and villains of popular melodrama. The mother is harassed with the obsession of loyalty — the self-induced conviction that her husband was innocent or at least that there must have been some flaw in the legal procedure which condemned him. Her son Elis, the young scholar, distrusts his friend and rival, frets over his lot in the most feebly womanish way, and lacks faith even in his betrothed, Christina, who tries to lift the depressing burden as best she may. Even little Benjamin, committed to the charge of the family because of the father's embezzlement of his property, is an indirect victim of the abnormal strain imparted to the family's vision — he fails at school in his examination. As Easter approaches, a crisis seems imminent; the "old gentleman" to whom they owe "so much money" is seen regarding the house fixidly, and a darker gloom settles down over the household in anticipation of the foreclosure. On Holy Thursday, the little daughter Eleanora, who has been confined to a home for the mentally deficient, suddenly returns, to work the holy miracle of faith, hope, resurrection. She is a psychic of marvellous powers of insight, whose former violence now takes the guise of spirituality, re-enforced by the wisdom of the Scriptures, mystic passages from which are ever upon her tongue. Under the ministration of this gentle spirit, the illusions of convention vanish away; the scales fall from the eyes of all. The old gentleman — with his terrifying blue document — breaks down the false pride of Elis by forcing him, under threat of foreclosure, to do the right, however bitterly his conventional pride and false sense of dignity may protest. This, truly, is one of the most impressive dramas of suggestion ever written — a work of genius in anticipation of the later variations on the same theme, of a more conventional symbolism, *The Servant in the House,* and *The Passing of the Third Floor Back.* This exquisite drama has the movement of psychic forces only — the material action is virtually nil. There is a profound life-lesson in this play — it is not the part of wisdom, nor even of sanity, in the larger signification, to live under the obsessions of self-pity, penny-plain convention, melodramatic views of conduct, false pride. As the glad mother exclaims: "Eleanora the child of sorrow, has come back with joy, but not the joy of this world! Her unrest has been turned into peace, which she shares. Sane or not, for me she is wise; for she understands how to bear the burdens of life as we do not."

Through the subtle suggestiveness of the spirit of faith, hope, charity, all regain in the end that happy balance which the sane life demands — and can look hopefully forward toward the future, a future of promise, of readjustment, of manful facing of life's grim realities. As Velma Swanston Howard, the sympathetic translator of *Easter* has said: "No trace of the old bitterness and hatred is to be found here. The author reveals a broad tolerance, a rare poetic tenderness augmented by an almost divine understanding of human frailties, as marking certain natural stages in the evolution of the soul. 'Clear thoughts, like clear fountains, do not seem as deep as they are; the turbid seem most profound.' These words of Richard Lander might well be applied to Strindberg. His finest and deepest thoughts are as simple as the Gospels whilst it is his turbid thoughts which seem the most profound."

VIII

The series of fairy plays, symbolic in guise and confessedly initiated under the influence of Maeterlinck, reveals the fundamental bent of Strindberg towards dramatic empiricism. Essentially an innovator, an experimentalist in form, Strindberg here exhibits his genius in appropriating a given genre, conceived in a chosen mood, and by a course of experimentation, more or less tentative and imitative, achieving a final form peculiarly his own. In *The Crown Bride,* a folk-lore play, reminiscent of Heijermanns in richness of local coloring, of Maeterlinck and Ibsen in the use of symbolic figures, we follow the bitter punishment of a young girl who has drowned her offspring before marriage. The poor creature is hounded down by her husband's relatives, and suffers the remorse and torture of the damned. There is an atmosphere of unreality about the incidents — Strindberg's persistent realism, his almost grotesque denotement of the grim naïveté and mediæval superstition of the fisher-folk accord ill with the symbolic paraphernalia of the piece. The finale is in brighter key, with its promise of salvation for the pitiful girl through the redemptive power of love. For her, " faith is born in hope," when she discovers the " greatest thing in life, the love of all living creatures, great and small."

The inequality so apparent in *The Crown Bride* is totally absent from *Swanwhite,* the " fairy drama " published in 1902, and intended as a medium for the histrionic genius of Strindberg's third wife, the actress, Harriet Bosse. The play has all the fanciful stage-properties so familiar in *The Princess Maleine* and other plays of Maeterlinck in his first period. Indeed, Strindberg is unusually lavish in stage directions; and one almost senses parody in his imperfect employment of the significant brevity, the almost puerile monosyllables of Maeterlinck. There is beauty here, faint yet tender; and as in *Joyzelle,* love is all-triumphant, redeeming even the " wicked stepmother " and recalling the " fairy prince " from the dead — a play, truly, for children, since the symbolism is of the most elementary and obvious sort. Produced by a Gordon Craig, with splendid scenic effects, *Swanwhite* might well win popular success in a Juvenile Theatre.

Through this experimental and imitative period, Strindberg was slowly forging towards a form of his own, far greater and more profound than the models before him. The realm of the higher fantasy had always beckoned to him — that realm where life in all its manifestations instinctively assumes the form of parable and prophecy. The most astounding testimony to the versatile greatness of Strindberg is that he, the most distinctive naturalist which the modern dramatic movement has furnished, could also write the marvellous fantasy entitled *The Dream Play*. Into it has gone at once his blighted faith in the consolations life can afford and his disillusionment over the sanctifying and redemptive aspects of existence. This philosophy of life takes mystic form through the unrollment of the panorama of human destiny — love, marriage, faith, science, religion — before the eyes of a daughter of the gods who descends to earth. The infinite sadness of human life, the eternal recurrence of its devastating duties, the everlasting return of self on self, the rythmic dissonance and discord, the perpetual bafflement and struggle — all this is revealed through the strangest of mediums. It is the macrocosm in the microcosm — the dream within a dream. All is inconsequence; thoughts ramble concentrically. Strange designs emerge with singular distinctness from the crazy-quilt patch-work of life.

The atmosphere is perfectly reflected in the author's Prefatory Note: "Anything may happen; everything is possible and probable. Time and space do not exist. On an insignificant background of reality, imagination designs and embroiders novel patterns: a medley of memories, experiences, free fancies, absurdities and improvisations. The characters split, double, multiply, vanish, solidify, blur, clarify. But one consciousness reigns above them all — that of the dreamer; and before it there are no secrets, no incongruities, no scruples, no laws. There is neither judgment nor exoneration, but merely narration. And as the dream is mostly painful, rarely pleasant, a note of melancholy and of pity with all living things runs right through the wabbly tale." The play transpires in the hazy, twilight zone of mystic feeling. It is the dramatization of unconscious cerebration. The daughter of the gods feels in all their force the pangs of life — and returns to heaven to lay all human grievance before the throne. There seems to be no conception here of life as creative evolution, pushing towards higher spheres. Life, as Strindberg sees it, is hopeless because it is static, immutable — the same yesterday, to-day, and forever. In the depth and reach of the imagination, the genius to interpret reality through the medium of unreality, this is assuredly one of the most marvellous dramatic achievements of modern times — unique, incomparable.

In the key of *The Dream Play* are written also two other plays of his, so singular in their treatment, so fascinating in their power, as to set them apart from all the rest of his work. First of these is *There are Crimes and Crimes,* where fantasy and inconsequence play their crucial rôles, though with subtle unobtrusiveness. This play, along with *Advent,* was originally published under the title *In a Higher Court* — a title singularly apt in expressing the quintessential meaning. The play is rich with the seductive brilliance of life at its most effervescent moments — a symbol of that intoxication which shatters balance and causes man madly to sin against the light. "The 'higher court,' in which are tried the crimes of *Maurice, Adolphe,* and *Henriette,*" says Mr. Björkman, the translator, "is, of course, the highest one that man can imagine. And the crimes of which they have all become guilty are those which, as *Adolphe* remarks, 'are not mentioned in the criminal code'— in a word, crimes against the spirit, against the impalpable power that moves us, against God. The play, seen in this light, pictures a deep-reaching spiritual change, leading us step by step from the soul adrift on the waters of life to the state where it is definitely oriented and impelled." This play is deserving of the popularity which it has achieved — of high constructive power, instinct with a profoundly salutary injunction for human guidance. It is a dramatization of the workings of conscience — a realization of that universal phenomenon to which all human nature is heir, the revolutionary illumination of the soul which comes through divination of the distinction between right and wrong. It has rare interest, subjectively, as a reflection of the revolution wrought in Strindberg's own attitude — mirroring a sense of faith, hope and love — certitude in the higher reality of the divine. "Only through religion," Strindberg has confessed, "or the hope of something better, and the recognition of the innermost meaning of life as that of an ordeal, a school, or perhaps a penitentiary, will it be possible to bear the burden of life with sufficient resignation."

The second of these realistic dramas, transfused with mysticism, is *The Dance of Death* — a work so powerful in detail, yet so inconclusive in totality, as to leave one with a haunting sense of a masterpiece unrealized. In stateliness, sweep, and grandeur, it ranks with the masterpieces of the Greek drama; in naturalism, modernity of outlook, and gripping power, it stands unsurpassed in the dramatic literature of the era. Life, in a setting of diabolical ferocity and hideous struggle, is set nakedly before us — in two separate plays, the second but the shadow, the reflection of the first. We see the drama of existence played out before our stricken gaze — the terrible struggles for self-realization, arising out of inequalities in condition, incompatibility in temperament; the duel of sex, a duel to the death, because of the futile struggle to realize unity through diversity, the foreordained tragedy inevitable when one individual strives to attain supremacy through the frenzied effort to shatter the integrity of another's character. Strindberg has not read his Darwin in vain — painting in garish colors the blind, relentless warfare of existence, waged upon the individual by the immitigable conditions of environment. Nor does the clue to life's hopelessness elude us ever — the pitiless monotony, the recurrence and repetition, of spiritual and mental experience in the face of all the chances and changes of this mortal life. There is no escape from the cyclic rhythm of life — as the *Captain* says: "Wipe out — and pass on." Marvellous, tragic image — wrought of the incoherence and pitiless sameness of experience — inconclusive, as life is inconclusive, without enduring, unshaken faith.

IX

There is one phase of Strindberg's monumental activity beyond the scope of the present inquiry — the field of national, historical drama. Time will show whether the vitality of Strindberg's characters will energize works dealing with remote, wellnigh forgotten periods of Swedish history. Certain it is that these plays are wonderful, not as re-creations of historical figures and epochs, but as verisimilar, life-like denotements of forceful character in epochal situations, individual and national. In every domain of art, Strindberg has always succeeded in projecting tremendously vital characters — tensely alive, subtly neuropathic, strenuous in mental and spiritual cerebration.

Nor can it profit us here to study the mystic wanderings and desert pilgrimages of that most profoundly philosophic work, most confusing medley of allegory, parable, autobiography, confession and self-exculpation, the trilogy *To Damascus*. Such a work defies even the genius of a Reinhardt in production — blurring the vision of the "average spectator" with its kinetoscopic heterogeneity of spiritual films. Yet from it, colossal in its incommensurability, we learn perhaps best of all the inner meaning of Strindberg's nature and soul.

Strindberg is the supreme universalist of our modern era. With all the virile force of his personality, the richness of his temperament as artist, Strindberg is in essence an analyst, a research-worker in the domain of the human spirit. In doubt, in the questioning, I had almost said the querulous, attitude towards life and the universe, Strindberg found the real clue to spiritual progress. Beginning as an individualist, with that supreme arrogance which he described as the last trace of Man's Godlike origin, Strindberg felt for a time the Socialist call of the era — only to lapse again into a more arrant and confirmed individualism, in his effort to realize the superhuman ideals of an age which produced a Nietzsche and a Blake. A confirmed sceptic, he frankly accepted the doctrine of the relativity of truth, and sought through experimentation and self-examination those spiritual realties which engender freedom of spirit and enfranchisement of soul. Ego-centric, jaundiced, moody, full of torturing discontent, he finally paid the penalty in the paranoia of that terrible five-year interval, obsessed with the chimera of exaggerated egoism, the delusion of referential ideas. In his search for the realities of the spiritual life, he achieved the miracle of resignation and acceptance — abandoning the search for happiness and seeking only the strength to endure his fate. Overmastered by his dominant weakness, which he described as "sensitiveness to pressure," he turned frantically, now this way, now that, in the blind effort to achieve moral certitude; but finally he came to rest, or at least resignation, in the consciousness that life is a complex of interaction, and that the individual, as part of the universe, has no inalienable personal "rights" to pleasure and happiness. His life-work is essentially moral in its nature; his nature was essentially Christian. However splenetic and arrogant his mood, however jaundiced and *macabre* his tone, we nevertheless recognize in him a supreme artist, whose ideal was cultural development; a moral force in the universe, seeking the ultimate redemption of the human soul. Reactionary, primitive in his attitude towards woman, at one period in his career painting woman as fiend in human form, he was none the less imbued with a love for his mother bordering on reverence, a sentiment of deep tenderness for his children. An idealist however misguided, it was his tragic fate never to realize or even to comprehend that the clue to human happiness is not strife, struggle, doubt and denial, but gently humorous acceptance of personal limitations and human frailties. Perhaps a vision came in the end; for on his deathbed, he said: "Now, everything personal is blotted out." Stroking his daughter's hand, he whispered, "Dear, dear Greta!" The Bible which he asked for being placed in his hand, he murmured: "Now I have finished with the book of this world!" His last words — the ultimate confession of the catholic Christian spirit — as he pressed the Bible to his heart, were: "Here is to be found the only true expression."

HENRIK IBSEN

"In reality my development is thoroughly consecutive. I myself can indicate the various threads in the whole course of my development, the unity of my ideas, and their gradual evolution and I . . . shall prove to the world that I am the same person to-day that I was on the day I first found myself."

Henrik Ibsen to Lorentz Dietrichson.

HENRIK IBSEN

The Evolution of His Mind and Art

I

From the standpoint of present-day America, with its gospel of the strenuous life, its tendency to hero-worship with the masterful captain of industry for hero, its Roosevelts and its Pearys, Henrik Ibsen may be said to have lived a singularly uneventful, marvellously secluded life. His future biographer — for no one has yet succeeded, or even made a legitimate attempt to succeed, in mirroring the features of this placid exterior life of crowded inner tumultuousness — must match Ibsen himself in patience, detachment and single-mindedness. Until now, it may fairly be said that the literature concerned with the life and art of Henrik Ibsen deals almost solely with a traditionary figure. This legendary being is a little crabbed old man, taciturn, uncommunicative, even bearish, who occasionally broke the silence only to advance his own interests, to lash out with envenomed rage at his enemies, or else to affront gratuitously the friends and admirers who sought to do him public honor. Now that we are left alone with memories — and reminiscences both kindly and malicious,— the spiritual lineaments of the Norwegian seer tend to define themselves to vision. For the first time, in the light of the reminiscences of his friends and acquaintances, is it becoming possible to discover the man in his works, and to trace some of the many vital threads in the close-meshed fabric of his art. In the light, too, of his literary remains — piously collected and astutely edited by Koht and Elias — one may at last follow his work consistently from first to last in a chain of unbroken sequence, and test the validity of Ibsen's claim that his development as artist is consistent, uniform, evolutional. Heretofore, the salient details of Ibsen's exterior life have been recorded with mediate accuracy; and numerous efforts, brilliant, mediocre, futile, have been made towards achieving the biography of Ibsen's mind. The great work which yet remains to be done is to relate the man to his work, to discover the real human being who lurks behind the cartoons of Vallotton, Laerum and Scotson-Clark, the real human heart beating beneath the formidable frock-coat of the "little buttoned-up man."

II

America has been prolific in studies which betray crass unfamiliarity with the surroundings from which Ibsen sprang, as well as imperfect comprehension of the streams of European thought which profoundly affected his spiritual development. The real contributions to the knowledge of Ibsen on the part of American scholars and critics have been concerned, in the main, with Ibsen's technical ability and with those inalienable qualities of his art which have rendered him, as a dramatist, unique and distinctive. To Ibsen, the countries which have shown most profound regard for his significance gave a defining title and character: Norway thought of him first as a conservative and later as a radical; Germany was widely divided between those who classed him, respectively, as naturalist, individualist, and socialist; and France abhorred his anarchy while celebrating his symbolism. Despite the admirable and scholarly work of Archer, Gosse, Herford, Wicksteed and others, the brilliant polemics of Bernard Shaw, the elevated but sporadic performances of Janet Achurch, Elizabeth Robins, and other exemplars of the modern school of acting, and lastly the dignified work of the societies for the promotion of the modern drama, Ibsen has never laid the "great public" in England under his spell nor assumed, in the eyes of the reading-public, the dignity of a classic.

There are many and cogent reasons why America has never profited by the lessons Ibsen presented so unmistakably to his own and to future generations. As individualist, Ibsen could hope to create no uproar in a country which surpasses the countries of the Ibsen social dramas in the production of self-assertive individualists. In America there was — and is — no school of acting, classic in finish, classic in tradition, to interpret the complex harmonies of the Ibsenian dramas. The New Theatre proved a failure. Mansfield's production of *Peer Gynt* was a half-hearted concession to what he regarded as a popular craze for the bizarre and the abnormal; and the brilliant performances of Mrs. Fiske as Hedda Gabler and of Miss Mary Shaw as Mrs. Alving, to mention the most notable achievements, reeked too strongly of the unhealthy and the distorted to conquer permanently the prejudices of American audiences which are nightly flattered with the display of brilliant costumes, beautiful but incompetent "stars," and heroic-looking, but wooden, "matinée idols" for their delectation. Nazimova demonstrated that there was an audience in America that really relished Ibsen; and the lists of the most popular books at public libraries in America contain the plays of Ibsen as a stock number.

In two notable respects, Ibsen should mean much for the present and for the future of American dramatic art. No fear of misunderstanding prevents the statement that Ibsen was the first and greatest of the literary muck-rakers of modern drama. From the turbulent squabbles of Norway as well as from the social ferment of Europe, Ibsen drew trenchant and immediate lessons from public conduct as well as from personal morals. The Plimsoll agitation in England for proper laws regulating the insurance of unseaworthy vessels, reflected in the press of Norway, was at the back of *The Pillars of Society;* and Thaulow's public propaganda against a local society which he deemed fraudulent eventuated in the fight of Dr. Stockmann for the purification of the baths of his native town. *John Gabriel Borkman* is rooted in the reality of the daily life of Norway; and *The League of Youth* fell afoul of Björnson and his coterie. It may be thought that Ibsen as champion of individual emancipation came too late for a country whose greatest boasts are its freedom and its scope for the free play of individuality. And yet, there are people so critically censorious as to maintain that there is no real freedom in America; and that we are bound hard and fast by the puritanical formulas of a provincial civilization. Freedom of thought in America has in no sense kept pace with license of conduct; and a country which cannot suppress night-riding, lynching and mob-violence should not throw stones at Gorki, Zola or *Mrs. Warren's Profession.* America, with its Morses and its Walshes, need seek no further for wounded titans of finance like Borkman; and the *Slocum* disaster dwarfs the *Indian Girl* of *The Pillars of Society* into trivial insignificance. In Dr. Charles W. Stiles America can point to a Dr. Stockmann with a nation, rather than a minor watering-place, for the field of his inquiry. The most significant lesson of modern democracy in America, learned not from Ibsen but from the dire example of the American Sugar Company, and a thousand other scandals, is that, in its fullest significance, eternal vigilance is the price of liberty. The literature of exposure is never *mal à propos* in a civilization whose protection rests upon perpetual publicity.

The buoyant youth of America, impressing alike a Van Eeden and a Ferrero, is both its strength and its weakness. It bespeaks at once America's inexperience in self-control and her optimism of outlook. America can furnish towns as provincial in tone as ever won the amused contempt of European audiences at the performance of Ibsen's plays of Norwegian life; and her political life furnishes types of half-baked political leaders no less contemptible and inexperienced than Stensgaard and his young men's league. But America is young and hopeful, at least; it is not peopled, we are confidently assured, with soul-sick tragedians mouthing their futile protests against the iron vice of environment, the ineradicable scar of heredity, the fell clutch of circumstance. Ibsen's pathological preoccupations should have no meaning for America — his dalliance with sick consciences, obsessed personalities, wounded souls, disillusioned fatalists. But America should take to heart Ibsen's bold challenge for individual freedom, his insistence upon moral duties, his concern for marriage founded upon equitable relations between husband and wife, his claim of the individual's right to develop fully and without trammel, and lastly, his faith that human love and the happiness that it secures for the individual transcend all the glories of the palace of art,— all the victories that vaulting ambition can achieve. All that is needed for a real appreciation of Ibsen in America is a re-application of these inspiring lessons to our youthful, buoyant, optimistic yet inchoate society.

As man, as social thinker, Ibsen has for America these distinct and salutary lessons. As artist and craftsman, his message is no less signal and imperative. Ibsen's technique is one of the supreme glories of his art; and there can be little doubt that, in certain plays, the technique displayed is inextricably bound up with the dramatic genius which devised it. But no would-be dramatist of modern life to-day, in its limited environment and in its circumscribed sphere, can afford to neglect the study of the technique of Henrik Ibsen. In order to mirror the real life of to-day in perfect naturalness, the dramatist must realize the evolutional trend of the drama and study carefully the models set by Ibsen for our day and generation. Thus will he be the better enabled to realize Ibsen's ideal: "to produce the impression on the reader that what he was reading was something that had really happened." The great secret to be learned from a study of Ibsen's craftsmanship is the way he bridges over the gap between art and life by identifying the action and the exposition. As Bernard Shaw admirably expressed it: "What we might have learned from Ibsen was that our fashionable dramatic material was worn out as far as cultivated modern people are concerned; that what really interests such people on the stage is not what we call action — meaning two well-known and rather short-sighted actors pretending to fight a duel without their glasses, or a handsome leading man chasing a beauteous leading lady round the stage with threats, obviously not feasible, of immediate rapine — but stories of lives, discussion of conduct, unveiling of motives, conflict of characters in talk, laying bare of souls, discovery of pitfalls — in short, *illumination* of life. . . ."

III

It has often been said that the drama can never be the same again, now that Ibsen has lived and written. It may be said with even greater truth that the world can never be the same again, since Ibsen has lived and written. The spirit of modern times, the form and pressure of the age, the most fruitful germs of modern culture are embodied in the dramas of Ibsen. It should be the purpose of the drama to crystallize and body forth ideals for the human race, and thus to inform reality with the ideal. For the age of Shakspere, the ideal of art was "to hold, as 'twere, the mirror up to nature; to show virtue her own feature, scorn her own image, and the very age and body of the time his form and pressure." The nineteenth century brought forth a man who boldly declared that we are no longer living in the time of Shakspere. He clearly realized that the artist's attitude toward life must be redemptive as well as revelative. Every man shares the reponsibility and the guilt of the society to which he belongs. The function of contemporary art, of dramatic art *par excellence,* is something higher than mere reflection. It is not enough merely to catch the surface sheen of life. Modern art concerns itself, must concern itself, with penetrative interpretation. The drama is not only a mirror to reflect the surface of things, but also a Röntgen ray to penetrate the surface and reveal, beneath the outer integument, the fundamental frame-work and structure of modern life. The great dramatists are the brief and abstract chronometers of the time. "It is surely the great use of modern drama," says Pincro, "that while in its day it provides a rational entertainment, in the future it may serve as a history of the hour which gives it birth." This is perhaps the least service rendered by the drama: to serve as an historical record of the age. Many realistic critics maintain that the only works of art worth considering as historical are not those written in one epoch to give a view of the life or the events of some earlier epoch, but those which deal with the life of the time at which they are written, and have grown truly historical through the lapse of years. Ibsen's supremacy springs, not from his so-called historical dramas, of the type which Maeterlinck defines as "artificial poems that arise from the impossible marriage of past and present," but from his real historical dramas — his personal and social dramas of contemporary life.

All great minds, in contemplating the riddle of the human chimera and the disquieting mystery of life, must have realized, with Leibniz, that "every present is laden with the past and big with the future." A world-dramatist like Ibsen is the child of the past, the companion of the present, the progenitor of the future — trinity indissoluble. That he is the heir of the ages but increases his obligation to body forth with convincing truth the age in which he lives. Goethe maintained that, in order to know the man, it is necessary to know the age in which he lived. To no time in the world's history is this truth so apposite as to the present. The feeling of cosmic unity and the sentiment of social solidarity have so penetrated and informed the thought of to-day that no one questions the statement, as applied to the dominant personality, that the age helps to create the man and the man helps to create the age. Every epoch-making mind, it has been said, is at the same time child and father, disciple and master, of his age. The more fully he surrenders himself to it, the more fully will he control it. "Our pride and sense of human independence rebel against the belief that men of genius obey a movement quite as much as they control it, and even more than they create it," says John Addington Symonds. "We gain a new sense of the vitality and spiritual solidarity of human thought. At first sight the individual lessens; but the race, the mass from which the individual emerges and of which he becomes the spokesman and interpreter, gains in dignity and greatness. Shakspere is not less than he is, because we know him as necessary to a series. His eminence remains his own."

In this light, the masterpieces of modern drama appear, not as detached monuments of literary art, but as symbols of a growing world-spirit. We see in the evolution of the individual the evolution of the race, in the regeneration of the individual the regeneration of society. The study of the interpreter of life to-day resolves itself into a study of the vital phases of the struggle that is going on in humanity to-day.

IV

We are living to-day in an age of transition — the transition between criticism and faith. The nineteenth century was called the age of perhaps the greatest doubt and the greatest faith the world has ever known. Science, with its transforming theories, its destructive and far-reaching criticism, swept the world with the force of an avalanche. The world has had to be reconstituted. The new world is just now beginning to emerge, like the phoenix, from the ashes of the old. The laboratory method, the dissecting fever, the analytic spirit have permeated and given new form to every department of human life. Nothing was accepted as fact until placed under the microscope, or perhaps subjected to the bombardment of X-rays, or analyzed in a retort. So, to-day, we have a new psychology, a new art, a new medicine, a new sociology, a new religion. Everywhere modification and alteration, redistribution and readjustment.

The world demands the Truth to-day, for it has scientifically demonstrated the Biblical theorem that the truth shall make you free.

Under the influence of the conception of cosmic unity, tracing its origin to Auguste Comte and permeating all modern thought, society has grown to symbolize a vast wave which carries along the individual with it. The laws of its motion are fixed: if the individual resists, he is submerged. The individual is but a tiny atom tossed upon the surface of this turbulent wave. Government in many cases appears to mean the stifling of the wise and enlightened few by the will of the ignorant and thoughtless many.

The social compact often robs the individual of freedom.

From the standpoint of evolution, the individual is at war with his fellows. The long line of scientists, from Lamarck to Spencer, from Huxley to Haeckel, from Darwin to De Vries have held their solemn clinics and registered their stern verdict. The theories of unlimited competition, of the invariability of species, of the mutability of organic forms, of the survival of the fittest (or is it, perhaps, the survival of the most unscrupulous?) are pronounced by the vast majority to be laws as sure, inevitable and relentless as the facts of life and death. The struggle for existence is the stern reality the individual cannot shirk. This struggle is sharpened in direct proportion to the increase in the cost of the staple commodities of life. Competition becomes so fierce as to amount, in many cases, to oppression, elimination, destruction.

In certain lights, life takes on the guise of a brutal fight.

From the side of modern medicine and modern biology, a more sinister spectre robs the world of peaceful sleep. The scientist, the surgeon, the physician play the leading rôles in the drama of our life. Nerve strain, neurasthenia, mental collapse, physical ills of every sort beset and menace on all sides a world which has already passed the first flush of youth. The ghost of Hamlet's father is a less terrifying apparition than the spectres of our own brain. All men are not born free and equal — not even those born in the same rank of society. Do what we will, we cannot escape the influence of the past. Heredity lays its skeleton hand upon us and we enter the struggle for existence with the ineradicable taint of hereditary weakness or degeneracy gnawing like a vulture at our very vitals.

The sins of the fathers are visited upon the children even unto the third and fourth generation.

The modern theories of spiritualism, thought-transference and hypnotic suggestion fill our souls with awe and disquiet, and tend to depress our sense of human vitality. Such scientists as Myers, Hyslop, Lombroso, Lodge and a score of others, working both independently and through reputable societies for psychical research, are making slow, but persistent efforts to fret away the thin veil — if such there be! — between matter and spirit. In the minds of many, there remains little room for doubt, not simply of the control of mind over matter, but of the control of mind over mind, of spirit over spirit. The dominant will comes into the sphere of our life, exerts upon us its occult influence, and our weaker will succumbs.

Humanity is the dynamo of potential forces which

we cannot fathom. Hypnotism is the thief of individuality.

Ever since the beginning of the world until the last century, two different standards of conduct prevailed for men and women. For the two sexes there obtained two different sets of laws, two different codes of ethics, two different philosophies of life. Ever since Mary Wollstonecraft awoke the world with her *Vindication of the Rights of Woman;* ever since John Stuart Mill animadverted against the subjection of woman; ever since Henrik Ibsen declared in burning words that in the Workers and the Women he placed all his hopes for the future, and that for them he would work with all his strength — this age has won the right to the title: the age of Woman's Emancipation. Through the slow but titanic pressure of the feminist movement, woman is at last beginning to gain the freedom — economic, intellectual, moral, and even political! — which has so long been denied her. The true relation between man and woman as co-ordinate factors in human progress is at last coming to light.

The emancipation of woman, in the completest sense, is on the way.

This is an age marked by unsettled and conflicting views in regard to standards of morality. "Social progress," it has been said, "takes effect through the replacement of old institutions by new ones; and since every institution involves the recognition of the duty of conforming to it, progress must involve the repudiation of an established duty at every turn." The world has had its eyes opened to the flaws in our rough-and-ready morality by the rhapsodic invective of Nietzsche, the mordant irony of Ibsen, the impassioned zeal of Tolstoi, the enlightening satire of Bernard Shaw, the lightning humor of Mark Twain. Inequality of divorce laws in the different States of America, for example, makes a man who is a scoundrel in one State a respectable gentleman in another. Murders under the specious excuse of the "unwritten law" are only too tragically frequent. In some States, children, even before birth, may be willed or deeded away like chattels. The fundamental principles of right and wrong — whatever they are, no one seems to know them! — are, of course, eternal; but the conventional code of conduct, the "morality of custom," as Nietzsche termed it, cannot with justice be applied invariably and unexceptionally.

Conventional morality is a very untrustworthy standard for distinguishing between right and wrong. The great discovery of modern life is that society, not the individual, is at fault. Democratic government is on trial. We no longer boast, with Shakspere, of Man: noble in reason, infinite in faculty, in form and moving express and admirable, in action like an angel, in apprehension like a god, for we realize the sad botch he has made of the actual affairs of life. The humanizing influences of fraternal sympathy, of social pity and social justice must replace the more personal and selfish interests of the individual. Social criticism is the sign-manual of the age. Redemption for the individual is to be attained through a recognition of the intolerable injustices of modern society, and through consistent efforts at remedial and constructive measures for its reorganization. "There still remains in the depths of every heart of loyal intention," says Maeterlinck, "a great duty of charity and justice that eclipses all others. And it is perhaps from the struggle of this duty against our egoism and ignorance that the veritable drama of our century shall spring."

The sociologist, the social reformer, is destined to be the hero of the future.

With science as the active and dominant spirit of the age, to whose tests all questions are now-a-days subjected, we begin to gain some sort of perspective of the complex character of contemporary existence with which the interpreter of life has to deal. The insistent problems of the social complex, the evolution of the individual under the operation of the law of the survival of the fittest, the sociological doctrine of environment, the biological theories of heredity and temperament, the psychic phenomena of hypnotism and spiritualism, the great gulf fixed between social influence and social impotence, the hideous corruption of politics, business and finance, the increasing unrest and discontent of the laboring classes, the growing artificiality of metropolitan life, distrust in conventional standards of morality, partial and imperfect justice meted out to woman, widespread dissatisfaction with the grosser injustices and inequalities of society and its organization, and, permeating all, the relentless criticism of science and sociology — these are, in sum, the momentous problems of chiefest significance in contemporary life which demand adequate treatment, with the prospect of eventual solution, at the hands of the conscientious student of present-day conditions.

It is through his masterful exposition and treatment of many of these deep and ever-widening problems that Henrik Ibsen has attained to supreme eminence and authority in the drama of our time.

V

No extravagance lurks in the statement that Henrik Ibsen is the greatest Teutonic dramatist since Shakspere, and the greatest dramatist of any race or clime, of our modern era. Not until he served an apprenticeship of decades did he earn the right to that comprehensive characterization. It became his due only after years of preparatory preoccupation with the legendary, the poetic, the historical, and the romantic. Henrik Johan Ibsen was born on March 28, 1828, at Skien, Norway. Ibsen and Björnson are customarily classed together as the great Norwegian geniuses; and Ibsen has long borne the title of the Norwegian Seer. A Scoto-Dano-Teuton seems a more fitting, if more cumbrous, characterization for this so-called Norwegian. Genealogical researches, extending as far back as Ibsen's great-great-grandparents, indicate that Ibsen had not a drop of Norwegian blood in his veins. The three strains in his ancestry are Scotch, Danish and German. It is perhaps attaching no undue importance to hereditary influence to attribute the lyric delicacy and sensitiveness of his poetry to the Danish element in his blood, his uncompromising morality and high ethical standards to Scotch influence, and his passion for abstract logic to the threefold German strain.

The Stockmann house in which Ibsen was born faced an open square, on one side of which stood the town-pillory, on the other the mad-house and the lock-up; while the Latin school, the grammar schools and the church looked on as if in protest. It was under the shadow of such surroundings, with their oppressive atmosphere of solemnity and gloom, that the first years of Ibsen's youth were spent. The Ibsen family was prosperous, moved in the "best circles," and were inclined to the lavish in their hospitality. When Henrik was eight years old, financial disaster overtook the family, and they were forced to withdraw to a small farm house on the outskirts of the little town, where they lived in poverty and retirement. This sudden transition from affluence to poverty made a profound impression upon the eight-year-old child. Ibsen afterwards remarked that those who had taken most advantage of his parents' hospitality in their prosperous days were precisely those who now most markedly turned to them the cold shoulder. Ibsen never quite forgot the lesson thus early learned of the shallowness and insincerity of society. This was doubtless the initial influence in bringing to pass that crushing indictment of modern society which runs through all his middle and later dramas.

There was nothing full-blooded or athletic about the youthful Ibsen; he seems to have cared nothing for outdoor sports. His chief distraction came from shutting himself away in a private little room of his own, and poring for hours over musty tomes, rare prints, old engravings, and the like. According to his sister's account, the only outdoor amusement in which he indulged was the building of houses — of what material she does not say. As a boy, he loved to play the part of magician, to mystify his elders, and to perform, with his brother's aid, tricks of legerdemain. It is noteworthy that he had a passion for cutting out fantastically dressed little figures in pasteboard, attaching them to wooden blocks, and arranging them in groups or tableaux. It requires little imagination to see the dramatist in embryo here — the play of the constructive faculty, the passion for technical sleight-of-hand, the fundamental interest in the manipulation of fictitious characters. There is strong reason to believe that Ibsen kept up this early child's play — identifying imaginary characters with little material models — throughout his entire life.

Considerable talent for painting showed itself in the youthful Ibsen; and like Bernard Shaw after him, he had an ambition to be a great painter. But financial exigency forbade; and at the age of sixteen, Ibsen was apprenticed, not to a Norwegian Raphael or Danish Titian, but — to an apothecary. The anarchist in Ibsen, so often displayed in later years, was first aroused to literary expression by the Revolution of 1848. The ferment in Europe, Ibsen himself confessed, "had a strong and ripening effect on my development, immature though it remained both then and long afterwards. I wrote clangorous poems of encouragement to the Magyars, adjuring them, for the sake of freedom and humanity, not to falter in their righteous war against 'the tyrant'; and I composed a long series of sonnets to King Oscar — urging him to set aside all petty considerations, and march without delay, at the head of his army, to the assistance of our Danish brothers on the Slesvig frontier."

In the meantime, he devoted his time to preparing for his matriculation examination at Christiania University, where he purposed studying medicine. By a remarkable chance, the subject assigned him by the

University for examination was the Conspiracy of Catiline, to be studied in the history of Sallust and the oration of Cæsar. Ibsen relates that he "devoured these documents greedily"; and a few months later his first drama, *Catiline,* was finished. The opening lines of this play might serve as the prophecy of Ibsen's whole life work:

> "I must, I must; a voice is crying to me
> From my Soul's depths, and I will follow it."

This youth, so "spectral" as his companions called him, going about like an enigma sealed with seven seals, found a most congenial subject in the story of Catiline. For Ibsen felt himself at odds with the community in which he lived, and was fired to do something bold and daring. This play contained in vague outlines many of the features identified with his later work: "the opposition between power and enterprise, between will and potentiality, alike the tragedy and the comedy of humanity." His future methods are previsaged here in his employment of his own individual technique — a dark and ancient secret inaugurates the action and causes the catastrophe; while two women, the one all passion, the other all gentleness, struggle for the love of the hero. Sallust may have influenced Ibsen far more than did Cæsar, as Mr. Gosse suggests; but behind all, lurk the influences of the most important prose-writer of Norwegian romanticism, Mauritz Hansen, and of the distinguished poet and dramatist, Henrik Wergeland. The edition of *Catiline* with the exception of thirty copies which, strangely enough, found purchasers, was disposed of as waste paper to a huckster. "For the next few days," Ibsen laconically remarks, "we (his room-mate Schulrud, who published *Catiline* at his own expense, and himself) lacked none of the first necessities of life!"

The little one-act drama, *The Warrior's Tomb*, which Ibsen brought with him in an unfinished state from Bergen, was finally completed and accepted by the Christiania Theatre. Though little financial aid came from the three productions given at Christiania, Ibsen was greatly encouraged by the acceptance of the play. This trivial play, with its exterior comparisons between the South and the North, is noteworthy solely for its traces of Oehlenschlager's influence; if it were the sole extant fragment of Ibsen's work, he would never have been heard of. Its closing lines:

> "Dem Grab ensteigt dann Nordland hell und hehr:
> Zur Geistesthat auf des Gedankens Meer!"

foreshadow his youthful confidence in his own future. His poverty was extreme; had it not been for his exceptionally strong constitution, his health must inevitably have suffered. One of his acquaintances at this time recently wrote that "when Ibsen's financial condition compelled him to practice the most stringent economy, he tried to do without underclothing, and finally even without stockings. In these experiments he succeeded; and in winter he went without an overcoat; yet without being troubled by colds or other bodily ills."

In preparing for the University, Ibsen met Björnson, who described him at this time in the words (no wonder!):

> "languid and lean, with a complexion like gypsum,
> Behind an immense coal-black beard — Henrik Ibsen."

This was the beginning of that long acquaintance between the two great geniuses, blighted for a time rather by the misunderstandings of partisans than of the principals, but afterwards renewed with larger appreciation and deeper comprehension — a relation cemented by the marriage of Ibsen's son to Björnson's daughter. It is worth mentioning that Ibsen warmly espoused the labor movement at this early period, at one time narrowly escaping arrest and imprisonment. From this time until his death, though not active in its display, he felt a deep and abiding interest in the labor movement.

The financial siege was temporarily raised when Ole Bull, the great violinist, offered Ibsen the post of "theatre-poet" at the newly constituted National Theatre in Bergen. Though Ibsen's salary was less than $350 a year, it was eked out by travelling grants, and gave him his first real start in the world as a dramatist. In Grimstad, Ibsen had written *Catiline,* perhaps partly under the influence of Schiller; *The Warrior's Mound,* originally entitled *The Normans,* after the manner of Oehlenschlager, though with ruder touch; and in 1849, he had actually begun his work on *Olaf Trygvesön.* In 1850, probably in Christiania, Ibsen chose a motive from Faye's book of Norwegian folk-lore as the theme for *The Ptarmigan of Justedal;* but on the appearance of Landstad's book of Norwegian folk-songs, and after Ibsen had completed one act and part of another, he re-worked his material into the final form of *Olaf Liljekrans.* He later made a brief attempt at an opera, under the title of *The Ptarmigan;* but only one act and a tiny fragment of another was ever completed. The fragments of *The Ptarmigan of Justedal,* and of the opera-text *The Ptarmigan,* now for the first time published in Ibsen's *Posthumous Works,* are interesting solely from the biographical side.

It was one of Ibsen's duties as " theatre-poct " to have a new play ready for each recurrence of January 2, the " Foundation Day " of the theatre. On that day, in 1853, Ibsen produced his own romantic comedy of *St. John's Night.* Under the spell of the punch seasoned by a nixie with malicious intent, the two young people who are engaged find that, in reality, they love someone else — quite after the manner of *A Midsummer Night's Dream.* As in many future dramas of Ibsen, for instance, in *The League of Youth,* and *The Wild Duck,* an ancient wrong plays a decisive rôle in the play — in this case, cutting the Gordian knot, dissolving the betrothal, and sending all away happy, each Jack with his Jill. It betrays Ibsen's first attempt at an artful intrigue, so admirably achieved later in *Lady Inger of Oestraat,* the best of Ibsen's dramas written under French influence. Julius Poulsen, the mildly ludicrous poet and nationalist, in his own person reduces to absurdity the æsthetics of Heiberg; in him we recognize the prototype of both Peer Gynt and Hjalmar Ekdal. The whole drama may be construed as an effort to distinguish between true romance and false romanticism. Juliane's words:

> "I must suffer and be silent — ah! that is woman's lot in this world."

foreshadow Ingeborg's memorable words in *The Pretenders*:

> "To love, to sacrifice all, and be forgotten, that is woman's saga."

And clear prevision of *A Comedy of Love* lurks in Poulsen's words:

> "In the state of amorousness, one treats love theoretically. Betrothal and marriage on the other hand — you see — those are practical affairs — and in practice, as we know, theories do not always hold good."

PROPERTY OF
St. Joseph College Library
WEST HARTFORD, CONN.

Though not produced until 1857, *Olaf Liljekrans* had its first conception seven years earlier. It is woven from the ballad of Sir Olaf, lured away by a fairy just as he is on the way to bring home his bride, and the folk-tale of the wild, graceful young maiden of Justedal valley, roaming the woods like the shy ptarmigan. The story is trivial; and the characters are insipid. There is only one incident which points forward to the Ibsen of a maturer phase of art, the scene in which Hemming and Ingeborg, the impractical lovers, discover after their flight together that they are incapable of the sort of love which will sustain them through all privations. This motive was, in a later year, to furnish the impulse for the like predicament of Falk and Svanhild in *A Comedy of Love.*

The publication of Ibsen's *Posthumous Works* brings to light Ibsen's hitherto unpublished skit on current political affairs in Norway — much the sort of thing one frequently reads in New York *Life;* it is deserving of a word before entering into the deeper current of Ibsen's development as a dramatist in *Lady Inger of Oestraat.* When Ibsen came to Christiania in March, 1850, he was full of revolutionary ideas; and a year later he observed with satirical contempt the new Storthing abandoning the advanced position they had taken in 1848. One morning he visited the Tribune of the Storthing, and the same evening, while attending a performance of

Bellini's opera *Norma,* the idea of the political satire came into his head. In the little satire, Severus — otherwise Herr Stabell — flirts now with Norma (the Opposition), now with Adalgisa (the party in power); various other members of the Storthing are openly satirized. All the vaunted pretensions of adherence that Severus first makes to Norma are proven insincere in the end when Adalgisa throws around him her protection and transforms him into a demigod — or in other words, a Minister! The effect is magical: all, even Norma, bow down reverentially before him, acknowledging in the position of Minister, gained at whatever sacrifice of party fealty, the true goal of the legislator. Slight as it is, the little skit shows Ibsen in a lightly satirical mood; and points forward to the time when he will pour out the vials of his wrath and contempt upon compromise and half-heartedness in his own nation. It stands as a signpost to the Ibsen of *The League of Youth* and *An Enemy of the People.*

In 1854 Ibsen revived *The Warrior's Mound* at the National Theatre, without popular success; and in 1855, he presented at the same theatre *Lady Inger of Oestraat,* his first drama which possesses significance, not only as a link in his artistic development, but for its own striking and signal merits.

Lady Inger of Oestraat, a long, five-act play, is really a remarkable imaginative re-vitalization of the spirit of an epoch centuries past. Comparison of the drama with the facts of history reveals Ibsen's faculty for discovering a splendid dramatic situation in an unpromising historical episode. There is something mystic and crepuscular in the atmosphere of this dark tragedy; and yet its mystery is less the spell of mood, than the confusion that results from imperfect and mystifying technique. "Go back to Lady Inger," says Bernard Shaw, "and you will be tempted to believe that Ibsen was deliberately burlesquing the absurdities of Richardson's booth; for the action is carried on mostly in impossible asides." For the first time in his career, Ibsen reveals the influence of his studies, both of classic and contemporary drama. The Greek element imbues the story itself — the retributive justice of secret sin committed long anterior to the opening of the play — that retrospective method which Ibsen afterwards made so peculiarly his own. The complications and intrigues show the diligence with which Ibsen has studied the artificial methods of that dexterous contriver, Scribe. For the first time also in his career Ibsen displays real genius for deep characterization — alike in the queenly woman, apparently destined to free her people from the tyrant, yet harassed by the thought of her past transgressions; in Nils Lykke, the fascinating libertine, purified through his love for a high-souled, gentle woman; and Elina, Ibsen's first genuinely appealing female character. *Lady Inger of Oestraat* was not a success — failing to please the playgoers of Bergen and not wholly satisfying Ibsen himself. Nor is this to be wondered at; for Ibsen was fumbling with technical methods, obsolescent and derivative, not yet having discovered his own original fingering for the dramatic keyboard. This dark drama, reminiscent now of *Macbeth,* now of Websterian violence and blood, now of German romanticism, now of Scribe, is striking, but imperfectly conceived. Genuinely interesting as a strong link in the evolution of Ibsen's art, as a step in the historical development of contemporary drama it is virtually negligible.

In *The Feast at Solhaug,* produced at the Bergen Theatre on January 2, 1856, Ibsen achieved his first genuine local success. He was recalled again and again to the footlights, was serenaded, made a speech, and afterwards confessed that he was quite happy over it all. The play spread abroad his fame throughout the Scandinavian countries and Denmark. Its popularity is scarcely explainable to-day, except from the fact that the play is in the line of classic Norwegian development. The extravagant and melodramatic plot possesses no permanent human interest; and the only noteworthy feature it possesses, in its relation to the development of Ibsen's art, is the situation which Ibsen employs again and again in later plays; the placing of a man between two women who struggle for his love, the one fiery and passionate, the other gentle and tender. It lends confirmation to the belief that, instead of enlarging his horizon, Ibsen tends rather to intensification of method — digging deeper and ever deeper into the sub-stratum of human feeling and human consciousness.

We come now to a turning-point in Ibsen's career as a dramatic artist. He has abandoned forever the romantic ballad — it has given him all it had to give. His career as director of the theatre at Bergen is at an end, and he has only one notable play to his credit — *Lady Inger of Oestraat.* And yet this five-years' apprenticeship at Bergen may be said to mark the turning-point in Ibsen's life. This blind step in the dark, taken in the magnificent rashness of youth, was the definitive step in his career as a dramatist. The Bergen apprenticeship enabled him, through experimenting with and discarding the technical methods of others, to discover his own individual and unique methods of dramatic procedure. Like Antoine, Clarètie or Granville Barker, Ibsen has learned, through precept, practice and example, the arts of theatre management, of stage technique, of dramaturgy. From this time forward we discover in Ibsen, not a Norwegian bungler in drama, but a great world-dramatist. Ibsen's drama now belongs to the future.

VI

In 1857, Ibsen was appointed director of the Norwegian Theatre at Christiania. Now began another six-year period, the most painful in Ibsen's life. He had to fight not only for the existence of himself and his family — for he was married in 1856 — but actually for the very existence of Norwegian poetry and the Norwegian stage. While looking for a subject that would display, in broad and primitive forms, the clash of characters in an ancient Norwegian family, he fell upon the *Volsung Saga.* By dramatizing a particular episode, he hoped to raise the national epic material to a higher degree of artistic valuation. It is a mark of the struggle between Ibsen's realistic mind and his romantic temperament that the aim evolved was to present, not the mythic world, but the life of Norway in primitive times. Ibsen accomplished his purpose by employing prose as a medium instead of poetry, discovering in the event that the play was more poetical in prose than in verse. The result was an authentically dramatic, finely executed achievement.

The Vikings at Helgeland is the tragedy of the man who has taken the credit of another man's deed — a theme of vicarious sacrifice exploited by Rostand with notable success in *Cyrano de Bergerac.* In Ibsen's play, the strong, passionate heroic woman, Hjördis, whose father was killed in a viking raid, has lived from girlhood in the conqueror's home. Sigurd and his friend Gunnar come, see and are conquered by her; she, secretly loving the fearless Sigurd, promises herself to him who kills the bear. Disguised in Gunnar's armor, Sigurd wins the maid for his friend.

The tragedy begins when Gunnar, committed to the secret, has to suffer the torment of listening to the praises of his deed — a deed which he has not only not performed, but which he was incapable of performing. His secret becomes a ghastly burden. The tragedy sharpens in intensity when, as Gunnar's wife, Hjördis discovers that the man she loves was he who really won her. There is a limit to self-sacrifice, she proudly tells him — and no man may with impunity give to his friend the woman he loves. Hjördis is most cruel to him she most loves, slaying him that they may go out together upon the winds.

There is something of the sublime horror of ancient days — as well as of its primitive strength and unsullied emotions — in this play. And doubtless Ibsen meant it as a tonic, an invigorant for a generation sated with cheap emotionalism, rank insincerity and forgotten loyalty. The play aroused violent opposition, was decried on all sides, and left Ibsen more depressed than ever. Next he turns to *The Comedy of Love* — only to rouse a tempest about his ears. Once more he returns to the sagas, in the hope of bettering his former effort and winning real renown. The new play is known as *The Pretenders,* though a more correct translation would be *The Stuff from which Kings are Made.* Here we have the tragedy of the man who steals the thought of another — just as, in *The Vikings at Helgeland,* we have the tragedy of the man who steals the deed of another. Georg Brandes says in a classic passage:

"In *The Pretenders* two figures again stand opposed to one another as the superior and the inferior beings . . . It is towards this contrast that Ibsen has hitherto unconsciously directed his endeavors, just as Nature feels her way in her blind preliminary attempts to form new types. Hakon and Skule are pretenders to the same throne, scions of royalty out of which a king may be made. But the first is the incarnation of fortune, victory, right and confidence; the second — the principal figure in the play, masterly in its truth and originality — is the brooder, a prey to inward struggles and endless distrust, brave and ambitious, with perhaps every qualification and claim to be king, but lacking the inexpressible somewhat that would give a value to all the rest. . . . 'I am a king's arm,' he says, 'mayhap a king's brain as well; but Hakon is the whole king.' 'You have wisdom and courage, and all noble gifts of the mind,' says Hakon to him; 'you are born to stand nearest a king, but not to be a king yourself.'"

There is one signally momentous passage in the

play deserving of quotation. Skule eagerly asks the old Skald:

"What gift do I need to become a King?"

"My lord," replied the Skald, "you *are* a King!"

Then Skule utters the thought that is eating its cankerous way into his soul:

"Have you, at all times, full faith that you *are* a Skald?"

Here is a strange mingling of that truth and poetry, that *Wahrheit* and *Dichtung* of which Goethe wrote so eloquently. As Gosse says: "It is by no means extravagant to see in the noble emulation of the dukes in *The Pretenders* some reflection of Ibsen's attitude toward the youthful and brilliant Björnson. The luminous self-reliance, the ardor and confidence and good fortune of Björnson-Hakon could not but offer a violent contrast with the gloom and hesitation, the sick revulsions of hope and final lack of conviction of Ibsen-Skule. . . . 'The luckiest man is the greatest man,' says Bishop Nicholas in the play, and Björnson seemed in those melancholy years as lucky as Ibsen was unlucky." Björnson was upborne by the favor of the populace; Ibsen worked without favor and without support. And yet, as Rudyard Kipling says, "He rides fastest who rides alone." This was Ibsen's darkest hour. The end is not yet.

VII

Henrik Ibsen began his trilogy of satires with a play as provocative, as piquant as it is satirical. It is the work of a prisoner of hope, a baffled idealist: Ibsen is seeking to chastise his own Norwegian people by painting them just as he saw them, without fear or favor. A daring novel, *The Sheriff's Daughters,* by Camilla Collett, was creating a profound sensation in Norway. This novel, a harbinger of the new thought movement in Norway, was a vigorous attack upon the marriage of convenience. That no marriage not based on love can be happy, was the book's thesis. Depressed by meagre success, harassed by financial embarrassment, Ibsen was in no mood to accept so roseate a view belied so utterly by the conditions he saw around him. No play of Ibsen's has been handled so crudely by the critics as *The Comedy of Love,* this most diaphanous structure of light satire. *Svanhild,* now for the first time spread before us in the *Nachgelassene Schriften,* was begun as early as 1856; the play was finally completed in 1862. It was begun in prose, and completed in rhymed iambics; and the original draft contains nothing critically noteworthy. But it is of the highest importance to note that in a letter to Clemens Petersen (Aug. 10, 1863), lately published, Ibsen frankly confesses: "As to *The Comedy of Love,* I can assure you that if ever it was necessary for an author to rid himself of a sentiment and a subject it was so with me when I began that work." *The Comedy of Love* is the image of an evanescent mood: it was Ibsen's way of getting rid of it.

Perhaps the most noteworthy passage in the play, is a scene which may have furnished the model for the "auction-scene" in Bernard Shaw's *Candida*. Guldstad, the wealthy, shrewd old merchant, gives the counsel of golden common sense, which induces the lovers — the poet Falk and the idealistic Svanhild — to part.

> Hear a golden counsel, then.
> Use your experience; watch your fellow-men,
> How every loving couple struts and swaggers
> Like millionaires among a world of beggars.
> They scamper to the altar, lad and lass,
> They make a home, and drunk with exultation,
> Dwell for awhile within its walls of glass.
> Then comes the day of reckoning — but, alas,
> They're bankrupt, and their house in liquidation!
> Bankrupt the bloom of youth on woman's brow;
> Bankrupt the flower of passion in her breast,
> Bankrupt the husband's battle-ardor now,
> Bankrupt each spark of passion he possessed.
> Bankrupt the whole estate, below, above —
> And yet this broken pair were once confessed
> A first-class house in all the wares of love.

Tennyson says that it is better to have loved and lost than never to have loved at all. Ibsen maintained — not in a general philosophical way, but with respect to the conditions he saw immediately around him — that it is better, if youthfully, romantically in love, to separate, rather than to marry. Ibsen is in agreement with the brilliant Frenchman who asserted that all comedies end with a wedding, because it is then that the tragedy begins! Ibsen was so much the observer, with the added divination of the poet, that in this play he almost achieved the distinction of a philosophical distillation of the real essence of love. Mirrored in his mood at the moment, love appeared to Ibsen as one of two things: either a dead, dull thing, a mere surfeit; or else the evanescent flame of the moment, or, to change the figure, a glass of champagne upon the board of life. There was, in Ibsen's vision, another deeper love, which he found not until *When We Dead Awaken* — if Falk and Svanhild had only possessed the true faith in the self-sustaining power of love, Ibsen means, they would never have parted. This is the materialistic flaw in the structure of modern life. For the inevitable erotic illusion, Ibsen betrays no scorn; he reserves his contempt for the decay of character consequent to the acceptance of the vulgar convention of the legal union, by this frail and weak-hearted generation. The play is a comedy, *not* a philosophy; Ibsen sought only, to use his own accurate words, to represent "the contrast in our present state of society between the actual and the ideal in all that relates to love and marriage." It is futile and beside the mark to point out Ibsen's one-sidedness in making no allowance for the vast number of happy marriages based upon love, and in valuing the memory of a beautiful love above the humanizing responsibilities of consecrated marriage, the enfranchising bonds of partnership and parenthood. How stupid — in face of the parting between Falk and Svanhild:

Falk (softly to Svanhild) —

God bless thee, bride of my life's dawn;
Where'er I be, to nobler deed thou'lt wake me.

Svanhild (looks after him a moment, then says softly, firmly:)

Now over is my life, by lea and lawn.
The leaves are falling — now the world may take me.

Ibsen clearly points out that, in the life around him, creature comforts are valued far above the sustaining power of love — and when Georg Brandes, urging the claim of ideal engagements eventuating in ideal marriages, remarked: "You know there are sound potatoes and rotten potatoes in the world," Ibsen replied with a cynicism, as light as it is sharp: "I am afraid none of the sound potatoes have come under my observation." The tone of *The Comedy of Love* as an attack on love and marriage branded Ibsen as an "immoral" (!) writer — a charge which a lifetime of blameless conduct alone could dissipate.

From Rome, after a space, came a momentous message. The frustration of an idealistic human spirit by the savage irony of reality is the theme of *Brand;* and its artistic temper at once ranges it in the category of *Hamlet, Manfred* and *Faust.* The epic-fragment discovered by Pontoppidan and recently published, with its souvenirs of Heiberg and Welhaven, prompts the wish that Ibsen had adhered to his original intention. For whatever the medium, *Brand* is essentially an epic. Brand himself is a figure of heroic, even Titanic mold, arraigning all compromise with his ideals of Christianity before the bar of Heaven. The God of his worship is the God of the Old Testament, animated with wrath and indignation against a faltering generation. What Brand (like Ibsen himself — who confessed that he *was* Brand, in his best moments) desires is so radical a revolution of the spirit of man that the spirit of compromise in man will be chained and buried forever from sight. As priest and man, he is determined to champion at any and all costs the cause of things, not as they seem, not even as they are, but as he is convinced they *should* be. Man's self-development is his highest duty; concessions to the world take the form of evil and temptation. The only way to develop one's self is to stand free and to stand alone. Brand's motto, "All or Nothing," is the logical epitome of his point of view.

Brand is a terrible arraignment of the half-hearted pietism of the Norwegian people. And yet Brand's ideal of pietism is an ideal unattainable: it cannot survive the shock of reality. Brand is the pictorial projection of a splendidly hopeless, idealistic dream. Cervantes in *Don Quixote* portrayed the bankruptcy of chivalry in collision with the brutal facts of life; so Ibsen in *Brand* portrays the bankruptcy of the pietistic ideal as soon as it is brought into collision with sordid reality. As soon as he put his faith to the test of acts, Brand brought nothing but suffering upon all whom he loved; he had reared a castle in the clouds which none — not even himself — might inhabit.

In Peer Gynt, the brilliant, formless, parti-colored pendant to *Brand,* Ibsen shows to the world the other side of the Norwegian people. Peer Gynt has for ideal the utterly selfish gratification of his own individuality — regardless of all the rest of the world. He glows with the desire to be romantic, but he has not the will or the courage to do the romantic thing; so he takes it all out in romancing. His ideal of man is a sort of demi-god and super-braggart combined, of all-conquering will — a masterful fellow, a "magerful man," a fascinating dog whom no woman can refuse, a born fighter, a gallant knight. But Peer soon discovers that no such bird of paradise has ever sung in the world-concert. The only thing left for him, in his disillusion, is to weave illusions about himself, and even to imagine that he is the hero of his own romantic lies. Peer Gynt is the tremendous prototype of Sentimental Tommy. After many adventures, by sea and by land, Peer returns home in the end, a pitiful and hopeless failure in all save worldly goods. He cannot gain admittance even to hell; for even as a sinner, he is only second-rate. He has lacked the greatness to sin greatly. He must go at once into the crucible of the great Button-Molder, be melted down and cast again. For, after all, he is only base metal.

Ibsen's effort is to arouse the world, to open its eyes to a freer, richer future, to point out the need for ridding itself of false ideals — ideals which cannot be realized in acts. Not the least strange feature of Ibsen's career is the fact that he started from the innermost depths of romanticism. Only gradually and painfully did he work himself up and out of the slough of romanticism on to the firm ground of realism, and into the pure air of freedom and truth. Ibsen has come now to the end of romanticism. All his discouragements and disappointments, the apathy, indifference and hostility he experienced, bred in him a spirit of discontent and revolt. This revolt is going to find expression in a long and detailed exposure of modern civilization, its venerable and antiquated institutions, its shallow and outworn ideals, its feebly conventional morals, its pettiness, weakness and hypocrisy. Hereafter we see Ibsen probing the secrets of the age. "My vocation is to question, not to answer;" so he expresses the world-thoughts that are in the air, voices the spirit of the age, taps the moral coin of the era only to find it debased or counterfeit. Ibsen now begins a new career: the breach with his country sounds in his sardonic lines, written in July, 1872:

My countrymen, who filled for me deep bowls
Of wholesome bitter medicine, such as gave
The poet, on the margin of his grave,
Fresh force to fight where broken twilight rolls,—
My countrymen, who sped me o'er the wave,
An exile, with my griefs for pilgrim-robes,
My fears for burdens, doubts for staff, to roam,—
From the wide world I send you greeting home.

* * * * * * * *

I send you thanks for gifts that help and harden,
  Thanks for each hour of purifying pain;
Each plant that springs in my poetic garden
  Is rooted where your harshness poured its rain;
Each shoot in which it blooms and burgeons forth
It owes to that gray weather from the North;
The sun relaxes, but the fog secures!
My country, thanks! My life's best gifts were yours.

VIII

Artificial as it is under any exalted standard of dramatic art, *The League of Youth* marks a point of departure of incalculable importance in Ibsen's career. At last he has discovered the true medium for the society comedy — the terse, pliant prose of daily speech. While this play exhibits all the earmarks of Ibsen's apprenticeship in the school of Scribe, it betrays marked independence and originality — in the realistic coloring of the dialogue, the prosaic naturalness of the conversations, and the omission of all monologues and asides. It is what Ibsen calls a "peaceful work" — the product, not of wine and walnuts, so to speak, but of Budweiser and Bologna. This satire upon the prevailing political conditions in Norway is provincial, indeed suburban, in tone; and gives an excellent handle to Ibsen's detractors. No wonder it caused an uproar — being a blow at Björnson, or at least, as Ibsen claimed, at his lie-steeped clique! One cannot blame Björnson for royal indignation over what he termed Ibsen's "attempted assassination." The play is a complex of intrigues; and misunderstandings and mishaps play a large part in the action. The greatest merit of the play is its foreshadowing of the modern woman. At one point, little Selma Bratsberg vehemently exclaims: "Oh, how you have maltreated me — shamefully maltreated me, all of you together! You have always compelled me to receive, and never permitted me to give. You have never required the least sacrifice of me, nor laid upon me the slightest weight of care.

When I asked to share your burdens, you put me off with a flattering jest. How I hate and detest you! You have brought me up to be dandled like a doll, and to be played with, as one plays with a child." In this speech is found the seed of that revolt against the false standard for women then in vogue. Brandes told Ibsen that the character of Selma did not have sufficient scope, and urged Ibsen to write another play to that end. Ibsen brooded over that suggestion, and in Nora, of *A Doll's House,* he created a Selma with the wide world for scope.

Professor Lorenz Dietrichson, Ibsen's life-long friend, once told me, when I visited him in Rome, that it was he who first directed Ibsen's attention to the career of the Emperor Julian. In this monumental work of imagination and philosophic conflict, the labor of years, Ibsen achieved neither a great drama for the stage, in which the characters " stand solidly in the light of their time," nor a fundamentally coherent philosophical synthesis. This " world-historic " drama, in two parts of five acts each, *Cæsar's Apostasy* and *The Emperor Julian,* purports to portray Ibsen's deepest spiritual experiences through the medium of the soul of Julian, the theatre for the warring religious tenets of the ancient and modern worlds. Instead of showing us a supreme world-figure, consistently evolving under the pressure of profound conviction, Ibsen projects a colossal egomaniac, victim of philosophic dilettantism. As *Brand* stood for rigorous fidelity to an idea, and *Peer Gynt* for the disciplinary bankruptcy of laxity, *Emperor and Galilean* stands for the struggle towards the golden mean, the higher synthesis of truth. In his effort at the reconciliation of pagan beauty and Christian Truth, Julian is a tragic failure — for, having repudiated his mission, he cannot achieve the "vision splendid" of the "Third Empire, in which the twin-natured shall reign."

One prose play intervenes between *The League of Youth* and *A Doll's House* — the play with which Ibsen conquered Germany. German critics extravagantly confessed: "We found our æsthetic creed — our young eyes were opened by it to all the theatric artificiality of the day. We trembled with joy." How strangely these words sound — in view of the theatric artificiality so patent to-day in *The Pillars of Society,* Ibsen's first attempt at the "photography by comedy" which Björnson had urged on Ibsen eight years before.

Consul Bernick, the protagonist of the play, is a pillar of society in his native town — its leading citizen and financier. His is a model home; his firm enjoys an established reputation; he himself is looked up to as a man of high honor and business integrity. But this pillar of society has for foundation the treacherous sands of sham, hypocrisy and lies. In his youth, Bernick had been guilty of grave indiscretions, financial and sexual, the blame for which he succeeded in foisting upon his brother-in-law. In his youth, Bernick betrayed the woman he loved in order to marry an heiress. He builds his house and reputation upon this insecure foundation. He lives a triple lie — to his wife, to his brother-in-law, to the sweetheart of his youth. In the end, his early sweetheart, aided by circumstances, brings him to a realization of the hypocrisy of his position; and he is brought sharply face to face with the alternative of silence and success, or revelation and ruin. Fortified by the noble counsel of his former sweetheart he confesses all — to his wife, and to his fellow-townsmen assembled *en masse* to do him honor. In the end, he declares that the true and faithful women are the pillars of society; but his former sweetheart replies: "No, no; the spirits of Truth and Freedom — these are the Pillars of Society." These spirits Ibsen invokes again and again in his later plays — that truth which means unfaltering recognition of fact and unflinching facing of reality, that freedom which connotes enfranchisement from the false ideals of a false society.

As a realistic picture of modern life, *The Pillars of Society* is noteworthy; and it is deserving of record that the crucial incident of *The Indian Girl* found its origin in Samuel Plimsoll's agitation in England, fully reflected in the press of Norway, for proper legal regulations concerning insurance upon unseaworthy crafts. As a drama, its technique is very vulnerable: Ibsen has not yet written his complete declaration of independence from the school of Scribe. Moreover, it is conventional, both in treatment and solution. Misrepresentation, evil and intrigue prevail for a time; wrong rules while waiting justice sleeps. In the end comes retribution — right prevails and truth is triumphant. But in reality Bernick is reformed, not by conflict with fate, but by providential intervention with a sort of death-bed-repentance effect at the end. Not otherwise are reformed the fascinating villains of the Adelphi. *The Pillars of Society* is a melodrama of the morals.

In *A Doll's House,* Ibsen first definitively sounded the trumpet-call of woman's freedom. This is his first drama wholly modern in tendency. The *dénouement* is so startling, so tremendous, so anti-social that when Francisque Sarcey first saw it in Paris, he threw up his hands in horror, declaring that he didn't understand a word of it. Here, in advanced maturity of technique, we behold the struggle of the modern woman against the vitiating influence of her environment, her heredity, and the social conventions which retard her development as an individual and as a human being.

The story is so familiar that it needs no recital here. The real significance of the play consists as

HENRIK IBSEN

much in Ibsen's attitude towards the "Woman Question" as in Nora's method of solution. Ibsen entered the lists as woman's champion, not in a partisan spirit, but because he realized that the cause of woman was the cause of humanity. It was an evolutionary growth of his spirit from the days when he tragically pictured woman as under the necessity of self-sacrifice and service for others. The "Woman Question," with Ibsen, was not a mere question of the vote — he wished women to secure such representation whenever her talents and sense of responsibility entitled her thereto. But to Ibsen, the "Woman Question" meant primarily the question as to the position of woman in marriage — as exemplified in *A Doll's House, Ghosts* and *The Wild Duck*. Even in the preliminary draft for *A Doll's House,* Nora observes that the laws are made by man, and that contemporary society means a society for men, not a society for human beings. It is a mark of Ibsen's human insight, as well as of his artistic detachment, that, in Nora, he reveals the New Woman still deeply rooted in the old Eve. She still employs all the arts of cajolery, of waywardness, of personal fascination for securing her own ends. And yet, even in the midst of that mad, despairing tarantella, we know that the old Eve is about to tear away the mask which conceals the modern woman. From Schopenhauer, Ibsen passed under the influence of the evolutionary theories of

Darwin and Spencer. In *A Doll's House,* Nora furnishes a striking illustration of the inheritance of characteristics; and we feel very strongly that, in another environment, Krogstad might have been an honorable citizen of society. From the tragic spectacle of Dr. Rank, Nora first grasps the principle of hereditary responsibility; and her spiritual development springs from the fixed conviction that she can become responsible for the welfare of her children only by gaining responsibility for herself and acquiring knowledge of society through contact with the great world. Environment, the treatment she has received from her father and her husband, has cultivated in her all the weaker and none of the stronger elements of her nature. She realizes, in Ibsen's own words, that everyone " shares the responsibility and guilt of the society to which he (or she!) belongs."

The continuity of Ibsen's development is strikingly revealed in one artistic quality. Later entire dramas are foreshadowed in single characters and episodes of some preceding play. John Gabriel Borkman is prefigured in Consul Bernick; the auxiliary figure of Ellida Wangel in *The Lady From the Sea* becomes the heroine of *The Master-Builder;* the tragic figure of Dr. Rank as the victim of parental incontinence becomes the more poignantly tragic figure of Oswald Alving in *Ghosts.* Society held up its hands in holy horror because Nora abandoned her children rather than surrender her individuality; but instead of shaking, this only confirmed Ibsen in his conviction that "the time had come for some boundary posts to be removed." In *Ghosts,* Ibsen gives his terrible answer to the question: "Do the children really benefit by the mother's surrender in living a lie in marriage?" The conditions of Nora Helmer and Helen Alving are by no means identical; nor were any such disastrous consequences prophesied for the children of the morally upright Helmer as fell to the lot of the son of the dissolute Chamberlain Alving. Nor is it at all clear that Helen Alving was acting with poise and entire sanity in throwing herself at the head of Pastor Manders. But it is perfectly clear that Helen Alving, by remaining in the hideous bonds of a bargain-and-sale marriage forced upon her by the pressure of her mother, her two aunts and her minister, committed a great wrong. And her final revolt was so subversive, so wide a swing of the pendulum from the mark of sanity, as to accentuate her feminine extravagance to the detriment of the purposed import of the play.

Ghosts aroused a tornado of abuse unequalled, it may be, in the history of the drama. Even to-day this play is forbidden production in Great Britain; and the King's Reader of Plays, before a Parliamentary Commission, recently expressed the conviction that it would never be allowed production in Great Britain. It is generally conceded to be the strongest, most terrible play of the nineteenth century. In 1898, Otto Brahm, the distinguished German critic, wrote: "The gates to the most modern German drama were opened when *Ghosts* first appeared on a German stage." William Archer termed *Ghosts* the harbinger of the whole dramatic movement in Europe, and Georg Brandes said that it was, if not the greatest achievement, at any rate the noblest action of the poet's career. In it, Ibsen finally concretizes his faith in the human being's right to happiness. Its basis is found, not in Kirkegaard, Schopenhauer or any European thinker, but in John Stuart Mill who, in his *Utilitarianism* (translated into Danish by Georg Brandes in 1872), posits "an existence, possibly free from sorrow and possibly rich in joy, in quality as well as in quantity." To Mill is doubtless attributable Ibsen's dramatic formulation of man's right to happiness. In dramatic technique, *Ghosts* is superb — the retrospective method of Greek tragedy brought to perfection. A performance I once witnessed in Christiania, by a notable cast, left a most profound impression upon me; and yet the most significant features of the play as then presented were its marked provincialism in that peculiarly local setting, and the interpretation, in Manders, of the normal Norwegian parson of half a century or more ago as an incredibly snivelling and contemptible hypocrite. One of the most profoundly moving exhibitions of human emotion I can conceive of was given in the interpretation of Helen Alving, not by Ola Hansson, but by Miss Mary Shaw. In *Ghosts*, Ibsen gives enduring dramatic exemplification to the memorable words of Maurice Maeterlinck: "We know that the dead do not die. We know that it is not in our churches they are to be found, but in the houses, the habits of us all."

When *Ghosts* awoke in Norway a positive howl of execration that resounded throughout Europe, Ibsen could restrain himself no longer. He had come to the limit of his endurance of the obloquy that had been heaped upon him ever since the days of *The Comedy of Love*. His conception of the function of the dramatist had gradually enlarged; he now unfalteringly assumed responsibility for the morals of others. Hitherto, with solemn periodicity, Ibsen's plays had followed each other at intervals of two years. *An Enemy of the People* was conceived and executed with passionate haste in the spring and summer months of 1882. This gay, yet intense play, so humorous and yet so trenchant, is devoid of all genuine "love-interest"; it is Ibsen's most polemic play.

The impulsive, choleric Dr. Stockmann discovers that the baths of his native town, a celebrated health resort, are contaminated. Instead of possessing healing and life-giving properties, in reality the mineral water spreads contagion and disease. Scornfully disregarding the fact that the baths are the greatest source of revenue for the town, Stockmann exposes to the leaders of the community his discovery of the crime they are committing against society. But the most valued possession of the pillars of society hangs in the balance: their "graft" will dwindle to nothing, if they are forced to vast expenditure for the purpose of ascertaining and obliterating the source of contamination. With sublime effrontery, characteristic of a Tweed or a Ruef, the owners of the baths disregard Stockmann's revelations; and through clever but specious arguments, they secure the support of the majority of the community. "It will disturb business" and "threaten prosperity"— ah, what familiar words here in America! Then only does Stockmann awake to a realization that, not merely are the baths contaminated, but the very well-springs of the society in which he lives are poisoned at their sources. This he bravely and defiantly proclaims with all the force of a scientific muck-raker at a tremendous mass-meeting. He is declared an enemy of the people, ostracized, stoned.

An Enemy of the People is Ibsen's dramatic incarnation of his gradually matured theory that the minority is always right. He had a firm faith in that "saving remnant," the minority; he rested his hope, as he said, upon the "minority which leads the van and pushes on to points which the majority has not yet reached." It is not Public Opinion, the Majority, which improves the prevailing order of the world, but

> "Tall men, sun-crowned, who live above the fog,
> In public duty and in private thinking."

Ibsen regarded himself as a "solitary franc-tireur at the outposts"; and he wrote to Brandes from Rome on January 3, 1882: "I receive more and more corroboration of my conviction that there is something demoralizing in engaging in politics and in joining parties. It will never, in my case, be possible for me to join a party that has the majority on its side. Björnson says: 'The majority is always right.' And as a practical politician he is bound, I suppose, to say so. I, on the contrary, must of necessity say: 'The minority is always right.'"

Strangely enough, Ibsen has confessed that Björnson, as well as Jonas Lie, was in his mind when he drew the picture of the bluff, spontaneous, genial Stockmann. Ibsen confessed to Hegel that he got along famously with Stockmann: "We agree on so many subjects. But the doctor is a more muddle-headed person that I am." He may even have had Brandes in mind, at times. But it has recently come to light that the most obvious model for Stockmann was Harold Thaulow, the father of the painter and the cousin of Henrik Wergeland. He was by nature an agitator, a reformer, who deeply loved his people and yet was continually in hot water through his effort to reform them. Only two weeks before his death, at the General Assembly of February 23, 1881, he made a violent attack upon the society known as "Dampf-Küche." He declared that there was no greater humbug in Christiania than this society, and continued for three-quarters of an hour in this strain. The colloquy which ensued, reproduced in the *Aftenpost,* leaves no doubt as to Ibsen's source for the leading feature of *An Enemy of the People.*

Thaulow: I won't permit my mouth to be shut (continues his address).

Consul Heftye: Herr Thaulow must stop!

Thaulow (reads on). Some express their disapproval by ostentatiously walking around the hall.

The president asks the assembly whether it recognizes his right to refuse Herr Thaulow the floor. Unanimous assent.

The president again requests Herr Thaulow to desist.

Thaulow: I won't permit my mouth to be shut.

President: Then we will proceed with the order of the day —

Thaulow: I will cut it very short (reads on).

Heftye: May he read on?

Thaulow (continues): "The splendid result of the Christiania 'Dampf-Küche' . . ." I'm almost through —

Heftye: At this rate the General Assembly will go to pieces.

President: I am sorry I have to interrupt Herr Thaulow. You mustn't speak —

Thaulow reads on.

Heftye: Stop — or you must leave the hall.

Thaulow: Just one word more (sinks exhausted into a chair).

The president now proceeds with the reading of the official report.

Thaulow listens grumblingly to the report, and several times makes an effort to gain a hearing.

When the opposition became too strong, he finally gave up the struggle and went away with the words: "I will have nothing more to do with you. I am tired of casting pearls before swine. This is infernal misuse among a free people in a free society. Well — my respects to you — go on, then, to your family meal!"

IX

The Wild Duck is Ibsen's first step along a new path. This is true in a double sense. Heretofore, Ibsen has been giving very positive, very defiant solutions to the questions he himself has posed. In many cases, he even goes so far as to formulate his solution of the dramatic complex in a single momentous action or even in a memorable, solitary phrase. *The Wild Duck* first fully justifies Ibsen's statement that his vocation was to question rather than to answer. No one was so sure of this as

Ibsen himself; he said that, to all, this play offered "problems worth the solving." Moreover, its point of departure, in another striking phase, is proclaimed by Ibsen in the words: "This new play in some ways occupies a place apart among my productions; its method of development is in many respects divergent from that of its predecessors." To Mr. Archer, *The Wild Duck* is a consummation rather than a new departure. A strange judgment, in view not only of Ibsen's own words, but also in view of the patent fact that here, for the first time, Ibsen sets his foot in the alien path of symbolism,—that symbolism so strangely interwoven in *Rosmersholm,* so mystic in *Little Eyolf,* so magically potent in *The Lady From the Sea!* The disquieting figure of the wounded wild duck, suggested to Ibsen as a dramatic symbol by Welhaven's beautiful poem *The Sea Bird,* flutters mysteriously through this disturbing play — symbolizing now the wounded soul of Werle, now the "evil genius of the house" (baldly stated in the "forework"), now the symbolic adumbration of the fateful secret of Hedwig's parentage bequeathed by the old Werle to the Ekdal family.

It is usual for critics to find in *The Wild Duck* an expression of Ibsen's dark pessimism, distrust in his mission, incipient disbelief in "the claim of the ideal." It is interpreted as a reaction against the dogmatic "All or Nothing" of *Brand,* against

Stockmann's cocksureness in the virtue of his mission in *An Enemy of the People*. In *The Wild Duck,* does Ibsen merely question whether "the bitter tonic-draught of truth" is the fundamental pre-requisite for the happiness and well-being of humanity, as it now is, or even as it may be for Heaven knows how long yet to come? This seems to me to be a superficial judgment. The real problem around which Ibsen's mind continually hovered was the problem, for the individual, of discovering himself in life. In the very year in which he wrote *The Wild Duck,* Ibsen spoke, not once, but twice, in letters, of "the duty and the right, of realizing one's self." Self-realization, in its amplest sense, for Ibsen, means not only the discovery of one's mission, but also the discovery of the great meaning, the great happiness even, that life holds for the individual soul. *The Wild Duck* is a dark and ironic commentary upon the wrong-headed reformer, who would turn the world upside down in a mad and meddlesome effort to realize his own extravagant ideals. This play is as little a *reduction ad absurdum* of Ibsen's own doctrine and ideal of the efficacy of truth as *How He Lied to Her Husband* is a caricature of *Candida.* In Hjalmar Ekdal's attitude towards Gina is satirized the absolute moral demand of Svava Riis in Björnson's *A Glove* (September, 1883), as Elias and Koht have pointed out.

And in Gregers Werle is mordantly satirized that "untutored idealism"—of which we have recently heard so much in America.

Gregers Werle is in pursuit of illusions. He is that "sick conscience" which subsequently found such memorable incarnation in Halvard Solness. He is the inevitable product of his own environment and his own heredity. In his reaction against the Life Lie of his own father, he absorbs the *idée fixe* of a mother rendered morbid and hysterical by her own domestic tragedy. With a grotesque mania for hero-worship and a ludicrous misapprehension of the moral bankruptcy of Hjalmar Ekdal, Gregers Werle flourishes aloft the banner of the ideal and revels in bearing heedless witness to the truth. In his misguided efforts to force upon weaker vessels, made of common clay, that which they are unable to hold, he succeeds only in shattering them into fragments. His passion for communicating to others his "fever for doing right" leaves disaster and death in his wake. "Oh, life would be quite tolerable, after all," says Relling—the real Ibsen speaking, undoubtedly *in propria persona*—"if only we could be rid of the confounded duns that keep on pestering us, in our poverty, with the claim of the ideal."

Nowhere has Ibsen's power of minute and veracious characterization showed itself so supreme. Gregers Werle is the classic embodiment of the misguided reformer. Hjalmar Ekdal is Ibsen's most striking embodiment of the pitiable moral bankrupt, self-deceiving, self-deceived — grotesquely failing to live up to standards inconsiderately applied from without. He is the tragic figure of the average sensual man, betrayed by ideals he has not really made his own — feeding upon his illusions, those illusions by which his very peace of mind, his happiness, are conditioned. Gina Ekdal, without any ideals save the eminently materialistic, eminently prosaic desire to preserve the comfortable *status quo,* is irresistibly natural and likable — perhaps because she is so utterly of the earth earthy. The gentle Hedwig, tender, appealing, young enough to make a hero of her selfish father, too young to detect his glaring faults, is Ibsen's most poetic feminine figure. Björnson acknowledged, after learning to know Ibsen's sister Hedwig, who served as the model for the Hedwig of the play, that he at last understood what a debt Ibsen's bent towards mysticism owed to heredity. *The Wild Duck* has been regarded as a perfect example of Ibsen's individual technique. But its most lamentable technical fault has been succinctly pointed out by Bernard Shaw: "The logic by which Gregers Werle persuades Hedwig to kill the wild duck in order that she may be provided with a pistol to kill herself, strains my credulity."

From this time forward, Ibsen's plays concern themselves less and less with society, more and more with individual problems of character and conscience. Just as *The Wild Duck* marks the transition from realism to symbolism, so *Rosmersholm* marks the transition from society to the individual. After this point, Ibsen's dramas are no longer sociological. They are psychological, and at times psychic, concern themselves with the inner life of thought and conscience, and verge ever towards symbolicism, mysticism and poetry. It is mediately true that we find the sociological Ibsen in Bernard Shaw, the symbolical Ibsen in Maurice Maeterlinck, the psychological Ibsen in Gerhart Hauptmann. Many years ago, Georg Brandes declared that at one period of his career, Ibsen had had a lyric Pegasus killed under him. After reading *The Lady From the Sea, The Master-Builder* and *When We Dead Awaken,* we realize that Brandes saw no further than the present. Wounded and dormant lay the winged steed through the middle years; but in time its strength returned, its pinions were once more unfurled, and it bore its rider over the lower slopes of later life.

In *The Wild Duck* Ibsen reaches the extreme point of his realism. Here he brings us face to face with "cheap, earthenware souls"; here he paints, in garish colors, the unromantic hero — that ludicrous contradiction in terms. At last we have the true *bourgeois* drama, dealing with the thoughts and passions, the loves and hates, the comedies and tragedies, of people such as we brush against every day in the street. The protagonist of to-day has "lost the last gleam from the sunset of the heroes." Here is the hero *manqué,* struggling in vain against the overwhelming pressure of environment, the brand of heredity, the coil of circumstance, the chains of character, the damning verdict of self-mockery, self-distrust, and self-contempt. In *Rosmersholm,* the leading characters lose none of their absorbing interest because one is a pseudo-reformer, weak-kneed if high-minded, and the other a criminal adventuress. This play brings Ibsen into juxtaposition with Nietzsche; for the real drama takes place in a spiritual region of quasi-ethical consciousness beyond good and evil.

"The call to work," wrote Ibsen on February 13, 1887, "is certainly distinguishable throughout *Rosmersholm.* But the play also deals with the struggle with himself which every serious-minded man must face in order to bring his life into harmony with his convictions. For the different spiritual functions do not develop evenly and side by side in any human being. The acquisitive instinct hastens on from conquest to conquest. The moral consciousness, the conscience, on the other hand, is very conservative. It has deep roots and traditions in the past generally. Hence arises the conflict in the individual. But first and foremost, of course, the play is a creative work, dealing with human beings and human destinies." In this succinct exposition, Ibsen, as it were, disengages the various leading motives; from it, we may learn the motive forces of the action of the play. The call to work is less generally human than specially local: it refers more distinctly to the situation in Norway. The secondary motive constitutes the play's inner meaning: the struggle to bring one's life into conformity with one's ideals — the old Ibsen strugle for self-realization. And fundamentally, the play does not so much point a conclusive moral, as exhibit a drama of the struggle of human souls, a picture of fainting and aspiring humanity.

Johannes Rosmer is a far more impressive victim of heredity, in his "tender-minded" conscience which, even in an atmosphere of pure scepticism, looks back to the revengeful standards of an Old Testament God, than ever was Oswald Alving with his tainted body. He has read John Stuart Mill; and, like Mill, has written (see the "forework") a book in which he proclaims happiness as the goal of existence. And yet he has not made the thoughts and ideas of the new time his own; they have laid their hold on him, less by virtue of their own inherent logic and efficacy, than by reason of the influence of Rebekka West's artful insinuations. What these thoughts and ideas are, other than those of Mill, it is difficult to say; but certain it is, from the evidence of the preliminary draft, that Rosmer and Rebekka had been reading together Henry George's *Progress* and *Poverty* (1880) which appeared in a Norwegian translation in 1885-1886 under the title *Fremskridt og fattigdom*. Paul Rée's book on the genesis of conscience (1885) must have been read by Ibsen during the progress of *Rosmersholm;* Rosmer carries too many traits accentuated by Rée. The tender-minded Rosmer must have been drawn in the light of Rée's theorem: "Anyone who, from his youth up, has been thoroughly accustomed to the thought that there is a God and that it is sinful to say: 'The conception of God is absurd,' will in later life, even after his belief has turned to unbelief, seldom mention the fact and then only with reluctance and distaste."

In *Rosmersholm,* Ibsen has penetrated more deeply into the soil of human conscience than in any other of his works. He knows each one of his characters down to the last convolution of the brain, down to the ultimate fold of the soul. Rebekka West is Ibsen's most intense female figure — alike in the clarity of her vision, the scope of her purpose, and the development of her character. She stands under the curse of the past — the past which the "white horse" of Rosmersholm mysteriously symbolizes. She scornfully holds herself superior to the obligations of conscience; and even in the end, we feel that her spirit, not her conviction, is broken. She wields every weapon of intrigue, artifice and cunning to accomplish her purpose, all under the specious guise of a champion of freedom — the freedom of truth; and yet, at last, she goes to her doom because she feels that such freedom can only be attained by one whose soul is pure. She is a radical broken upon the wheel of Rosmer's conservatism.

Fantasy plays its part in this drama of the interior life; and Ulrik Brendel belongs in the category of the "Rat Wife" in *Little Eyolf* and "the Stranger" in *The Lady From the Sea.* He speaks with veiled wisdom in the language of a visitant from a fantastic, supersensible world — the Ibsen chorus in full swing. To those living in a country where wealth accumulates and men decay, where fortune and fame seem in themselves to be the sole aim of existence, the words of Brendel come with poignant significance: "Peter Mortensgaard has the secret of omnipotence. He can do whatever he will. For Peter Mortensgaard never wills more than he can do. Peter Mortensgaard is capable of living his life without ideals. And that, do you see — that is just the mighty secret of action and of victory. It is the sum of the whole world's wisdom."

If Mr. Courtney is correct in positing the failure to achieve one's mission on earth as the quintessence of contemporary tragedy, then *Rosmersholm* is Ibsen's most tragic drama. It prefigures an ideal; and conditions its attainment upon the destruction of the only possible means thereto. Nothing short of Rebekka's sacrificial death can revive in Rosmer his lost faith in the possibility of ennobling humanity; and this sacrifice destroys, for him, the possibility of remaining in life and accomplishing the work, which he might now be capable of. Perplexing, tragic antinomy!

The Lady From the Sea, Ibsen's most genial and charming play, embodies the spiritual realization of the longings and ideals for which Ibsen's heroes continually struggle — that " something other and greater than life " which is at stake. It is a poem in psychotherapeutics, veiled in the garb of mysticism. In Haeckel's *Natürlicher Schöpfunggeschichte,* or perhaps in Darwin's *Descent of Man,* Ibsen must have read of that fish-species, the *Amphioxus Lanceolatus,* which in his own words (in the " forework ") " forms the primordial link in the evolutionary chain." *The Lady From the Sea* finds its origin in Ibsen's perhaps not wholly fantastic supposition that rudiments of it survive in human beings, or at least in the nature of some of us. The importance of this origin is memorable. *The Lady From the Sea* stems from Darwin and Haeckel. And this fact lends additional weight to the ingenious theory of Jules de Gaultier to the effect that Ibsen's effort is to reconcile and conciliate the two biological hypotheses: the invariability of species and the mutability of organic forms. Perhaps the reason why Ibsen is less successful in bridging the chasm between the outer and the inner life is because his fundamental standpoint here is not mystical, but biological. Heretofore Ibsen has shown the individual chiefly struggling with social forces and moral standards which prevail in the world. In *The Lady From the Sea,* Ellida Wangel struggles against a force of Nature which has its rudiments deep-seated in her own nature. "The sea exercises over people the power of a mood, which works like a will," says Ibsen in his memoranda for this play. "The sea can hypnotize. Above all, Nature can. The great mystery is man's dependence upon the 'will-less.'" Herein lies the explanation of Ellida's strange and dramatic struggle.

In *Rosmersholm,* Johannes and Rebekka go down together in death because they have been unable to reconcile themselves with their environment. *The Lady From the Sea* has an enfranchising, sublimating quality — showing the other side, the happy side, of the recurring problem of self-realization — Ellida's ultimate reconcilement with her environment. In the preliminary draft, Wangel is an attorney-at-law; what a wonderfully dramatic heightening of the effect Ibsen achieves by making him a physician in the final form of the play! Wangel may be a comparatively unskilled physician of the body; but he is an incomparable physician of the soul. Through his selfless adoration for his wife, he achieves that "miracle of manly love" for which

Nora Helmer longed in vain. His love for Ellida teaches him the secret of alienism: that yielding alone can help the sick soul. He employs the familiar experiment: humoring the patient's fancies, and thereby lightening the forces of the past and of nature which become a positive obsession of the unknown.

The problem lies deeper than this. Nature has its roots deeper than this: morality has behind it natural claims which transcend it. In a curious note Ibsen once made on a loose sheet of paper, he prefigures the real solution for Ellida's psychiatric obsession: "Freedom consists in securing to the individual the right to free himself — each according to his own particular need." The dramatic climax of the third act is complete and convincing, when Ellida says to Wangel, softly — and trembling: "Oh! Wangel — save me from myself." Wangel opens the way for Ellida's salvation from herself by cancelling the law's bargain. He secures to her the inner, spiritual right to freedom — freedom to act upon her own responsibility. The real dramatic conflict of the play takes on a schematic cast; and perhaps it is the absence of any resort to physical action, in order to accentuate Ellida's crucial decision, which weakens, dramatically, the ultimate climax. Even Ibsen found it difficult to vitalize the victory of psychology over hypnosis!

The Lady From the Sea is Ibsen's most romantic,

most poetic prose drama. Ellida is a mermaid who defies domestication, symbolizing and catching up within herself all the sheen, vacillation and mystery of the wild, restless sea. Ibsen's symbolism is essentially romantic; and he harks back to the mysterious, nameless lover, beloved of romance throughout the history of art. "Nobody should know what he is," Ibsen said to Hoffory in a letter recently published; "just as little should anybody know who he is or what he is really called. This *uncertainty* is just the chief point in the method chosen by me for the occasion." This stranger, about whom so much romantic uncertainty hovers, seems to be the symbolic object of woman's longing for freedom, woman's tremulous and fearful passion for the unknown.

What a contrast we find in *Hedda Gabler!* Ibsen turns from imaginative poetry to irreducible fact, from mysticism to the hard coldness of electrically brilliant realism. In *The Lady From the Sea,* Ibsen's hand falters — the pronounced subplots are extraneous and subsidiary, unmotived by vital relation to the forward movement of the central action. In *Hedda Gabler,* Ibsen's technical virtuosity once more shines out undimmed. "The title of the play is *Hedda Gabler* (not *Tesman*)," Ibsen wrote on December 4, 1890. "My intention in giving it this name was to indicate that Hedda, as a personality, is to be regarded rather as her father's daughter than as her husband's wife. It was not my desire to deal in this play with so-called problems. What I principally wanted to do was to depict human beings, human emotions, and human destinies, upon a groundwork of certain of the social conditions and principles of the present day." *Hedda Gabler* is not a problem play: it is a portrait play; the full-length portrait, in all its cold fascination, of the most repellently attractive woman in the modern drama. Bernard Shaw once blithely said that if people knew all that a dramatist thought, they would kill him; and Ibsen, like Sargent, always means infinitely more than he says. "These are no mere portrait busts . . ." says Rubek of his sculptures. "There is something equivocal, cryptic, lurking in and behind these busts — a secret something that the people themselves cannot see." In the full-length statue of Hedda, we detect that "something equivocal, cryptic" lurking behind the dimly realized likeness to a vampire. Hedda is the horrifying image of, not the *Ewig Weibliche,* but the temporal womanly — which drives men backward and downward. In her are the traits of the treacherous Lorelei painted by Heine — faithless, inhuman, reptilian — luring man to destruction in the sea of sensuality. She reminds us of Philip Burne-Jones's picture — with a dash of Wedekind's *Erdgeist.* And yet she excites our mournful pity, if only we are sufficiently detached to reflect that Hedda, like

Rank, Oswald, Hedwig and the rest, is a victim of heredity. This woman who stems from a worn-out race is vastly interesting as a problem in eugenics; when her father married, he was already a man old in years who had drained to the dregs the cup of sensual pleasure. "Perhaps that has left its mark upon me," says Hedda significantly,— in the fore-work; but so direct an allusion is omitted by Ibsen in the final draft. She gives pointed significance to the Biblical aphorism: "The fathers have eaten sour grapes; and the children's teeth are set on edge." The appositeness of the phrase is immense: Hedda's tastes are all set on edge. With all the gifts that life can give, Hedda is the incarnation of ennui. Her tragedy is not that she fails to achieve her mission, but that she has no mission to achieve.

From the little model of Gossensass, Emilie Bardach, Ibsen perhaps learned one trait for Hedda: that her desire to win the adoration of others is not for the sake of adoration, but for the thrill which the sense of possession and domination over others awakens in her. The other characters — the dæmonic Lövborg, self-pitying, self-destroyed; Tesman, the quintessence of the methodical second-hand; Thea, this second childish Nora whose experiment so piteously fails — all dwindle into insignificance in the face of the characterless personality of Hedda. With intricately lascivious instincts, the sensual *stigmata* of a degenerate father, Hedda "hath already committed adultery in her heart." But the fear of the world's judgment mocks and terrifies her; she lacks the courage even of her own instincts. The play has been aptly termed the picture of a condition, not an action; and Ibsen has shown the utter depravity of Hedda by laying bare her distorted soul at the very moment when woman's instincts are most sacred — in the face of coming motherhood. Flaubert's words, of an earlier day, give a final judgment of the marvellous art of Ibsen as displayed in this terrible play: "The author in his work must be like God in the universe, present everywhere, and visible nowhere; art being a second nature, the creator of this nature must act by an analogous procedure; must make us feel in all the atoms, under all aspects, an impassibility secret, infinite; the effect for the spectator must be a species of amazement. How is it all done? one must ask, and one feels shattered without knowing why. . . ."

X

"You are essentially right," wrote Ibsen to Count Prozor in March, 1900, "when you say that the series which closes with the Epilogue (*When We Dead Awaken*) began with *The Master-Builder.*" And yet it must be realized that the "new method," upon which Ibsen relied in his later years, really began with *The Lady From the Sea;* and it is in this very play that Ibsen's master hand first wavers.

Ibsen seems slowly to lose his powers when he leaves the domain of social relationship, and enters the untried fields of hypnotism and supernatural phenomena. And yet it cannot be denied that *The Master-Builder* is, of all Ibsen's plays, the densest in content, the one most provocative to a rich and ever richer measure of interpretation. Goethe once said he was inclined to believe that the more "incommensurable" a work of art, the greater it is likely to prove. *Incommensurable* is the magic word for *The Master-Builder*. If the meaning of *Hamlet, Macbeth* or *King Lear* could be explained in a few words, it is reasonable to conclude that they would not rank as three of the greatest dramas ever written. In them are magic "over-tones," muted harmonics, which can be heard only by ears delicately attuned to their music. It is this profound and elusive quality, this power of stimulating the far reaches of mentality and imagination, which informs and irradiates *The Master-Builder*. No one will ever see down all the dim vistas of the imagination opened up by the speculative and brooding Hamlet, the crime-obsessed Macbeth, the palsied prophet of a cosmic ruin, King Lear, and the tottering idealist Solness, sent climbing to his fall.

The Master-Builder reveals Ibsen hovering fascinated around the problem to which Nietzsche devoted his life — a problem with which Ibsen had occupied himself before, and independently of

Nietzsche. The motto of *The Master-Builder* might well be the words of Browning:

> "Ah, but a man's reach should exceed his grasp,
> Or what's a heaven for?"

And yet it is no heaven for which Solness longs, but that savage mundane time, that era of the "roaming blond beast," when man's instincts shall be given feral freedom. He aspires to live in the fierce light of the high noon of egoism — the day of Zarathustra, unbeclouded by the restraints of conscience. *The Master-Builder* is Ibsen's true tragedy of the guilty conscience. Hilda, naïve, fresh, imperious, is Ibsen's fascinating projection of the Superwoman in spirit: a keen-eyed bird of prey, like a young falcon pouncing upon its marked-down victim. And yet in the end, like Rebekka, her predatory instinct wavers before the imminent sense of moral responsibility. Solness, like Rosmer, sets too great store by that "glad guiltlessness" of the moral conservative, ever to do more than fail nobly. He believes, this mystic epileptic, that some people are "elect"; that a certain "grace" is vouchsafed to them, whereby they may, by concentrating all the forces of their being upon the desired end, succeed in achieving it. Yet one cannot accomplish great things alone: one must call to his aid mysterious powers, "helpers and servers," from the very depths of his being. These come forth and subject themselves to the master will. This is what people mean by having *Luck*. And yet, this master over the destinies of others, finally, tragically fails; for he is neither master of himself nor free from the disquieting pangs of a sick conscience. "Let us not invoke the illimitable law of the universe, the intentions of history, the will of the worlds, the justice of the stars," says Maeterlinck in his essay on *Luck*. "These powers exist: we submit to them, as we submit to the might of the sun. But they act without knowing us; and within the wide circle of their influence there remains to us still a liberty that is probably immense. They have better work on hand than to be forever bending over us to lift a blade of grass or drop a leaf in the little paths of our ant-hill. Since we ourselves are here the persons concerned, it is, I imagine, *within ourselves* that the key of the mystery shall be found; for it is probable that every creature carries within him the best solution of the problem that he presents."

Ibsen's last three dramas exhibit a gradual loosening of the dramatist's hold upon vitally dramatic phases of human existence. Ibsen recedes farther and farther from the stage, and penetrates ever deeper into spheres of moral contemplation, self-examination, and introspection —"wild with all regret." *Little Eyolf* is a poignant study of the mental reactions from the problem of moral responsibility set up in the souls of a husband and wife through the neglect and loss of their little son, and the consequent struggles of conscience. With a certain large-minded tolerance, Ibsen does not shrink from exhibiting, in a spirit of calm justice, the distortions imparted to sane existence by the single-idea-d passion to "live one's own life"—superficially classed as Ibsen's pet theory—irrespective of the larger social reactions. I felt that Nazimova, fortified by a consistent conception, endowed the character of Rita with a sort of alluring naturalism, and this in face of the fact that Ibsen's Rita is the repellent type of the exclusively carnal instinct. Because of just such patchwork characters as Allmers, with his fine-spun theories, mouth-filling phrases, and petty conduct, Ibsen's repute as a dramatist suffers most. In this play are scenes most poignantly moving in tragic revelation, dark soul interiors suddenly illumined with lightning flashes of intuition. Yet we cannot share the sad optimism of Rita and Allmers in the sincerity of their altruistic purpose—the craving of the animal only slumbers, amateur idealism shall suffer attenuation through the sophistry of the theorist.

John Gabriel Borkman is Ibsen's most quiescent, most perfectly static drama. One may best describe it as an evocation of a state of mind. Ibsen here paints the peculiarly modern type of the megalomaniac, the logical product of the industrial brigandage of the late nineteenth century. Borkman is a wounded Napoleon of finance shown in the last phase, fretting out his great mad soul in the St. Helena of his little room. He is the tragic victim of colossal egotism; the Nietzschean exemplar of the "higher morality" shattered upon the rock of inexorable legal justice. *When We Dead Awaken,* Ibsen's sad epilogue, is at once a Calvary and a Resurrection. Like Nietzsche, Ibsen burned for great exhibitions of full-blooded egoism, aspired to tremendous struggles for that moral freedom which is beyond good and evil. And yet, like Solness, neither could climb as high as he built. In the life of daily actuality both were incapable of standing "high and free." Nietzsche's life and letters show it only too clearly; Ibsen's life, his experience with the little falcon of Gossensass, his moral reflections poured out in his latest plays, are all too circumstantial. In Rebekka West, in Hedda Gabler, in Halvard Solness, in Ellida Wangel, we see the nascent and maturing impulses of the "Will to Power"; but Ibsen breaks down upon the frontiers of the kingdom; he can never escape the eternal question: Has one the moral right? *When We Dead Awaken* is the tragedy of life's disillusion: the discovery when it is too late that life's best gifts have been wasted in pursuit of the illusory, rather than of the enduring real. Great is Eros; and Ibsen, even Ibsen, is his prophet. The lesson of *When We Dead Awaken,* perhaps the meaning of Ibsen's

" high, painful happiness " in old age, the hopeless longing for the irrevocably unattainable, is caught up in Robert Browning's memorable words from *Youth and Art:*

> " Each life's unfulfilled, you see,
> It hangs still, patchy and scrappy:
> We have not sighed deep, laughed free,
> Starved, feasted, despaired, been happy,
> And nobody calls you a dunce,
> And people suppose me clever:
> This could not have happened once,
> And we missed it, lost it forever."

XI

Exaggeration lurks in the statement that Henrik Ibsen laid the foundations of a new school of art by enlisting naturalism in the service of social reforms. Rather is it true that, by veracious portraiture of contemporary life, Ibsen sought the moral regeneration of the individual, and, indirectly, of society. The ideal is the eternal sovereign of the palace of life. Man perishes, but the ideal endures. " The ideal is dead, long live the ideal! " is the epitome of all human progress. In the evolutionary trend of human progress Ibsen rested his profoundest hope. The charge of nihilism he resented with the utmost bitterness. His heresy consisted in regarding morality as fluid, evolutional; he insisted that ideals were functions of civilization. "It has been asserted on various occasions that I am a pessimist," Ibsen once remarked. "So I am to this extent — that I do not believe human ideals to be eternal. But I am also an optimist, for I believe firmly in the power of those ideals to propagate and develop." The cry of progress, in all ages, is the disillusioned cry of one of Ibsen's own characters: "The old beauty is no longer beautiful, the new truth no longer true." Ibsen preferred to dedicate himself to the future; he sacrificed friends because he regarded them as an expensive luxury, and once was heard to quote approvingly Arthur Symons' line: "The long, intolerable monotony of friends." It is always the future in which Ibsen puts his trust; and historical optimism describes his personal angle of vision. Like Nietzsche's fierce prophet Zarathustra, Ibsen might well say of himself: "I am of to-day and of the past; but something is within me that is of to-morrow, and the day after to-morrow, and the far future."

In matters of conduct, Ibsen has no golden rule for the governance of society. Bernard Shaw says of Ibsen's philosophy: "The golden rule is that there is no golden rule." Individual responsibility is the sole and ultimate test of conduct. Ibsen's whole ideal of life may be expressed in the words of Polonius in *Hamlet:*

> "To thine own self be true
> And it doth follow, as the night the day,
> Thou canst not then be false to any man."

Ibsen advocates the naked assertion of the human will; but he never escapes the unsolved problem of moral right.

His own Brand implacably declares:

> "Beggar or rich,— with all my soul
> I *will;* and that one thing's the whole."

And yet Brand is Ibsen's most colossal, most tragic failure. Self-realization through conscious self-examination and active assertion of the human will — this is the lesson of the Ibsenic dramas. Ibsen is an evolutionist; and evolution teaches, if indirectly, that self-development, self-realization, if you will, should be the aim, both of the individual and of the race. "The expression of our own individuality is our first duty," Ibsen once said; and this doctrine he has exemplified in all his social dramas. If only every man be true to himself, if only every individual will seek his own highest development, there need be no fear for the future. It is in that future that the "third kingdom" shall come. Ibsen once rose at a banquet and, in a toast as holy as a benediction, as solemn as a sacrifice, drank deep to *das Werdende, das Kommende.* When someone once remarked to Ibsen, in his latter years, that he would be fully understood in the distant future, Ibsen eagerly replied: *"Ja, wenn wir d a s nur glauben könnten!"*— Yes, if we only could believe *that!*

What Ibsen desired was a revolution of the spirit of man. He fully recognized the moral quality of all human experience. And morality, as Nordau shrewdly puts it, is essentially optimistic, presupposing conscious and rational efforts towards the realization of the maximum of human happiness. With the force of the moral ever at work within him, Ibsen has taught us in the school of our own lives. Before us he has held the mirror of his art-works; and therein we have recognized, sometimes with amazement, sometimes with horrified fascination, sometimes with cursings and revilings, our own moral features, our own spiritual lineaments. None but ourselves have we met on the highway of fate. As Goethe said of Molière, so say we of Ibsen: he has chastized us by painting us just as we are. His appeal is to the restless, disturbing life of our own day. And his dramas are his tentatives at the question which Tolstoi claims Shakspere never consciously proposed to himself: "What are we alive for?"

Ibsen's plays, his greatest plays, are universal because they are laid in the inner life, the region of moral consciousness. His whole drama, from one aspect, may be regarded as a microscopic analysis of the morbid self-consciousness of modern life. The immediate effect of Ibsen's plays is to awaken thought, to induce reflection, to compel people to analyze and ponder grave questions of individual and social morality. Here we have a striking example of that desiderated publicity so widely heralded to-day as the salvation of the business and commercial honor of democratic government. Ibsen does not summon to immediate action: his appeal to what we are accustomed to call "the passions" is practically nil. His appeal is to that great and growing moral passion for social enlightenment which is permeating the entire civilized world. Ibsen starts within the individual a train of meditation and reflection which may alter a life, which may even influence the whole world. Emerson says: *To think is to act.*

Ibsen once said: "It should be the endeavor of every dramatist to improve the prevailing order of the world." Ibsen's aim is to aid in the perfecting of individual and civil life. It seems, indeed, as Brunetière says, that we of to-day are marching towards the socialization, the moralization of literature. Since Ibsen has lived and written, literature has thrilled with a new joy — the passion for individual self-realization, the passion for a more just and perfect social order.

The Genesis of His Dramas

"To dramatize is to see."
Henrik Ibsen to Johann Paulsen.

I

Like Goethe, like George Eliot, Henrik Ibsen was that rarest of products, an artistic temperament endowed with a scientific brain. Along with Edgar Allan Poe, Ibsen must be ranked as a strange composite of scientific worker and artistic thinker. With unexampled frankness, he once likened himself to a surgeon holding the feverish pulse of society in the interests of universal sanity. And yet his art seems like the work of a magician; and about the composition of his well-nigh flawless plays there is something of the air of prestidigitation. The cloak of mystery in which he veiled himself from all the world, even from his wife and son, well served Ibsen's purpose of exciting endless speculations as to the manner of creation of those marvellous dramas which give positive character and quality to the age in which we live.

When Ibsen was incubating the ideas for a new play, he displayed the most delicate art of finesse in directing the conversation of everyone to the theme over which he was brooding, without leading the speakers to suspect his own vital interest therein. From his wife, Ibsen jealously concealed every faintest indication of his dramatic "whimsies" as he was fond of calling them; but once the play was entirely finished, she it was who read it first. On one occasion, his wife and son were very curious about the new play, concerning which Ibsen had let fall not the slightest hint. One day, on leaving the *coupé* at the station, Ibsen dropped a tiny piece of paper, which his wife surreptitiously picked up. Upon it was written: "The doctor says—" that was all. Having confided to Sigurd, in advance, her playful intention of teasing Ibsen, she knowingly remarked to him: "What sort of doctor is that who takes part in your new play? He certainly has many interesting things to say!" For a moment, Ibsen was speechless with amazement and rage. Then the deluge: What was the meaning of this? Was he no longer secure in his own home? Surrounded by spies? His desk rifled, his sanctuary defiled? Imagine the silent humiliation with which he heard the true explanation!

At last, the secrets of this abnormally secretive genius have been disclosed. And perhaps no more interesting, no more unique, no more novel documents in the field of literary evolution have ever been given to the world. "The doctor says—"

read that enigmatic slip which so piqued Fru Ibsen's curiosity. It is an enigma no longer, for in the volumes of his *Nachgelassene Schriften* the Doctor has indeed spoken.

At several periods in his career, Ibsen contemplated writing an autobiographical account of the outward and inward conditions under which each one of his works came into being. Discreet and taciturn as he was by nature and by cultivation, Ibsen yet realized the advisability of some form of concession to the vastly greedy public who resented his extreme reserve and were genuinely interested in learning the history of the psychological evolution of the great dramatist. Delighting in a sphinx-like attitude and deliberately fostering the accumulating legends of his mysterious wizardry, Ibsen wished to tell only of the circumstances and conditions under which he wrote, " observing the utmost discretion, and leaving a wide field for all kinds of surmises." Unfortunately for the world, Frederik Hegel, Ibsen's publisher, dissuaded him from his unusually suggestive project. The experiment with *Catiline* had aroused the public interest; to do the same for all his plays seemed to Ibsen eminently worth while. This idea of writing some form of autobiography seems for many years to have lurked just below the surface of Ibsen's mind. The divergence of opinion in regard to certain of his works, the repeated assertions by the critics of the contradictoriness of his philosophy and its lack of any sort of logical continuity, impressed Ibsen with the necessity of writing a book dealing with the gradual development of his mind and exhibiting the intimate connection between the philosophical and psychological motives of his successive plays. " In reality," he once confessed to Lorentz Dietrichson, " my development is thoroughly consecutive. I myself can indicate the various threads in the whole course of my development, the unity of my ideas, and their gradual evolution, and I am on the point of writing down some notes, which shall prove to the world that I am the same person to-day that I was on the day I first found myself." His little book, of from 160 to 200 pages, and to be entitled *From Skien to Norway,* has never come to light. Certain it is that for some time prior to November, 1881, he had been working upon this book, portions of which he actually offered to Olaf Skavlan for his magazine *Nyt Tidsskrift.* A fragment alone survives. In lieu of that work, of which a merest beginning was made, now appear the precious volumes (three in the Scandinavian, four in the German edition) of his *Nachgelassene Schriften.* There can be little question that these volumes, exhibiting as they do the intricate workings of Ibsen's mind in the actual process of the composition of his plays, are of far more universal and permanent interest than any form of autobiography or self-analysis he may have contemplated or even, in part, committed to writing. It cannot be said that the few examples we have of Ibsen's attempts at critical self-analysis are particularly successful, or, indeed — to the critical student — wholly convincing. There lurks behind them something of the equivocal and the disingenuous — for Ibsen had a way of denying, when charged with it by the critics, the most patent indebtedness to others.

II

To the human mind there is an indescribable fascination in searching out the secrets of the great masters of literature in the composition of their masterpieces. Perhaps the poet, as Poe suggests, voluntarily encourages the popular opinion that he composes in a series of lightning-flashes of ecstatic intuition:

"His eye in a fine frenzy rolling."

Incidents in support of this fantastic and sentimental conception frequently run the gamut of publicity; and strange stories of magic feats of composition impress alike the sceptical and the credulous. Long and elaborate works of art require profound reflection, minute analysis and prolonged study. To peep into the workshop of the great master's brain and assist at the precise balancing of the arguments *pro* and *con*, to observe how an idea first finds lodgment in the brain, and to note the gradual symmetrical accretion of the fundamental nuclei for the final creation — this is a privilege that has perhaps never fully been realized by any observer. Poe, for the first time in the world's history, elaborates the various mental processes, the successive reflections, by which a poet — himself — arrives at the philosophical and structural bases of a poetic masterpiece — *The Raven.* He draws the curtain and lets the people take a peep behind the scenes

> at the elaborate and vacillating crudities of thought — at the true purposes seized only at the last moment — at the innumerable glimpses of idea that arrived not at the maturity of full view — at the fully matured fancies discarded in despair as unmanageable — at the cautious selections and rejections — at the painful erasures and interpolations — in a word, at the wheels and pinions — the tackle for scene-shifting — the step-ladders and demon-traps —the cock's feathers, which, in ninety-nine cases out of a hundred, constitute the properties of the literary *histrio.*

So lucid, so logical is Poe's analysis of the considerations which gave him the fundamental motives for *The Raven,* that it has been customary for the critics to point out the discrepancy between Poe's cold-bloodedly scientific explanation and the romantic glamour of his magic poetry. The world has been inclined to judge Poe's exposition as a brilliant scientific analysis of poetic intuition and inspiration — *after the fact* — a mathematical recreation in the category of cipher-solving. And yet, there is good reason for believing that Poe, with his marvellous faculty of analysis, must have experienced some such succession of mental states as those he so succinctly describes, though doubtless not in the elaborately articulated and logical sequence upon which he lays so much stress. Even granting the validity of all that he says, he still holds something back. We have not yet plucked the heart out of his mystery; the last veil is yet unpierced, the veil which conceals the inner shrine of his poetic genius — the secrets of his haunting music, his dæmonic magic, his creative imagination.

Nothing so piques the fancy as the image of the great master-craftsman spinning out the threads of his creative imagination and weaving the magic patterns of human life which shall enrapture thousands in that palace of light and sound, the theatre. The curiosity of the inquisitive has recently been given official sanction by a great educational institution — in the case of the investigations, by Hodell, of that "Yellow Book" which first awoke in Robert Browning the idea of the many-sided complex of confession, recrimination and exculpation embodied in *The Ring and the Book.* The documents which Henrik Ibsen, the greatest dramatic craftsman since Molière, religiously preserved and which are now brought to light, at last furnish to the world the most elaborate, most veraciously authentic record of the evolutionary genesis of the masterpieces of a great genius, that the world has ever known. These literary remains, be it noted, consist not of Ibsen's possibly supposititious accounts of the brain processes which gave rise to his dramaturgic masterpieces, but of the actual documental memoranda of the successive states of Ibsen's mind in the creation and development of his plays. Here we find the first original jottings of the thoughts which clustered together around some burning point in modern social philosophy; the original scenarios which project a vivid picture in little of the dramatic conjuncture; the genetic states of mind through which Ibsen passed in creating and re-creating human experience; and finally the penultimate drafts of his plays, just prior to that last marvellous polishing, filing and chiselling upon the dexterously fashioned material of his own creation. These documents, which Ibsen called "foreworks," are given to the world with his authorization; he looked upon them much as a great painter regards the original sketches and preparatory designs for his completed pictures. And it is noteworthy that, more than once during the latter years of his life, Ibsen, pointing to this packet of manuscripts, remarked to his wife and son: "These are very important things — perhaps the most important of all." Ferdinand Brunetière has applied the complex machinery of Darwinian evolution to literary forms, and shown the successive stages by which a literary type reached its present state of development. In his "foreworks," Ibsen exhibits the successive stages in the evolution of a particular specimen of art-form, the modern drama, the most difficult, most recalcitrant of the forms of creative composition. Here we may observe, as it were, the Darwinian process modified by the mutation theory of De Vries — the gradual evolutionary process of infinitely small changes modified by the "evolution by explosion" of the human, experiential factor. A marvellous composite of the dual, mutually interacting operations of the analytic faculty with the synthetic genius, of the scientific method with the poetic vision.

III

Upon Ibsen's table, it has been related, there stood beside his inkstand a small tray, containing a lot of extraordinary toys — some little carved wooden Swiss bears, a diminutive black devil, small cats, dogs and rabbits made of copper, one of which was playing the violin. "I never write a single line of any of my dramas unless that tray and its occupants are before me on the table," Ibsen is said to have remarked. "I could not write without them. It may seem strange — perhaps it is — but I cannot write without them." And with a quiet laugh, he mysteriously added, "Why I use them is my own secret." There is one other remark of Ibsen's which, taken in connection with this perhaps fanciful story, serves to give the clue to Ibsen's real attitude towards his work and the methods he employed. "Everything that I have written," he said in a letter to Ludwig Passarge in 1880, "has the closest possible connection with what I have lived through, even if it has not been my own personal experience; in every new poem or play I have aimed at my own spiritual emancipation and purification — for a man shares the responsibility and the guilt of the society to which he belongs. Hence I wrote the following dedicatory lines in a copy of one of my books:

> "To *live* — is to war with fiends
> That infest the brain and the heart;
> To *write* — is to summon one's self,
> And play the judge's part."

Ibsen succeeded in packing his plays with the utmost of thought content, in that he deliberately made it a rule never to speak polemically save through the medium of his dramatic characters. Contrary to the popular impression that the successful dramatist must write always with "his eye on the stage," Ibsen seldom visited the stage save when his presence was imperatively required at the rehearsals of one of his own plays. And yet he was peculiarly sensitive to scenic effects, such as the color of carpet and wall-paper, to proper intonation, and even to such an apparently insignificant detail as the size of an actress's hands. Brandes relates a significant incident which took place at a dinner given to Ibsen. One of the banqueters, who had escorted the beautiful actress, Fräulein Constance Brunn, arose at the banquet and said, "My partner requests me to present to you, Dr. Ibsen, the thanks of the actresses of the Christiania Theatre and to tell you that there are no rôles which she would rather play, or from which she can learn more, than yours." To which Ibsen immediately replied, "I must state at the outset that I do not write rôles, but represent human beings; and that never in my life during the creation of a play have I had before my eyes an actor or actress." It was Ibsen's remarkable power of visualizing the stage sets which enabled him to dispense with the actual theatre and the actual player. "Since I have a strong imaginative feeling for the dramatic," he once wrote, "I can see before me most vividly everything that is really credible, trustworthy, true." Like the great French magician, Houdin, Ibsen possessed a faculty for minute observation trained to a supreme degree. His genius for detail confirms his significant statement to Paulsen: "To dramatize is to *see*."

IV

Before Ibsen wrote a single line bearing upon a play, he gave himself over to isolated contemplation and reflection. In long solitary walks, in the sanctuary of his study, in hours-long motionless contemplation of the sea or of the landscape, in minute reading of the newspapers down to the smallest advertisement, in dumb contemplation of the human pageant in the mirror before him as he sat at meals in his restaurant — Ibsen slowly and patiently allowed the ferment of ideas to go on in his brain until, as by a chemical reaction, there occurred the intellectual precipitation of some generality of moral import and sociologic bearing. He never put pen to paper, as he once confessed to Alfred Sinding-Larsen, until he had a clear picture of everything in his head — even down to the versification and rough details of the dialogue. When he actually began to write, he exhibited the marvellous spectacle of proceeding as uninterruptedly as if he were writing to dictation. The act of dressing was a long and laborious process with Ibsen; according to his own confessions, he was revolving in his mind, while dressing himself, the incidents and scenes of the play then in progress. It piques the fancy to wonder if the "auction" of *The Lady From the Sea*, Solness' ascent to the tower, or Nora's argument with Helmer, occurred to Ibsen while he was pulling on his trousers! When he left off work for the day, he took pains to keep in mind some fragment of dialogue for a starting point on the morrow. If, however, this bit of dialogue did not set his thoughts flowing readily through his pen, he abandoned writing for the time being, and quietly brooded over the problem, the characters, or the situation.

First of all, Ibsen jotted down memoranda (Auszeichnungen), by which he clarified the intellectual problem and set the drama in embryo, as under a microscope, before his eyes. These memoranda are usually of a philosophical, psychological or sociological nature: pungent observations upon life, criticisms of contemporary society, epigrams, thumb-nail sketches of character, *je ne sais quoi du tout.* They were written upon the most haphazard material — odd slips of paper, the backs of envelopes, newspaper wrappers, any loose sheets of paper. These noted ideas gradually seemed to group themselves, as if with subconscious design, around some generality of thought — a nuclear accretion around some central point.

After a time, the principal characters of his projected play, minutely observed from life but always transmuted in his poetic consciousness, began to assume definite psychological character and highly individual attributes. Then Ibsen seems to have brought this experiential conception to bear upon the epigrammatic idea-forms preserved in haphazard memoranda. This intrusion of his dramatic conception into the field of his general ideas produced a remarkable effect — much like that caused by a magnet brought to bear upon metal filings scattered upon a glass plate. At once the general ideas began to group themselves into symmetrical designs of definite contour.

These notes are preserved to us in various states of nuclear accretion; and examples may best exhibit the types of these various states. The following epigrams point directly to the plays bracketed after them.

Modern society is no human society; it is solely a society for males.—(*A Doll's House.*)

"Free-born men" is a mere flowery phrase. There aren't any. Marriage, the relation between man and woman, has destroyed the race, has fixed upon every one the marks of slavery.—(*Ghosts*)

This tomfoolery! We acknowledge the right of the majority; and yet those who exercise the ballot constitute a small, arbitrarily limited minority.—(*An Enemy of the People.*)

Freedom consists in securing for the individual the right to free himself — every one according to his needs.—(*The Lady From the Sea.*)

People say that suicide is immoral. But what about living a life of prolonged suicide — out of regard for one's environment?—(*Hedda Gabler.*)

A new nobility will come into being. It will not be the nobility of birth or of wealth, nor yet the nobility of endowment or of knowledge. The nobility of the future will be the nobility of soul and of will.—(*Rosmersholm.*)[1]

[1] Ibsen used almost these identical words in a speech to the workingmen of Trondhjem, June 14, 1885.

Those among us who have the vote are in the minority. Is the minority right? —(*An Enemy of the People.*)

At a slightly later stage in the evolution of his dramatic conception, Ibsen's ideas, as caught in consecutive memoranda, began to converge towards some general fable of human experience. The best example of this stage is the collection of the first memoranda for *Ghosts;* and to show the unsystematic way in which these ideas first found expression, it may be pointed out that some are found upon the back of an envelope addressed to "Madame Ibsen, 75 via Capo la Case, Citta (Rome)", others upon the back of a newspaper addressed to "Herr Dr. Ibsen, Swedish Consulate at Rome," date 1881.

The piece will be like an image of life. Faith undermined. But it does not do to say so. "The Asylum"—for the sake of others. They shall be happy — but this also is only an appearance — it is all ghosts —

One main point. She has been believing and romantic — this is not wholly obliterated by the standpoint afterward attained — "It is all ghosts."

It brings a Nemesis on the offspring to marry for external reasons, even if they be religious or moral.

She, the illegitimate child, may be saved by being married to — the son — but then —?

He was in his youth dissipated and worn out; then she, the religiously awakened, appeared; she saved him; she was rich. He had wanted to marry a girl who was thought unworthy. He had a son in his marriage; then he returned to the girl: a daughter —

These women of to-day, ill-treated as daughters, as sisters, as wives, not educated according to their gifts, withheld from their vocation, deprived of their heritage, embittered in mind — these it is who furnish the mothers of the new generation. What will be the consequence?

The fundamental note shall be: the richly flourishing spiritual life among us in literature, art, etc.— and then as a contrast: all humanity astray on wrong paths.

The complete human being is no longer a natural product, but a product of art, as corn is, and fruit trees, and the creole race, and the higher breeds of horses and dogs, the vine, etc.

The fault lies in the fact that all humanity has miscarried. When man demands to live and develop humanly, it is megalomania. All humanity, and most of all the Christians, suffer from megalomania.

Among us we place monuments over the dead, for we recognize duties toward them; we allow people only fit for the hospital (literally lepers) to marry; but their offspring —? the unborn —?

A more finished state of memorandum, immediately precedent to the actual elaboration of the definite scenario, is preserved in reference to the play of *A Doll's House*. It is important to observe — and this with absolute certainty —, that undoubtedly at *one* stage in the development of the material, the drama developed from quite general ideas. Ibsen himself confessed to M. G. Conrad that he always used the individual as his starting point; and he probably never worked his general ideas into a play solely for their own sake. Ibsen always insisted that he was much more the creative artist than the philosopher the public seemed bent upon finding in him. And his plays must be thought of, not as thesis-plays merely embodying one germ-idea, but as artistic re-creations of human experience. With these reflections in mind may now be cited Ibsen's "Notes for the Tragedy of To-day," the preliminary memorandum for *A Doll's House,* bearing the inscription "Rome, 10-19-'78."

There are two kinds of spiritual laws, two kinds of conscience, one in men and a quite different one in women. They do not understand each other; but the woman is judged in practical life according to the man's law, as if she were not a woman, but a man.

The wife in the play finds herself at last entirely at sea as to what is right and what wrong; natural feeling on one side and belief in authority on the other leave her in utter bewilderment.

A woman cannot be herself in the society of to-day, which is exclusively a masculine society, with laws written by men, and with accusers and judges who judge feminine conduct from the masculine standpoint.

She has committed forgery, and it is her pride; for she did it for love of her husband, and to save his life. But this husband, full of everyday rectitude, stands on the basis of the law, and regards the matter with a masculine eye.

Soul-struggles. Oppressed and bewildered by the belief in authority, she loses her faith in her own moral right and ability to bring up her children. Bitterness. A mother in the society of to-day, like certain insects (ought to) go away and die when she has done her duty toward the continuance of the species. Love of life, of home, of husband and children and kin. Now and then a woman-like shaking-off of cares. Then a sudden return of apprehension and dread. She must bear it all alone. The catastrophe approaches, inexorably, inevitably. Despair, struggle and disaster.

After the general outlines of the play had taken on finished shape, as revealed in the above memorandum for *A Doll's House,* for example, Ibsen next proceeded to the elaboration of the scenario. Ibsen worked from the scenario forward, in a manner highly scientific; this was always his practice, even the manuscript of the original version of Ibsen's first play, *Catiline,* of date "25-2-'49," exhibiting an elaborate scenario. Indeed, Ibsen had no respect for any dramatist who proceeded otherwise. Once besought by a young dramatist to read the manuscript of his new play, Ibsen curtly asked for the scenario. When the young man proudly replied that he needed no scenario, having followed his inspiration whithersoever it led him from scene to scene, Ibsen grew furious and showed the pseudo-dramatist the door, declaring that anyone who dispensed with a scenario didn't know what a drama was and couldn't possibly write one. And yet, after all, the scenario as first outlined by Ibsen may best be regarded as an experimental foreshadowing, subject to radical modification as the writing of the play itself proceeds. It serves as the skeleton framework for Ibsen's subsequent ideation. Not infrequently a whole act — as in the case of *Peer Gynt* — is written before Ibsen has definitely decided just what rôle some leading character is destined to play. The fragments of *A Doll's House* indicate clearly that Ibsen discarded the original plan for each act, when he came to the actual writing of it. While it is true, then, that the material took shape in his mind long before he wrote a word of actual dialogue, yet Ibsen expressly acknowledged that it never took such unalterable shape in his mind as to permit him to write the last act first and the first act last. During the course of the work, the details emerged by degrees.

In this respect, the creation of the drama, as exemplified by Ibsen, exhibits an excellent contrast to the creation of the Short-story, as exemplified by Maupassant or Poe. In the Short-story, the lines of action initially converge to the final goal. As Stevenson put it, the end is bone of the bone and flesh of the flesh of the beginning. The conception must be retained throughout. In the drama, the lines of interest are continually set anew to converge, now here, now there. The totality of effect, the *Stimmung,* with Ibsen is created after the "story" is mapped out in skeleton dialogue. Ibsen at will broke through his original plan in the gradual development of a play. *The Lady From the Sea* in its original outline, with its wealth of characters, its unique rôle for Arnholm and the "Strange Passenger," and its situation in a much smaller place than in the completed play, exhibits the digressions from his original scenario which Ibsen at times made in the final form. In many instances there is less a digression than an actual fusion or re-casting of adjacent parts under the fire of his creative imagination. Both *The Pillars of Society* and *Rosmersholm,* for example, are four-act plays, though originally planned, and in part written, to have five acts.[1] Ibsen possessed a remarkable faculty for rejecting the superfluous; he welds together allied yet technically dissociate elements, and by the formation of a concrete whole, projects us into the midst of the catastrophe itself.

Parts of the scenario of *The Lady From the Sea* in a most striking way exhibit at once the riotous play of Ibsen's fancies, and the initial fantastic form of his conception. Originally the scene of the play is a small watering place, shut in by steep, high, overshadowing cliffs, and the play begins at the

[1] In *Rosmersholm,* the first two acts are fused into one.

time of the last voyage of the year. Slowly, the ships pass at midnight, noiselessly slipping into the bay and then out again.

The life is clearly gay, buoyant and fine up there in the shadow of the mountains and in the monotony of seclusion. There thoughts are thrown away: this sort of life is a shadow-life. No active power; no struggle for freedom. Only longing and wishes. Thus passes away the brief, bright summer. And after — into the gloom. Then awakes the longing for the great world without. But what is to be gained by it? With the situation, with the spiritual development arise claims and longings and wishes. He or she, who stands upon the heights, desires the secrets of the future and share in the life of the future and association with the distant world. Limitation everywhere. Hence dejection like a mute song over the whole of human existence and human action. A bright summer day, with the great darkness behind — that is the sum total.

Is there some gap in man's evolution: Why must we belong to the dry land: Why not to the air? Why not to the sea? The longing to have wings. The strange dreams that one can fly without wondering over it,— what is the meaning of all this?

We shall gain control over the sea. Launch floating cities. Tow them northwards or southwards according to the season. Learn to control storms and weather. Something happy will come of it. And *we* — we shall not be there to see it!

The seductive power of the sea. The longing for the sea. People who are akin to the sea. Bound to the sea.

Dependent on the sea. Must get back to the sea. One species of fish forms the primordial link in the evolutionary chain.[1] Do rudiments of it still lurk in man's nature? In the nature of particular individuals?

The fantasies of the unresting, churning life of the sea, and of that which "is lost forever." The sea exercises upon you the power of a mood, which works like a will. The sea can hypnotize. Above all, Nature can. The great mystery is man's dependence upon the "will-less."

V

With indefatigable industry, coral-like building row upon row, Ibsen slowly worked out the psychological features of his dramatic characters, first broadly sketched in the scenario. His power of imaginative incarnation was that of a magician indeed; and he never wrote about his characters until, as he himself phrased it, he had them wholly in his power and knew them down to the "last folds of their souls." The preliminary drafts, as a rule, lack dramatic emphasis or finality; and there is a certain stage in the incubation of a play, as Ibsen confessed to Mr. William Archer, when it might as easily turn into an essay as into a drama. Ibsen declared that the ability to project experience *mentally lived through* was the secret

[1] The species of fish, *Amphioxus lanceolatus,* is here doubtless referred to, indicating that Ibsen had given some study to the scientific treatment of the subject, probably in Darwin's *Descent of Man.*

of the literature of modern times. He looked around him and found models in abundance in actual life. He searched out the depths of his own soul and found there the confirmation of his hopes and dreams of future society. Starting from some crucial instance of contemporary human experience, Ibsen envisages for his creative fancy certain clearly marked, highly individual natures. Not the thesis, but the individual soul, is the prime subject of his ceaseless preoccupation. It was a source of genuine pride to him that he possessed a genius for utilizing his acquaintances as models for his dramatic figures, — a way of "getting hold of people," as he expressed it, for his plays. It is by no means improbable that Ibsen personified the little toys which stood upon his table. These were, perhaps, the *dramatis personæ;* he perhaps endowed each one of them with a name, conversed with them in the solitude of his study, and gave them their positions, their entrances and exits, in the play then preparing. The people of his fancy with whom he sometimes lived in solitude for decades before their final incarnation and inclusion in a play, were often more real to him than actual human beings; and he knew the characters almost from birth, in ancestral hereditament, in the features of their environment, in nascent qualities of soul. When someone remarked to Ibsen that Nora, in *A Doll's House,* had an odd name, Ibsen immediately replied: "Oh! her full name was Leonora; but that was shortened to Nora when she was quite a little girl. Of course, you know she was terribly spoiled by her parents." Sometimes he fumbles here and there with his figures, developing some trait, heightening some characteristic. Again, he broods over a figure for years before finally incorporating it in a play. Yet again, he finds the secret at once and knows his characters from the very beginning. Perhaps there is no better illustration than the description of the two leading figures in the first form of *Rosmersholm*.

> She is an *intrigante* and she loves him. She wishes to be his wife and tenaciously pursues this aim. He suspects it, and she freely acknowledges it. Now for him there is no longer any happiness in life. Sorrow and bitterness awake the dæmonic in him. He wishes to die, and she shall die with him. She does.

Here we have the situation outlined in the most laconic form. The genius of the ultimate creation is displayed in the utilization of the immitigable influence of ancestral traits; the invention of the means — the driving to death of Mrs. Rosmer by Rebekka — through which Rosmer's self-confidence is shattered and his happiness destroyed; individualistic youth, tainted with blood-guiltiness finally broken down under the pressure of ideals of life which lose themselves in the mists of ancient heredity. In the case of virtually all his prose plays, Ibsen was in the habit of tabulating a complete cast of characters before proceeding to any noteworthy development of the theme. And in some striking cases — notably in *Rosmersholm, The Lady From the Sea,* and *When We Dead Awaken* — he has noted the most important spiritual traits of the characters, and outlined in marvellous brevity of compression the inner meaning of their tragedy. This is well illustrated in Rosmersholm, as we have observed; but perhaps most strikingly in the preparatory notes for *When We Dead Awaken.*

First renowned through Irene. Then he wishes to live and enjoy a second youth with another. Then he changes the statue into a group. Irene becomes an auxiliary figure in the work, which has made him world-renowned —

First a single statue, then a group. Thereupon she left him.

Our life was not the life of two human beings.

What, then, was it?

Only the life of the artist and his model.

* * * * * * * *

When we dead awaken.

Yes, what see you there?

We see, that we have never lived.

We observe, again and again, Ibsen's stereoscopic imagination functioning brilliantly in the shaping and evolutional formation of character. With all the art of a finished worker in mosaic, Ibsen bit by bit discovers hidden traits and qualities, gives form and motive to his dramatic figures. The first drafts show the characters moving about with less volitional activity than they display in the completed play, much as a person acting under mesmeric control differs from the normally active individual.

Once Ibsen had grasped the individual in full significance, knew her or him as he might know his own flesh and blood, the rest came easily, almost mechanically. The inscenation, the dramatic *ensemble,* gradually took shape —" composed," to use the artist's term — as if of its own volition. It is this which makes the dramas of Ibsen so supremely great: the characters are not the creatures of the situation, as in Scribe and Sardou, but the situation — the plot — is the inevitable consequence of the characters. This it is, which gives to the plays of Ibsen, as Bernard Shaw has acutely put it, the quality of " illumination of life "— imparting final verisimilitude to the discussions of conduct, unveiling of motives, conflicts of characters, laying bare of souls. Here comes into full play what Rossetti termed " fundamental brain-work ": the working up of material in situation, in characterization and psychology. In the final forms, Ibsen eliminates the superfluous accessory figures, lops away auxiliary motives, heightens the dramatic effect of the situations, and rejects all that is coincidental and adventitious in the mechanism.

VI

A study of the prose plays brings to light the interesting fact that, in general, the complete meaning of a play was never definitely fixed in Ibsen's mind until the ultimate draft, in spotless purity and perfection of chirography was finished. In certain cases the original title which Ibsen employed was not the title he finally adopted: *Svanhild* for *The Comedy of Love, White Horses* for *Rosmersholm,* and *Resurrection Day* for *When We Dead Awaken.*[1] Ibsen once remarked to M. V. Conrad in connection with *The Lady From the Sea* — and it seems to have been true in general — that he did not know what the title was going to be, as he had one more act still to write. "I find my title at the end," he said. It is much the same with the names of his characters, which change with such rapidity in the rough drafts or fragments that one is continually brought up wondering at some new character, who yet seems so familiar. To cite a random illustration in *Rosmersholm,* Kroll first appears as Hekman, then as Gylling; Ulrik Brendel next takes the name of Hekman, borrows from Rosmer the name of Rosenhjelm, appears next as Sejerhjelm, and again as Hetman; Rosmer assumes in succession the names

[1] Ibsen abandoned the title of *White Horses* in favor of *Rosmersholm,* probably because, a short time before, he had employed a symbolic title for *The Wild Duck.*

of Boldt-Römer — a union of two old Norwegian noble names; Rosenhjelm; from Römer and Rosenhjelm in conjunction comes Rosmer — first with the surname Eilert Alfred (reminiscent of *Hedda Gabler* and *Little Eyolf,* forework), then with that of Johannes. In the first act the adventuress appears as Frau Rosmer, next changes to Fräulein Radeck, then Badeck; again appears as Frau Agatha Rosmer, next as Frau Rebekka, then as Fräulein Dankert, and in the third act finally as Fräulein Rebekka West. This matter of names may seem trivial; but it should be recalled that Ibsen expressed the conviction that there was a sort of hidden relation between name and character. And who has not remarked the appropriateness of *Stockmann* for the obstinate, stiff-necked doctor in *An Enemy of the People,* of *Rummel* for the noisy boaster in *The League of Youth,* of *Maja* for the blithe impersonation of the spring month in *When We Dead Awaken?* Ibsen left unstudied no detail which might contribute to the mood, the form, or the carrying power of his plays.

VII

The original fragments of dialogue, as they first occurred to Ibsen, seem not to have been preserved. But the fragments that are preserved show these bits of dialogue thrown together in the form of acts, scenes, or even portions of scenes. The fused portions of *The League of Youth*, *A Doll's House*, *The Lady From the Sea*, *Little Eyolf* and *When We Dead Awaken* are, almost certainly, first forms of this nature; probably this is also true of *Rosmersholm*, *The Master-Builder* and *John Gabriel Borkman*. After he had begun the development of a drama, Ibsen usually employed one or the other of two methods. One method was to take up each act singly, as soon as it was ready, work it over and write it out in final form before proceeding to the next act. The other method was to go straight through with his composition, and then go back and revise it. The mornings he was in the habit of devoting to the working-up of his dramatic material, the afternoons to the making of a "fair copy" of the completed portions. Ibsen certainly employed the first method in *The League of Youth* — the traces of which may readily be discerned in the unevenness of the dialogue of the finished play. He actually made a fair copy of the first act of *The Pillars of Society* after the original working up of the whole play — with the disappointing result that he had to discard all his already worked-up material. In consequence of this disastrous experience, he ever afterwards seems to have employed the plan of completely finishing a play before proceeding to the final drafting.

VIII

The transcendent genius of Ibsen is revealed, not primarily in the sureness of instinct with which he rejected the superfluous, the marvellous taste revealed in the deletion of the obvious or the questionable, the lopping off of the auxiliary characters which diffuse rather than concentrate the action. Nor can it be said that Ibsen's technique, with all its finish and classic restraint, is his most remarkable quality as a dramatist. His plays, as Henry James phrased it, are "infinitely *noted,*" revealing the ultimate refinement of the critical and creative temperaments in fortunate conjunction. His observation was unerring; and his power of visualizing the scene was so perfected that he never felt the necessity to enter the theatre or to study the drama in its natural environment. These qualities, alone and in themselves, were sufficient to make of Ibsen perhaps the most deft technician, all things considered, that any age has known. Ibsen knew quite enough science for his purpose; and his grasp of the fundamental weakness of modern life gives to his plays the character of sociological documents. But the quality which gives permanence and enduring validity to Ibsen as a dramatist is the quality of psychological intuition. His power of penetrating into the brains and hearts of men, searching out their secrets, and projecting authentically veracious and human representations of human character far transcends all his other powers.

Nowhere does Ibsen's art as a dramatist more signally reveal itself than in the comparison of the preliminary studies for his modern social dramas with the completed plays themselves. Here we are enabled to espy the great dramatist like a spider in his den, spinning out the fine-drawn threads of the complicated web of dramatic conjuncture and spiritual crisis. The final forms, as compared with the " foreworks," display immense economy of material, compression of thought, and complication of motive. A situation which, in some rought draft, appears somewhat commonplace, begins gradually to take on lively significance. The atmosphere becomes surcharged with suppressed emotion; the characters thrill with tense excitement; and there are lapses and pauses full of implication to replace the diffuse explication of the original dialogue. The rough draft lacks color and atmosphere; the final form is a dramatized mood to which the human symphonic orchestra is delicately attuned.

An admirable example is furnished in the case of *A Doll's House*. It is noteworthy that Ibsen is here primarily concerned with the woman question; and his first inclination was to exhibit this clearly, at the same time showing Nora's ignorance of and indifference to this question as a burning social problem. In the final version, the following interesting bit of dialogue in the preliminary draft has been deleted — doubtless because it called attention too obviously, too extraneously, shall we say, to the play's thesis.

Nora: When an unhappy wife is separated from her husband she is not allowed to keep her children? Is that really so?

Mrs. Linden: Yes, I think so. That's to say, if she's guilty.

Nora: Oh, guilty, guilty; what does it mean to be guilty? Has a wife no right to love her husband?

Mrs. Linden: Yes, precisely, her husband — and him only.

Nora: Why, of course; who was thinking of anything else? But that law is unjust, Kristina. You can see clearly that it is the men that have made it.

Mrs. Linden: Aha! — so you have begun to take up the woman question?

Nora: No, I don't care *a bit* about it.

In *The League of Youth,* and even in *The Pillars of Society,* with their omnipresent intrigue, their occasional intervention of the long arm of coincidence, their elaborate auxiliary plots, Ibsen has not yet succeeded in freeing himself from the influence of the artificial methods of Scribe and the French school of drama. So, in the preliminary draft for *A Doll's House, Dr. Rank,* under the name of

Hank, appears as a perfectly needless character, mechanically filling in the gaps and having no organic relation to the plot. He is a weak survival of the classical confidant, a futile *raisonneur* of the most artificial kind. At the time he was writing *A Doll's House,* it seems that Ibsen was full of the ideas of Darwin, whose works he probably had recently read — the *Origin of Species* (1872) and the *Descent of Man* (1875) having both been translated by the Danish author, Jens Peter Jacobsen. So Ibsen employs Dr. Hank solely as the mouthpiece for the Darwinian ideas of evolution — as exhibited in the following two passages, both of which are deleted in the final version.

Hank: Hallo! what's this? A new carpet? I congratulate you! Now take, for example, a handsome carpet like this — is it a luxury? I say it isn't. Such a carpet is a paying investment; with it under foot, one has higher, subtler thoughts, and finer feelings, than when one moves over cold, creaking planks in a comfortless room. Especially where there are children in the house. The race ennobles itself in a beautiful environment.

Nora: Oh, how often I have felt the same, but could never express it!

Hank: No, I daresay not. It is an observation in spiritual statistics — a science as yet very little cultivated.

* * * * * * * *

If Krogstad's home had been, so to speak, on the sunny side of life, with all the spiritual windows opening toward the light — I daresay he might have been a decent enough fellow, like the rest of us.

Mrs. Linden: You mean that he is not —?

Hank: He cannot be. His marriage was not of the kind to make it possible. An unhappy marriage, Mrs. Linden, is like smallpox: It scars the soul.

Nora: And what does a happy marriage do?

Hank: It is like a "cure" at the baths; it expels all peccant humors, and makes all that is good and fine in a man grow and flourish.

It is a mark of Ibsen's skill that he invents Dr. Rank's malady — like Krogstad's moral downfall — as an illustration of his favorite theme in future drama, Responsibility. Thereby Nora's eyes are gradually opened to the significance of her responsibility to her children, and so, through this transformation Dr. Rank, as family physician and personal friend, takes on a unique relation to the development of Nora's conscience.

Many empty sayings, many superfluous motives in the earlier draft are transposed in the final form into terms of spiritual development and character exposure. In the first draft, after Helmer has read Krogstad's letter returning the forged note, he cries, "You are saved, Nora, you are saved"; in the final form, with what singular clarity is Helmer's irredeemable selfishness caught in the changed phrase, "*I* am saved, Nora, *I* am saved!" In the preliminary draft, there is no trace of the oft-quoted question and answer with which, as by a lightning flash, Ibsen reveals the abyss which has suddenly yawned between Nora and Helmer:

Helmer: I would gladly work for you night and day, Nora — bear sorrow and want for your sake. No man sacrifices his honor, even for one he loves.

Nora: Millions of women have done so.

Nora's inordinate fondness for macaroons, so indicative of her childish nature, is an afterthought; and there is but the barest indication of her tendency to fibbing, so admirably accentuated in the final form as an instance of the transmission of hereditary characteristics. In the final form, the incident of the tarantella is naturally introduced — whereas, in the preliminary draft, it appears to be lugged in as a mere concession to the popular taste for theatricality; and natural causes are finally assigned for Nora's success in deceiving Helmer about her furtive copying. Further instances are unnecessary for demonstrating Ibsen's perfection of craftsmanship in his transmutation and re-adaptation of the apparently trivial, yet character-revealing incidents in the play.

IX

A Doll's House, in the course of its development, exhibits admirably the various mental stages through which Ibsen passed in the creation of a drama.

We note how Ibsen makes experiments and acknowledges failure; goes into blind alleys and is forced to retrace his steps; gradually develops and complicates the motives of his characters; and ultimately exhibits the situation as the inevitable outcome of the psychology. A study of the foreworks reveals salient examples on every hand. In *The Pillars of Society* Ibsen exhibits his power of condensation, in dropping the figures of Mads Tönnesen, Johan's father, Consul Bernick's blind mother, and Dina Dorf's mother; and his economy of technique is portrayed in having Johan Tönnesen and Lona Hessel go to America together and return together, rather than act in the haphazard ways of the first draft. From a dull, simple child in the forework, Hedwig in *The Wild Duck* is transformed, as if by a magician's wand, into a sweet, loving, infinitely tender daughter; and the real poignancy of her tragedy is unforgettably fixed in the imagination by the introduction of the presaged darkness of her coming blindness. By this simple expedient, Ibsen vastly deepens the tragedy; and the suspicious connection of Hedwig's threatened blindness with the failing eyesight of the old Werle tightens the cords of suspicion already tense to bursting in Hjalmar's breast. In the cast of characters, in the foreworks to *Rosmersholm,* Rebekka is depicted merely as " somewhat unscrupulous, but in a refined way "; and in the preliminary memorandum, it is stated that, in Rebekka's pursuit of Rosmer, there is cause for misery and unhappiness. In the finished play, these two concepts are brought into psychological harmony, by making Rebekka the evil genius who, in her passion for Rosmer, does not scruple, by diabolic and repeated insinuations, to drive the weak-minded, sick-souled Beata into the mill race. In the first draft of *Little Eyolf,* Miss Varg, the old "were-wolf," is Johanna's (Rita's) aunt; and she possesses little of the symbolic meaning and hypnotic power of the finished figure. The subtlety with which Ibsen has made of the "rat-wife" a figure of lasting mystery and horror, an impersonation of Death itself, is an irresistible reminder of the weird magic of the author of *The Marble Faun.* The "secrets of the alcove" revealed in the completed play furnish the real cause and motive for the mutual estrangement of Eyolf's father and mother; and the memorable phrase, "There stood your champagne — and you tasted it not," was a brilliant, strong afterthought. The preliminary draft of *Hedda Gabler* is conspicuous for the absence of that magic phrase, "vine leaves in his hair," with which the erotic Hedda always conjures up a Bacchanalian image of the dæmonic Lövborg. And that potent formula, "Liberty with Responsibility," the one clue to the destruction of Ellida's obsession (though even in the finished play it gives a schematic note to the *dénouement*) *is* found nowhere in the forework to *The Lady From the Sea.* In many of the finished plays are memorable phrases and situations which fix the fancy and knit the action and the characters closer together; while from the preliminary drafts are gone numerous details which too strongly accentuate the thesis or are in themselves, though intrinsically interesting, dramatically extraneous.

Ibsen's efforts at the emancipation of modern society inevitably took the form of life-struggles. It is to the enduring profit of the stage that these life-struggles always presented themselves to Ibsen as dramas. And everywhere, in the study of his posthumous works, we gain the impression of a mighty intensity at work, creating, re-creating. Everywhere refinement, everywhere complication of motive, everywhere increase in psychological depth and richness. Superficial incidents of the exterior life are sublimated into vitally revealing incidents of the inner life. Ibsen now stands forth in a new light as a dramatist. Every play appears as a marvellous result of artistic compression and selection. Every play is individual and distinctive; and yet all are linked together with invisible, hidden motives. All rest upon the indestructible foundation of permanent, enduring art.

MAURICE MAETERLINCK

"Indeed, it is not in the actions but in the words that are found the beauty and greatness of tragedies that are truly beautiful and great; and this not solely in the words that accompany and explain the action, for there must perforce be another dialogue beside the one which is superficially necessary. And, indeed, the only words that count in the play are those that at first seemed useless, for it is therein that the essence lies. Side by side with the necessary dialogue will you almost always find another dialogue that seems superfluous; but examine it carefully, and it will be borne home to you that this is the only one that the soul can listen to profoundly, for here alone is it the soul that is being addressed."

Maurice Maeterlinck: *The Tragical in Daily Life;* from *The Treasure of the Humble;* p. 111.

MAURICE MAETERLINCK

The closing half of the nineteenth century exhibits no marvellous and immutable fixations in the sphere of consciousness. Like all the other epochs, it has been a period of flux and reflux, of ebb and flow, of mutation and transmutation. Any well-marked devolution in the forms of literary art, in the ethical and philosophical expressions of human consciousness, has been checked by countercurrents, setting contrariwise, towards light, freedom, spirituality, truth.

The keen psychologist, intent upon the analysis of the intricate and devious workings of the mind, the intellect, and the human heart, first held the world's gaze for a space; his day is not yet done. He was succeeded by the Naturalist — bare of arm, merciless knife in hand, waiting to dissect with surgical precision his human victim. Then came the dilettante poco-curantists, the pastel Impressionists, reproducing with effects of elusive significance the outermost details of life, with their suggestions of depths and abysms of thought and feeling. Here was change in literary art ideals; but was it a progression or a retrogression? Realism was followed by its bastard progeny, Naturalism, to be followed in its turn by Realism's remotest of artistic relations, Impressionism. Psychology is replaced by physiology, and subsequently by photography; there is devolution here, and the devolution is from the actual to the artificial — mind, body, integument.

Just as, in the physical world, to every action corresponds a reaction, so may we expect the law of tidal ebb and flow in the sphere of literary phenomena. Edmond Rostand arose in France with romance as his watchword. Forthwith the French world forsook Zolaism and crowned Rostand with the laurels of genius. Stephen Phillips in England, a shining apparition in a gray world of naturalism, only accentuated the swing of the pendulum away from the pseudo-social and imperfectly truthful drama of Pinero. A generation sated with honeyed sentiment and pointless pruriency sits up with renewed vigor to listen to the provocative quips, the sovereign satire of Bernard Shaw. Maurice Maeterlinck, at the very crest of the wave of reaction, marks the return from the coarse and the artificial to the spiritual and the true. He turns from the realism of Hauptmann and Sudermann to the mysticism of Marcus Aurelius, Ruysbroeck, Novalis, and Thomas à Kempis; from the naturalism of Zola and D'Annunzio to the supernaturalism of Guy de Maupassant and Edgar Allan Poe.

Individualism is the most resonant note in the

symphony of modern thought; and individualism and reaction in philosophy rang out the dying years of the last century. To-day the three names that are emblazoned on the oriflamme of Revolt are Friedrich Nietzsche, Henrik Ibsen, and Maurice Maeterlinck. Their supreme distinction is modernity — in art, in vitality of thought, in form of expression. Each in his particular sphere, they represent what Nietzsche has called the link between Man and Superman, between Man as he is and Man as they would have him to be. Under their guidance man may be enabled to "rise above himself to himself and cloudlessly to smile." They represent the restless, throbbing, unquiet spirit of the age. They stand forth as apostles of regeneration — the physical, mental and spiritual regeneration of the individual. Each one soars over the most novel spheres of thought, truth's red torch aflame within his brain. It is by that ruddy and clarifying light that we shall see our way clearly. Stockmann, Monna Vanna, and Zarathustra eloquently attest humanity's struggle towards the light.

Advancing along strikingly distinct paths and unique each in his view of life, nevertheless these three men — Nietzsche, Ibsen, Maeterlinck — in reality are following radiating lines which converge towards some far distant point. They follow the so-called parallel lines of human endeavor which are said to meet at some Utopian infinity. In his millennial philosophy of the *Uebermensch*, the late Friedrich Nietzsche — poet, philosopher, and prophet — symbolizes the reaction of dynamism from the mechanism of Darwin, of aristocratic anarchy against the levelism of the age. The divinity of Nietzsche's rhapsody is not a subject for Bertillon or Lombroso, but the "roaming, blond animal," created through the felicitous conjunction of man's cunning and Nature's process. The supreme exaltation of the individual, thus spake Zarathustra.

Henrik Ibsen in his dramas of revolt flung defiance in the teeth of modern society. That trenchant sentence, "The majority is always wrong," seems to sum up his message to humanity. He has taught the final efficacy and supremacy of will; but his doctrine involves the salutary concession that "submission is the base of perfection." He stands out in grim aloofness the apostle of individual freedom — freedom of choice, freedom of the will, freedom from the false conventions and trammels of society. He has etched his own personality into the century's page with the corrosive acid of his mordant irony.

Maurice Maeterlinck — poet, mystic, transcendentalist — comes with gentle words of wise and aspiring sincerity to impress upon the world the belief that the development and disclosure of the human soul is the ultimate aim and goal of existence.

Marking the spiritual reaction from the blatant bestiality of Zolaism, he seeks to realize the infinite, to know the unknowable, to express the inexpressible. "Oh, that this too, too solid flesh would melt!" is his eternal prayer. He is individualistic in the sense that he is unique and essentially modern, not explainable as a product of the age, but rather as a reactionary, hostile to all its materialistic tendencies. He heralds the dawn of a spiritual renascence.

I

Maeterlinck's first little volume of lyrics, *Serres Chaudes,* expressive of his initial manner, most completely identifies him with that band of poets and mystics in France known as the Symbolists. There is no greater mistake than that of supposing that the wide hearing he has gained is attributable to the peculiar eccentricities of his style, the novelties in literary form he has employed, or the seeming inanities or solemn mystifications of his poetry. At first there was about him a trace of the *fumisterie,* that air of solemn shamming, which has helped to make the Parisian "Cymbalists" (as Verlaine loved to call them) a jest and a mockery. Perhaps he first caught the most obvious tricks of his style, those very idiosyncrasies his own fine instinct has since taught him to discard from the school of Mallarmé, Vielé-Griffin and Régnier. Yet the reiterant ejaculations, the hyperethereal imaginings of the Symbolist manner, are the symptoms of a tentative talent, not of an authoritative art.

Symbolism — the casting of the immaterial thought into the material mold of speech, to use the word in a broad connotation — marks the correspondence between the outward visible sign and the inward spiritual idea. One must distinguish with the greatest care between the Symbolism of the French school and that of Ibsen, of Hauptmann, or of D'Annunzio. The point of departure for the art of the French Symbolists was the effort, by tricks of sound and rhythm, of figure and image, by allusion and suggestion, to cast a languorous spell over the reader, evoking rare and fleeting emotions, producing strange and indefinable impressions. As Henri de Régnier expresses it: "It is the function of the poet to express his own emotions. He realizes that his ideas are beautiful. He would convey them to the reader as they are. It is then that the power of common speech forces him to place known words in uncommon sequence or to resurrect an archaism that his idea may be better expressed. He is in no sense an analyst of the emotions but an artist, pure and simple; his function is not with life and nature, but with the imagination." A Symbolist in this sense is an artist who finds the words at his command inadequate clearly to express his emotions, and is therefore compelled to employ words as symbols, deeply suggestive in their meaning. It is apparent that, with the Symbolists, the simplest words, the homeliest figures, may take on untold significance. The poetry of the Symbolists is characterized by peculiar, haunting and elusive beauty and destined for the profoundest suggestiveness; but quite too often, it must be confessed, conveying no meaning at all to anyone save to the initiated.

To compare Maeterlinck's early poems with the "unrhymed, loose rhythmic prose" of Walt Whitman is to make a perfectly obvious and yet at the same time perfectly irrelevant criticism. While both are disjointed, formless, enumerative, Maeterlinck's every line is charged with a certain vague significance, suggestive of subtile and ever subtler possibilities of interest. Take a passage from *Serres Chaudes* like the following:

> "O hothouse in the midst of the forests!
> And your doors shut forever!
> And all that there is under your dome,
> And under my soul in your likeness!
> The thoughts of a princess an-hungered,
> The weariness of a sailor in the wilderness,
> Brazen music at the windows of incurables."

Is this pompous mystification or profound poetry? Is it sense? As Bernard Shaw would say: "Is it right, is it proper, is it decent?" And yet the morbid mind of modernity sighs through it all: he is excluded by very reason of his supersensitive, exotic soul from spontaneous and untrammelled communication with nature. Witness the poignant image of the princess, born in affluence suffering the unimagined pangs of hunger. The isolation and hopelessness are accentuated by the figure of the sailor, longing for the cool waves and bracing salt breezes of health, as he wanders with parched throat over the hot sand of the endless desert. What more laconically modern symbol than that of a brass band passing under the windows of a hospital for incurables! Lonely souls are these so laconically sketched, obsessed with world-weariness, harassed with morbid self-distrust and uncertain of a goal.

As an illustration of the beauty and finish and simplicity of Maeterlinck's art as a poet, at its highest and least symbolical pitch, may be cited Richard Hovey's translation of Maeterlinck's unnamed poem:

> "And if some day he come back
> What shall he be told?
> Tell him that I waited,
> Till my heart was cold.
>
> "And if he ask me yet again,
> Not recognizing me,
> Speak him fair and sisterly,
> His heart breaks, maybe.

"And if he asks me where you are,
What shall I reply?
Give him my golden ring
And make no reply.

"And if he should ask me
Why the hall is left desolate?
Show him the unlit lamp,
And point to the open gate.

"And if he should ask me
How you fell asleep?
Tell him that I smiled,
For fear lest he should weep."

II

M. Maeterlinck owes his world reputation, not to fad, to decadence or to symbolism. He is admired because he is the sincerest of literary artists, because he is ever striving for that Truth which is Beauty. His poetry, even when vaguest and most mysterious in its strangely symbolic vesture, leaves always upon the mind, or rather upon the senses, an ineffaccable impression of peculiar and unusual beauty. He cannot be said to have created any great, distinctive, or strikingly modern form of prose writing. Still his prose wears a gentle simplicity, and a pensive appeal that charms when the fulminations of the phantasmagoric imagination tire the senses and polished periods leave the heart unmoved. Such a book as *Wisdom and Destiny* — a book that may truly be called noble — marks a distinct epoch in spiritual and cosmic evolution. The calm philosophy of Marcus Aurelius; the longings after the Infinite, if haply they may find it, of the fourteenth century mystic, Ruysbroeck the admirable, and the gentle Novalis; the transcendentalism of the Greek spirit in our own literature, Emerson; the "second sphere," the realm of unconscious revelation of the Ibsen of *The Lady from the Sea* and *The Master Builder;* the brooding mysticism of the Shakspere of *Hamlet* — these and other inspiring influences mingle with and color Maeterlinck's own conception of the "inner life." If, in Maeterlinck's interpretation of the world-riddle, there is one charm more fascinating than another, it is his disinterested search for truth. He is never didactic, never even definitive in any ultimate sense. Quite often he is actually found contradicting himself, consciously doing so, in the hope of retracing his steps a little way, aided by the faint glimmer of some new light, until he enter once more the straight path to his goal. His books show that, in a sense rightly understood, he is a scientific worker, difficult as this is to reconcile with the vagueness and groping insecurity of his mysticism. From the evidence of his books, M. Maeterlinck has studied the modern theories of auto-suggestion, hypnotism, telepathy, psychology, and psychic phenomena. No reader of *The Life of the Bee* can doubt that M. Maeterlinck is a scientific worker, although this exquisite social history is the work of an artist and a *littérateur* as well as of a scientist. His works — poetry, prose, drama — all evidence his close study and deep comprehension of modern scientific theories, especially of a psychic or psychologic character, and these works evidence it concretely and suggestively, but more often by mere implication.

It would be a serious mistake to imagine M. Maeterlinck the mere mouthpiece of the mystics of other years. It is not to be doubted that his mysticism is based upon a long and loving acquaintance with the greatest mystics of the past. To find standards of comparison for a phenomenon like the rare mind of this new-century mystic, we have to seek, not in our own, but in another age. A comparison of M. Maeterlinck's philosophy with that of the mystics of the past shows similarity in fundamentals to exist between them. But to say that M. Maeterlinck follows Ruysbroeck here or Novalis there, is not an easy matter: with other mystics M. Maeterlinck has in common only mysticism. The point of vantage from which he views the world, the eyes with which he sees it, the transmuting mind, are all his own. Nor has he studied modern science — that of the body, the organism, that of the mind, the intelligence, that of the soul, the higher emotions — only to be thrown back upon himself in disappointment, disillusionment and despair. Rather, as someone has recently said: "There is evidence that his mysticism is not so much a refuge from the tyranny of scientific naturalism as the deliberate choice of a man who finds in it confirmations of countless hopes and suspicions science herself raised within him."

III

Much has been said in praise of the technique of Maeterlinck's first little no-plot plays — laudatory classification of them as forms of art absolutely new under the sun. Maeterlinck was intimately familiar with the cognate work of his countryman, Charles van Lerberghe; and to Maeterlinck, as to Baudelaire, Poe was the master. The art-form of which Maeterlinck's no-plot plays are mere dramatic transpositions is virtually a creation of the nineteenth century; and, with all their bizarre novelty, these little plays appear as little else, technically, than Short-stories cast in the dramatic mould. The Short-story, as formulated by Professor Brander Matthews, must always convey essential unity of impression — or, as Poe phrased it, a totality of effect. Intensive, cumulative force is the most significant distinction of this art-form. No one has ever succeeded as a writer of Short-stories who had not ingenuity, originality, the faculty of compression, and, in many instances, the touch of fantasy. As an example of Maeterlinck's early manner in the drama, consider, for example, that wonderfully convincing study in hallucination, Maeterlinck's *L'Intruse* — the most striking, awe-compelling, and, withal, most original of his no-plot plays.

The grandfather, blind and helpless, is seated in his arm-chair, with his three granddaughters around him. The old man's beloved daughter has given birth to a child, and lies ill in the inner chamber. The atmosphere is pregnant with catastrophe, the senses are chilled by the prevision of impending misfortune. Overbrooded by anticipant foreboding, the grandfather subconsciously feels the approach of death. His senses, subtile and acute beyond their wont — from his blindness, perhaps — give him unmistakable warning. The gradual approach of some unseen being, the fright of the swans, the sudden hush of nature, the sound as of the sharpening of a scythe, the ghostly creaking of the house door, the noise of footsteps on the stair, the fitful gleams and sudden extinguishing of the lamp — the significance of all these signs and portents is divined by the blind old grandfather alone. When finally someone is heard to rise in the pitchy blackness of the sitting-room, the old man shudders with peculiar horror. The door of the inner chamber opens, and a Sister of Charity mutely announces by a sign that his daughter is dead. The Intruder has gained admittance.

This little play, the dramtic production of which the late Richard Hovey confessed made an ineffaceable impression upon his consciousness, bears the clearest stamp of unity of impression, of totality of effect. The keynote of its mood is cumulative dread; while ingenuity and originality are displayed in every line of the conception. The art which well-nigh makes the impalpable invade the realm of the tangible, the supernatural to place one foot over the border line of the natural, attains here something very like perfection. Fantasy fills every interstice of the play. In *L'Intruse* as a psychic concept, a deep and penetrating insight into subjective states of mind in direct correspondence with movements in the supernatural world is revealed. It is not so much that Maeterlinck has created a new shiver, to quote Hugo on Baudelaire, as that he has evoked a shiver in a novel and startling way.

L'Intruse was chosen as an illustration of the dramatized Short-story because it excels all the other no-plot dramas in power and inevitableness. Perhaps *Les Aveugles,* because of the quiescence and paralyzed initiative of the groping blind man, and because, too, its conclusion is not "short, sharp, and shocking," comes nearer to a Sketch cast in dramatic form than a dramatized Short-story; but certainly *Les Sept Princesses* and *L'Intérieur* are examples of the latter form as clearly as is *L'Intruse.*

The artistic kinship of Maeterlinck with Maupassant and Poe becomes all the more patent when we recognize Maeterlinck's no-plot dramas not only as occult studies in hallucination but as dramatized versions of the perfected art-form of these masters of the Short-story.

IV

It is the fundamental faith of M. Maeterlinck that the theatre of to-day needs reorganization and reformation in order to conform to the subtler demands of the higher and more complex life of our epoch. The theatre, he affirms, has for its supreme mission the revelation of infinity, and of the grandeur as well as the secret beauty of life. He would have a theatre in accordance with modern psychic demands, giving a revelation of what the Parisian mystic Schuré calls the *abîmes* and *profondeurs* of the soul. Carlyle also pleaded for a recognition of what he called in his own speech the Eternities and the Immensities. M. Maeterlinck would bring the inner life of the soul closer to us; he would push the actors further off. Thus he regrets that he has ever seen *Hamlet* performed on the stage, since it robbed him of his own conception of its mystic significance. The actor, the spectre of an actor, dethroned his own image of the real Hamlet. From the printed page starts forth the old Hamlet of his dreams never again.

His regret is for the loss of the "second sphere," that subconscious realm where soul speaks to soul without the intermediary of words. He hails the coming of the Renascence of Wonder, the mystic epoch when men shall penetrate deep into the soil of their subliminal selves. The age, which, as Phillips Brooks once said, "stands off and looks at itself"—that age Maeterlinck heralds and summons. Ibsen, too, has dreamed of this dawning day: Julian perhaps in the end caught some faint prevision of the "third kingdom."

Silence is the pall that hangs over the earlier plays of Maeterlinck; the characters themselves are quiescent and immobile. It is only in silence that we can really know each other — in the fugitive look, the chance meeting, the sudden hand-clasp. Only in such moments do we truly come to know anything that is worth knowing. Half conscious of his deep-rooted faith in the meaning of presentiments, the significance of sub-conscious revelations, M. Maeterlinck wrote a number of plays surcharged with the impalpable and imponderable weight of pathos and groping nescience. "The keynote of these little plays," he once wrote, "is dread of the unknown that surrounds us. I, or rather some obscure poetical feeling within me (for with the sincerest of the poets a division must often be made between the instinctive feeling of their art and the thoughts of their real life) seemed to believe in a species of monstrous, invisible, fatal power that gave heed to our every action, and was hostile to our smile, to our life, to our peace and our love. Its intentions could not be divined, but the spirit of the drama assumed them to be malevolent always. In its essence, perhaps, this power was just, but only in anger; and it exercised justice in a manner so crooked, so secret, so sluggish and remote, that its punishments — for rewards there were never — took the semblance of inexplicable, arbitrary acts of fate. We had then more or less the idea of the God of the Christians, blent with that of fatality of old, lurking in nature's impenetrable twilight, whence it eagerly watched, contested, and saddened the projects, the feelings, the thoughts, and the happiness of man."

In those early plays the interest hangs upon the passage, rather than upon the victim, of fatality; our grief is not excited by the tragedy: we shudder with wide-eyed horror at the argument of the invisible, the evidence of things not seen. By the intuitive apprehensions of the soul, its instinctive gropings, the incomprehensible, disquieting movements in nature, the dark forebodings of dumb, shadowy events — by these means M. Maeterlinck made us aware of the adumbration, the gradual approach, and ultimate presence of the mysterious forces of Fate,

Terror, and Death. He objectified and concretized for us those moments of life.

> "When . . .
> In some nimble interchange of thought
> The silence enters and the talkers stare."

The unnamed presence was always Death — Death the intruder. In *L'Intruse* we waited with tense expectancy and strained senses for his coming; in *L'Intérieur* we accompanied him to the scene of the eternal tragedy; in *Les Aveugles* we awaken with a start to find Death in our very midst. Terror lurks behind a half-closed door, and all the poignant mystery of the Universe seems embodied in the figures of seven princesses sleeping in a dim castle beside the sounding sea. There was no escape from the obsession of some dire, inexpressibly dreadful unknown presence. "This unknown," M. Maeterlinck himself has said, "would most frequently appear in the shape of death. The presence of death — infinite, menacing, forever treacherously active — filled every interstice of the poem. The problem of existence was answered only by the enigma of annihilation. And it was a callous, inexorable death; blind, and groping its mysterious way with only chance to guide it; laying its hands preferentially on the youngest and least unhappy, for that those held themselves less motionless than others, and that every too sudden movement in the night arrested its attention. And round it were only poor, little, trembling, elementary creatures, who shivered for an instant and wept, on the brink of a gulf; and their words and their tears had importance only from the fact that each word they spoke and each tear they shed fell into this gulf, and resounded therein so strangely at times as to lead one to think that the gulf must be vast if tear or word, as it fell, could send forth so confused and muffled a sound."

A time came in M. Maeterlinck's career when he recognized the morbidness and unhealthiness of such a view of life, and realized that, in the transition, he had come out "on the other side of good and evil." This conception of life may be truth, he grants, but it is "one of those profound but sterile truths which the poet may salute as he passes on his way"; with it he should not abide. It is perhaps this early conception which led him to avow that he had written these plays for a theatre of marionettes. The characters all silently and unresistingly do the bidding of some unseen, unknown power. Duse said of Maeterlinck: "He gives you only figures in a mist — children and spirits." Even that "savage little legend" of the misfortunes of Maleine, M. Maeterlinck's first play, with all its violence, lust, bloodshed, tears and terror, is overbrooded by haunting and inexpressible misery.

Octave Mirabeau wrote of this play: "*M. Mau-*

rice Maeterlinck nous a donné l'œuvre la plus géniale de ce temps, et la plus extraordinaire et la plus naïve aussi, comparable et — oserai-je dire? — supérieure en beauté à ce qu'il y a de plus beau dans Shakspere . . . plus tragique que Macbeth, plus extraordinaire en pensée que Hamlet." Plus, plus, and again *plus!* Bernard Shaw delightedly, though unjustly, accused even the precise and careful Archer of conferring the "Order of the Swan" (the Swan of Avon) upon Maeterlinck.

There are many suggestions of Shaksperean characters in this little play — Hamlet, Ophelia, Juliet, Lear, the nurse in *Romeo and Juliet,* and Lady Macbeth; one rather feels, however, that the author of this play is in no sense a "Belgian Shakspere," but instead a rather morbid and immature young man, re-interpreting and rehandling the plots and personages of the master-poet, in the effort to express himself and his faith in terms of the psychic chirography of to-day. *Maleine* is full of the unnamed terrors of the Poe of *The House of Usher,* of ghost-haunted regions, of dark, pestilential tarns — the Poe of *Ulalume* and *The Haunted Palace.* It is not until M. Maeterlinck's second, or rather third, period is reached that his theories find plausibly human concretizations.

V

The late Richard Hovey once spoke of Maeterlinck as "the greatest living poet of love, if not the greatest poet of love that ever lived." The Maeterlinck of the second manner we recognize as essentially the celebrant and interpreter of Love.

In *Pelléas and Mélisande* we have a play of conventional plot — a modern revision of the Da Rimini story of Dante —; yet in Maeterlinck's play there is no such thing as local color, no trace of Italy, for example, no suggestion of the thirteenth century. So distant is the scene, so fanciful is the setting — a pathetic love-story projected against a gloomy background of old, forgotten castles — that we might almost think of it as taking place out of space and time. It is typical of the plays of this period, peopled with princes and princesses from No-Man's Land, named after the characters in the *Morte d'Arthur,* striking stained-glass attitudes of pre-Raphaelite grace; old men, symbolic of experience, wisdom, abstract justice; blind beggars, intoning the song of the world-malady; little wise children, whose instinctive divination gives new veracity to the words: "Out of the mouths of babes and sucklings . . ." There are castles in the depths of haunted forests, fountains playing softly in the misty moonshine of secret gardens, where errant princesses lose their golden crowns in magic pools, or their wedding-rings in caverns echoing with the murmur of the sea. These are pictures in which may faintly be traced the lineaments of humanity; but the figures are dim and confused, more abstract than vital. In *Pelléas and Mélisande* the accent is nowhere placed upon the human characters; the stress is thrown upon forces of a supersensible dreamland, beyond the frontier of the natural. Throughout every scene, in almost every speech, there lurks a hidden meaning, so suggestive, so elusive, so profound, that the unembodied forces of another world seem to adumbrate and control the destinies of humanity. Mélisande is a child-princess, wedded through no will of her own to the gaunt, rugged, silent Golaud. As soon as Mélisande and the young and handsome Pelléas, Golaud's half-brother, meet, their mutual insight tells them that they are destined for each other. Struggle as they will against fate, the coils are too strong for them and they succumb to the inevitable call of soul to soul. Through the little Yniold, his son by a former marriage, Golaud learns of Mélisande's infidelity, surprises the lovers in each others arms, strikes Pelléas dead, and gives Mélisande a mortal wound.

Throughout the whole play there breathes an atmosphere of the most profound symbolism. Even the simplest acts, the merest words of all the characters, are charged and freighted with symbolic meaning. The beautiful balcony episode, suggestive as it may be of *Romeo and Juliet,* is not only cast in exquisite poetic form, but is animate with tragic significance. The incident of the flight of Mélisande's doves, the fluttering of her hair to her lover's lips, the loss of the wedding-ring, the cavern scene, and the clandestine meetings beyond the walls of the castle loom large with hidden import. Nowhere is the novel dramatic method of M. Maeterlinck more manifest than in this play. The faintest movements of nature coöperate with the thoughts and deeds of the characters to suggest the overshadowing of that divinity which shapes our ends.

As presented by a wholly French cast at Covent Garden, London, in the season of 1910, Debussy's opera of *Pelléas and Mélisande* seemed to me a marvel of matchless beauty, of sight and sound. The eery strains of this strange music seemed magically devised to express the fateful sadness of Maeterlinck's poem. The characters move as in a dream through the exquisite scenes of their predestined fate — with a hopelessness, a sad sense of imminent misfortune incomparably poetic and tragic. Such collaboration is a miracle of art: Maeterlinck himself might have passed into the soul of Debussy and inspired him. An even more memorable performance — if such be possible! — was given in the latter part of August, 1910, at M. Maeterlinck's own home, the ancient Abbey of St. Wandrille. The changing scenes of this romantic play, with its antique setting, were all found in the Abbey itself and its environs. The few rapt spectators took their prearranged places of vantage and spied, like eavesdroppers, upon forlorn little Mélisande weeping in the forest over the loss of her golden crown; upon Golaud riding up to the castle gates on his white charger, joyously bearing his young bride in his arms; upon Pelléas and Mélisande engaging in gentle converse, now in the stillness of the lime trees, now beside the splashing waters of the fountain; upon the prophetic bedside scene when Golaud discovers the loss of Mélisande's betrothal ring; upon the tower scene where Pelléas bathes in the beauty of Mélisande's hair; upon the final tragic scenes of suspicion, surprised love, assassination, death. With such artists as M. René Maupré, M. Jean Durozat, M. Severin-Mars, Mme. Leblanc, Mlle. Jeanne Even, and Mlle. Gilberte Livettini, with such setting as the Abbey of Saint Wandrille, Maeterlinck's beautiful drama had a marvellous rendition that bids fair to remain unsurpassed in the history of the production of his plays.

In all Maeterlinck's love-dramas — *Alladine and Palomides, Pelléas and Mélisande,* and *Aglavaine and Sélysette* — the mood is ever individualistic, symptomatic of the modern thinker. The action, simple to the verge of bareness, is a frail framework through and beyond which we gaze into the depths of the human soul. Maeterlinck seems to throw faint gleams of light into the dark pool where humanity has lost its golden crown. The march of events is but a passing show, life is a tiny oasis in an illimitable desert, a narrow vale between two eternities. The characters do not bring things to pass; they are set in a magic maze of tragic destinies: through them are ever sweeping the impelling forces of the universe. Action is but the seeming; emotion is eternal reality. Deeds are but the evanescent expression of the temporary; feelings are the vital repository of immortal truth.

The realities, the crises of life, are found in silence and in sadness: "*sunt lacrimæ rerum.*" We see no vital, tremendous, self-captained soul, incarnate with the deep-seated elements of religion and Christian morality. Love is ever the victim, wantonly broken upon the wheel of fate. The supremacy of destiny is solemnly acknowledged, its decrees accepted. The call of soul to soul cannot be disregarded: the forces of Love and Chance conspire in the tragic outcome.

VI

To M. Maeterlinck, as both his plays and essays affirm, tragedy to-day is of necessity of a different cast from the tragedy of the past. Speaking of his art, Ibsen once significantly said: "We are no longer living in the time of Shakspere." However he may have carried his theory out, at least Gerhart

Hauptmann has said: " Action upon the stage will, I think, give way to the analysis of character and to the exhaustive consideration of the motives which prompt men to act. Passion does not move at such headlong speed as in Shakspere's day, so that we present not the actions themselves, but the psychological states which cause them." Maeterlinck believes that the bold bloodshed and gaudy theatricism of the conventional drama of the past must be replaced in this modern day of analysis and introspection by psychic suggestion and the silent conflicts of the soul. The " character in action " of Shakspere will be superseded by the inverted " action in character " of Maeterlinck. Or, to be more precise, life reveals its meaning to us only in static moments, in the passive intervals of our life. " It is no longer a violent, exceptional moment of life that passes before our eyes — it is life itself. Thousands and thousands of laws there are, mightier and more venerable than those of passion. . . . It is only in the twilight that they can be seen and heard, in the meditation that comes to us at the tranquil moments of life."

Maeterlinck's ideal mood is static. He protests against the false anachronism which so dominates the stage that dramatic art dates back as many years as the art of sculpture. He cites modern examples of the art of painting to prove that Marius triumphing over the Cymbrians, or the assassination of the

Copyright by Elliott & Fry, Ltd.

MAURICE MAETERLINCK

Duke of Guise, is no longer the type. The drama is no longer dependent upon the exhibition of violent convulsions of life: "Does the soul flower only on nights of storm?" It is only when man is at rest that we have time to observe him. "To me, Othello does not appear to live the august daily life of Hamlet, who has time to live, inasmuch as he does not act. Othello is admirably jealous. But is it not perhaps an ancient error to imagine that it is at the moments when this passion, or others of equal violence, possess us, that we live our true lives? I have grown to believe that an old man, seated in his arm-chair, waiting patiently, with his lamp beside him, giving unconscious ear to all the eternal laws that reign about his house, interpreting, without comprehending, the silence of doors and windows and the quivering voice of the light, submitting with bent head to the presence of his soul and his destiny — an old man who is conscious not that all the powers in this world, like so many heedful servants, are mingling and keeping vigil in his room, who suspects not that the very sun itself is supporting in space the little table against which he leans, or that every star in heaven and every fibre of the soul are directly concerned in the movement of an eyelid that closes or a thought that springs to birth,— I have grown to believe that he, motionless as he is, does yet live in reality a deeper, more human, and more universal life than the lover who strangles his mistress, the captain who conquers in battle, or 'the husband who avenges his honor.'"

VII

Preoccupied ceaselessly with the "disquiet of universal mystery," groping hesitatingly in that twilight zone which vaguely delimitates the real and intimates the over-real, Maeterlinck in his earlier fatalistic moods seemed content to look upon the legend of the human chimera with the "grave, wide-eyed gaze of an inspired child." He succeeded in diffusing through this twilight zone that strange "lunar brilliance" which Heine divined at times in Shakspere. In his symbols there is some audible, almost sensable revelation of the Infinite; in Carlyle's phrase, "the Infinite is made to blend itself with the Finite, to stand visible, and, as it were, attainable there." First, I think, in *Aglavaine and Sélysette* is there real descent to earth, a real adumbration of a primarily human problem. This play, along with *Sœur Béatrice* and *Ardiane et Barbe Bleu,* marks the actual transition stage in Maeterlinck's art from the drama of fatality, of pity and terror, to the drama of human interests, of real emotions, and of direct volitional activity. *Aglavaine and Sélysette* is an illuminating essay, though seen in a glass darkly, upon ideal possibilities in human relationship in a future state of elevated moral consciousness. The noble, soulful Aglavaine realizes that she loves, and is beloved by, Méléandre, already wedded to the childlike Sélysette. Through sympathetic communion with the lofty soul of Aglavaine, the little Sélysette awakes to a realization of the shallowness of her fruitless, butterfly existence. With her mate, there has been no high pilgrimage to those uplands of peace where the soul truly flowers. The unfolding, petal by petal, of this flower-like, primrose soul is intimated with an art as exquisite as it is finished. And yet the situation, humanly speaking, is perilous, untenable. "I love you," says Aglavaine; "I love Méléandre, Méléandre loves me, he loves you, too; you love us both, and yet we cannot live happily, because the hour has not yet come when human beings may be thus united." (Does the world offer no instances to the contrary?) With the resolution born of a hopeless certitude, Aglavaine attains the power of sincere resignation and offers to go away forever. Humanly consenting in the first glad rush of relief, Sélysette in the event attains the diviner resignation, resolutely going out into the night of despair and death that two souls, immemorially mated, may attain the foreordained consummation of their destiny.

Librettos for music — *Singspiele,* as the Germans say — *Sœur Béatrice* and *Ardiane et Barbe Bleu* serve more clearly to mark the transition in Maeterlinck's attitude towards problems which concern the interpreter of life. *Sœur Béatrice* is the Everywoman of human love — instinctive, sacrificial. She flees the convent with her lover, and though externally besmirched with earthly contacts, she returns in the end to sanctuary to find that the Virgin has kept her place inviolate — a subtle vindication of the sanctity of human impulse. When the Abbess intimates that love divine is a terrible burden, Béatrice replies, "Mother, no. It is the love of man that is the burden, the weary burden. . . . I have said often, when I was not happy, God would not punish if He once knew all. . . . In other days all folks ignored distress, in other days they cursed all those that sinned; but now all pardon, and all seem to know. . . ."

The self-reliant Ardiane, of Maeterlinck's version of the old Blue Beard legend of a thousand transformations, is the direct progenitress of the passionate Joyzelle and the heroic Giovanna. Her intuition is sure and supreme; for though she is free to open all doors but one, it is the forbidden door alone that she seeks. "Open the others if you will; but all that is permitted us will tell us naught." Truth lies not on the beaten path of convention, but in the secret recesses of the soul. Guilty for a moment of human yielding to the sparkling allurements of the senses, Ardiane recoils in time, and releases her imprisoned sisters in captivity — only to find that they are wedded to their chains. Without too violent reference to the concrete — the vaticinations of a Mary Wollstonecraft or the violences of a Christabel Pankhurst — it is obvious that Maeterlinck is envisaging here the present and coming revolt of woman against her subjection; and enunciating quite definitely, if delicately, satiric commentaries upon the "womanly woman."

VIII

The influence of much modern philosophy, of much modern drama, is unmistakable. There is a secret and abstract justice, a sphere of ethical equity, outside of and above the external domain of law, convention and authority. The arbiter of human conduct must be, not the merciless dictum of the world, but the mystical sense of justice deep-rooted in the consciousness of the race. To the question: Which of two forces which work within us, the one natural, the other ethical, is the more natural and necessary? Maeterlinck would doubtless answer, according to Lorenzo Ratto, "The great ideas of humanity belong to the species, not to the individual. Justice is perhaps an instinct whose tendency is the defence and conservation of humanity. Ideal justice is innate and is transformed by reason and will into moral force. Justice is within ourselves; outside of us is infinite injustice, which may rather be called justice incomplete, because exposed to all the errors and modifications which result from clashing interests. While we are benefited by following the dictates of this inner voice, its influence cannot extend to our surroundings and modify the laws of nature. Its sole result is an internal equilibrium, the balance of the conscience in which we may enjoy material well-being."

But how shall this human, instinctive justice, perpetually functioning within ourselves, find expression in a drama of nescience and fatalistic quietude? How shall such a drama exist in the world of spectators whose composite and aggregate passion is for character in visible action? After his long period of probative experimentalism followed by contemplation — the reverse operation to that of the pure theorist — Maeterlinck discovered and frankly acknowledged the obligation of the dramatist writing for the actual theatre of to-day. "To penetrate deeply into human consciousness," he says in *The Double Garden,* "is the privilege, even the duty of the thinker, the moralist, the historian, novelist, and, to a degree, of the lyric poet; but not of the dramatist. Whatever the temptation, he dare not sink into inactivity, become mere philosopher or observer. Do what one will, discover what marvels one may, the sovereign law of the stage, its essential demand, will always be *action.* With the rise of the curtain, the high intellectual desire within us undergoes transformation; and in place of the thinker, psychologist, mystic or moralist, there stands the mere instinctive spectator, the man electrified negatively by the crowd, the man whose one desire is to see something happen." Nowhere have I seen a more admirable and succinct formulation of the essential criterion of true drama — unless it be Brunetière's classical positing of the struggle of human wills; and this, in the light of contemporary specimens of drama, is subject to very wide modification and restatement. In Maeterlinck's case, it is peculiarly noteworthy that his practice accompanies the actual formulation of his hardly won discoveries.

Early in his career, Maeterlinck confessed that when he went to a theatre, he felt as though he were spending a few hours with his ancestors, who conceived life as something primitive, arid and brutal. In the dramas of the school of Dumas *fils*, he found the most elementary of moral conflicts brought on the stage — the husband avenging his honor, the promulgation of the rights of the illegitimate child, aspects of divorce, variations on the "unwritten law," and so on. It was not until he pondered the dramas of Ibsen and his followers that he discovered that "the further we penetrate into the consciousness of man, the less struggle do we discover." A mystic who has lost faith in the healing efficacies of revealed religion, Maeterlinck has undergone the inevitable attendant disillusion. And his dispassionate contemplation of the eternal enigma has fixed in his consciousness the irrevocable conviction that the great duties, faiths, obligations and responsibilities of the future will gently disengage themselves from the violent, bitter and all too human passions of to-day. "A consciousness that is truly enlightened will possess passions and desires infinitely less exacting, infinitely more peaceful and patient, more salutary, abstract and general, than are those that reside in the ordinary consciousness." In a world of human beings, emanating justice from within and living an interior life of rare calm and benignity, only the most pressing and most universal duties will possess the power to disturb the internal equilibrium of human consciousness.

IX

Monna Vanna is the summit of Maeterlinck's art as a dramatist; and *Joyzelle,* though following it in point of time, in reality is a link between *Monna Vanna* and his earlier works. Indeed, it is a sort of pendant to *Monna Vanna* and should be considered prior to and in connection with it. And I think that the theoretical considerations outlined above may serve to act as commentary upon both plays. *Joyzelle* is more imaginative, poetic and symbolic than *Monna Vanna,* as Maeterlinck himself said, but it is far less coherent and significant, relying upon such obvious symbolism. "It represents," said Maeterlinck, "the triumph of will and love over Destiny, or fatality as against the converse lesson of *Monna Vanna.*" In order to illustrate the possibility of such a result of the struggle between environment and personality, it was necessary, Maeterlinck further explained, to place the chief personages of the drama in very peculiar circumstances, and to invoke the aid of myth and symbolism. The grounds for such a necessity are clear only in the case of an artist of Maeterlinck's peculiar quality; and there can be no doubt that the circumstances in which the characters are placed are decidedly "peculiar." Merlin, the old seer, knowing the future through the intermediary of his familiar spirit, Arielle — symbolic incarnation of his faculty of divination — and realizing all that the future holds for his beloved son, determines to play the rôle of destiny in order to ensure his happiness. Joyzelle loves Lanceor, Merlin's son, with a perfectly human, instinctive passion; and acts under all the cruel and harrowing tests to which she is submitted by Merlin, with forthright decisiveness and simplicity. Maeterlinck fails to convince us that there is any real conflict — merely the successful, but foreseen, surmounting of all the tests imposed; and at the end as at the beginning, Joyzelle is identical with herself — fresh, spontaneous, loyal unto death. To win her Lanceor, she is nerved even to crime; but fate — or a mechanical symbol for fate! — intervenes. Maeterlinck loosely evades the moral implication of this incident; for when Joyzelle naïvely inquires, "Is it then ordained that love should strike and kill all that attempts to bar the road?" the answer is, "I do not know." It is interesting to observe that Joyzelle is submitted to the same test as Vanna, with this fundamental difference: upon the consent of Vanna to a sacrifice of her person is conditioned the material happiness and the lives of thousands; Joyzelle fights for the inner sanctity of individual and personal love. Lanceor is a mere lay figure — the dupe of a Maeterlinckian Midsummer Night's Dream; and in the strange story of this Ferdinand and Miranda, Joyzelle is struggling for a consummation of very dubious value. The play is noteworthy in one respect, viewed in the light it throws upon the evolution of Maeterlinck's art as a dramatist. Hitherto Maeterlinck has always vouchsafed to fate the victory over humanity. In *Joyzelle,* Maeterlinck has given the victory to love — a love of authentic finality and enduring strength.

X

Original and distinctive as Maeterlinck succeeds in remaining through all his tentatives and experiments, he is perhaps the most impressionable of modern artists. The influences that work in him are lost in the mists of antiquity and find solid ground in the most modern of the moderns. If at times he seems the incarnation of the Stoicism for which we have to go to Marcus Aurelius to find a parallel, at others he penetrates to the heart of modern problems, and challenges comparison, as moralist, even with Ibsen and Nietzsche.

Max Nordau contemptuously, though not inaptly, characterized *La Princesse Maleine* as a sort of cento out of Shakspere, a "Shaksperean anthology for children and Patagonians." Indeed, *La Princesse Maleine,* and *Joyzelle* with its *Tempest* setting, testify to Maeterlinck's preoccupation with the scenic accessories and romantic violences of the Shaksperean drama. *Monna Vanna,* as Professor W. L. Phelps pointed out, owes its setting and one of its structural features to Browning's *Luria;* and *Pelléas and Mélisande* finds its roots in the Dantean story of the two who go forever on the accursèd air. And yet, in every case, Maeterlinck's adaptation, modification, or amplification of the facts, material or spiritual, and his re-presentation of the characters he has chosen to reincarnate, reveal individuality, a distinctive habit of mind, and originality of depiction. These plays, in a sense, serve as Maeterlinck's personal impressions of his adventures among the masterpieces of Shakspere, Browning and Dante.

The most noteworthy influence visibly operant upon the art and thought and life of Maeterlinck came however, not from literature, but from life — in the person of that woman who was eventually to share all his joys and sorrows. *The Treasure of the Humble* was dedicated to Mlle. Georgette Leblanc; and it is significant that in the year of its publication,

1896, Maeterlinck leaves Flanders forever and enters the great cosmopolitan world of Paris. Behind him now lie the ancient spires, the dark canals, the sluggish waters, the floating swans, the gloomy atmosphere and phlegmatic spirit of his ancestral city. Behind him lie the strange and morbid fancies of his youthful days — the arabesque landscapes, hidden grottoes, haunted castles, noxious moonlit gardens; the pitiable, bloodless spectres, with their frantic gestures of despair and stammering incoherent protests against immitigable doom. The gray Stoic dons the bright colors of optimism; the poet of the ethereal becomes the celebrant of the humanly real.

Again in 1898, Maeterlinck dedicates a book, *Wisdom and Destiny,* to Mlle. Leblanc — in words eloquent of her influence: " I dedicate to you this book, which is, in effect, your work. There is a collaboration more lofty and more real than that of the pen; it is that of thought and example. I have not been obliged to imagine laboriously the resolutions and the actions of a wise ideal, or to extract from my heart the moral of a beautiful reverie necessarily a trifle vague. It has sufficed to listen to your words. It has sufficed that my eyes have followed you attentively in life; they followed thus the movements, the gestures, the habits of wisdom herself."

Lovingly celebrated in his *Portrait of a Lady,*

with its motto from La Bruyère: "He said that the intelligence of this fair lady was like a diamond in a handsome setting"— Mlle. Leblanc finds real incarnation in Monna Vanna, which she is destined to create with moving and magic force. *Monna Vanna* is Maeterlinck's great human challenge of mystic morality to the modern world — no fourth-dimensional drama of the spirit, "pinnacled dim in the intense inane," but a drama of flesh and blood, of heart as well as of soul. It bears all the hall-marks of the drama of to-day, even to its ideal spectator, its undulation of emotional process, its classic conflict of wills. It bears the pure Maeterlinckian stamp as well — but this time the glorious struggle of the ideal morality against the purely human passions of daily life. Monna Vanna is the apotheosis of womanhood — the fine flower of the virginal type become volitional, latent in Aglavaine, just stretching shining pinions in Ardiane. With such high-minded disinterestedness is it conceived that our heart, in turn, goes out to the passionately loving, but outraged husband, Guido; to the barbaric, but essentially noble Prinzivalle; to the old Marco, sacrificing the love of his son to the ideal demands of the loftier morality; to Vanna, in her evolution from blushing and tender femininity to decisive and noble womanhood. The unresolved cadence of its clamant finale is our concession to the mystic Maeterlinck. "With conscious strength," as Anselma Heine says, " Monna Vanna carries her fault upon her shoulders like a coronation mantle, and with uplifted gaze strides forth into happiness."

XI

The Blue Bird, Maeterlinck's " Fairy Play in Five Acts," is, on reflection, less a surprise than a confirmation. Here at last is the " anthology for children "— neither from Shakspere, nor for Patagonians — but pure Maeterlinck, an allegorical fantasy of that search for ideal happiness with which he is ever concerned. From the essay on Luck in *The Buried Temple* there is a significant passage which adumbrates this new fancy. " Let us unweariedly follow each path that leads from our consciousness to our unconsciousness. We shall thus succeed in hewing some kind of track through the great and as yet impassable roads that lead from the seen to the unseen, from man to God, from the individual to the universe. At the end of these roads lies hidden the general secret of life." *The Blue Bird* belongs to that modern literature of childhood's dreamland, which finds such tragic exemplification in Hauptmann's *The Assumption of Hannele,* such joyous celebration in Barrie's *Peter Pan.* Maeterlinck seems to be harking back to the ideas of his poet-friend, Charles Van Lerberghe; and in this new creation gives us a real play for marionettes that would have delighted the author of *A Child's Garden of Verses*.

It is a future possibility of Man to discover the soul of inanimate things, to conquer thus all the forces which are now veiled from him and arrayed against him, and to live in a pantheistic universe of life, freedom and light. And it is Man's destiny to pursue that "great secret of things and of happiness," which is the Blue Bird of the Maeterlinckian fantasy. Some such general idea as this lies back of the simple symbolism and allegory of this fairy play.

In dreamland, Tyltyl and Myltyl, the children of two old peasants, are visited by the fairy Bérylune who bids them start in search of the Blue Bird. This Blue Bird she must have for her little girl who is very ill. "We don't quite know what's the matter with her; she wants to be happy . . ."— thus the fairy Bérylune, who to the children seems to bear a strange resemblance to their neighbor, Madame Berlingot. The green hat with a diamond ornament, which Bérylune gives to Tyltyl, enables him, by turning it a certain way, to see the inside of things, and to summon the souls of the inanimate. No sooner has Tyltyl turned the diamond than a wonderful change comes over everything, and forth come trooping the Hours, dancing merrily to the sound of delicious music, the souls of the Quartern-loaves, of Man's one absolutely faithful servant, the Dog; the Cat, Water, "like a young girl, streaming, dishevelled and tearful," Milk, "a tall, white bashful figure who seems to be afraid of everything," sanctimonious Sugar, and a luminous creature of incomparable beauty, called Light. And now forthwith, with these strange and sprightly attendants, the children start on their quest for the Blue Bird.

At the fairy's palace, Bérylune explains to the children that if they can find the Blue Bird, they will know all, see all, at last dominate the universe — a Biblical reminder of that fruit of the tree of knowledge, eating which man shall know all things, both good and evil. They journey first to the Land of Memory, and there meet their grandparents and their long-lost brothers and sisters, who need only to be remembered to live again. Here Tyltyl captures a bird which seems "blue as a blue glass marble"; but alas! as soon as they leave the Land of Memory — for when we dwell on the past in loving memory we idealize all things there — the bird is no longer blue.

And so their pilgrimage continues to the palace of Night, who lives in terror for fear Man will capture all his mysteries, and vanquish all his terrors. Here Tyltyl takes a peep into the cavern of the Ghosts who, as Night explains, "have felt bored in there ever since Man ceased to take them seriously"; at the Sicknesses, who are not happy since "Man has been waging such a determined war upon them — especially since the discovery of the microbes. . . . The Doctors are so unkind to them." Though not yet winter, one of the smallest almost escapes, sneezing, coughing, and blowing its nose: it's Cold-in-the-Head. Nowhere can they find the Blue Bird — not among the Wars, the Shades and Terrors, the Mysteries, nor in the private locker where Night keeps the "unemployed Stars, my personal Perfumes, a few Glimmers that belong to me, such as Will-o'-the-Wisps, Glow-worms and Fireflies, also the Dew, the Song of the Nightingales, and so on . . ." Finally, though warned that it is not permitted to open one great door, Tyltyl musters up courage, to discover there

> "the most unexpected of gardens, unreal, infinite, and ineffable, a dream-garden bathed in nocturnal light, where, among stars and planets, illumining all that they touch, flying ceaselessly from jewel to jewel and from moonbeam to moonbeam, fairylike blue birds hover perpetually and harmoniously down to the confines of the horizon, birds innumerable to the point of appearing to be the breath, the azured atmosphere, the very substance of the wonderful garden."

Too easily dazzled by this glitter, they seize eagerly only those birds that are within reach — only to discover when they are held to the light that the birds are dead.

In the Forest, betrayed by the treacherous Cat, they are beset by all the trees and animals, who know that if the Blue Bird is captured, their last breath of freedom and independence of man expires. Though guarded zealously by the faithful Dog, the children are hard put to it to defend themselves, and are rescued in the end only by the intervention of Light. Next day they seek the Blue Bird in the Graveyard — but they are not accompanied by Light, who might terrify the dead, nor by Fire, " who would want to burn the dead, as of old; and that is no longer done . . ." Tyltyl turns the jewel, and

> " Then, from all the gaping tombs, there rises gradually an efflorescence at first frail and timid like steam; then white and virginal and more and more tufty, more and more tall and plentiful and marvellous. Little by little, irresistibly, invading all things, it transforms the graveyard into a sort of fairy-like and nuptial garden, over which rise the first rays of the dawn . . ."

Stunned and dazzled, Myltyl asks, looking in the grass, " Where are the dead? " And Tyltyl, looking, answers: " There are no dead . . ."

Once again they resume their pilgrimage, this time to the Kingdom of the Future peopled with the Blue Children, who await the hour of their birth. One prophesies that, once on earth, he will have to " invent the thing that gives happiness "; another will invent a " machine that flies in the air like a bird without wings " (whether a Blériot monoplane or a Wright biplane is left in doubt); another will " bring pure joy to the globe by means of ideas which people have not yet had." At last white-bearded Time, with scythe and hour-glass, appears upon the threshold; and one catches a glimpse of the " white and gold sails of a galley moored to a sort of quay, formed by the rosy mists of the Dawn." As the galley floats away to Earth, bearing the Blue Children, Tyltyl and Myltyl hear an extremely distant song of gladness and expectation. Tyltyl inquires, " What is that? . . . It sounds like other voices . . ." To which Light responds, " Yes, it is the song of the mothers coming out to meet them."

The children at last return to earth, for Light assures them that she has caught the Blue Bird and has it hidden under her cloak. They awake in the cottage of their parents, now illumined, as if by magic, with strange, fresh beauty; and they talk so strangely of their long dream-pilgrimage, more real than reality, that their mother is alarmed for fear they have discovered the hiding place of her husband's brandy-bottle. When Madame Berlingot enters, the children to her surprise call her Bérylune, and express sorrow that they have been unable to find the Blue Bird. But Tyltyl offers his own little turtle-dove for her sick child. She rapturously seizes it and runs to present it to the invalid. In a moment she returns, "holding by the hand a little girl of a fair and wonderful beauty, who carries Tyltyl's dove pressed in her arms." The miracle is wrought; here at last is the Blue Bird. But as Tyltyl, wishing to show her how to feed the dove, momentarily takes it from her, it escapes and flies away.

"Never mind, . . . don't cry . . . I will catch him again," says Tyltyl reassuringly. And with all the grace of a Peter Pan appealing to the public for their belief in fairies, Tyltyl steps to the front of the stage and addresses the audience:

"If any of you should find him, would you be so kind as to give him back to us? . . . We need him for our happiness, later on . . ."

Maeterlinck's marvellous imaginative faculty for evocation of images of rare, strange beauty plays through the scenic directions. That greatest of living stage-managers, the Russian Stanislavsky, has already realized Maeterlinck's intention in a production notable for the magic beauty of its setting. *The Blue Bird* was played in Moscow for considerably more than a year, and has been produced all over Russia literally by scores of companies. It was most fitting that *The Blue Bird* should have been successfully produced in London; for M. Maeterlinck has gracefully acknowledged Mr. Barrie as "the father of *Peter Pan,* and the grandfather of *The Blue Bird.*" Fantastically, if somewhat conventionally imaginative, were the designs for The Palace of the Night with its stately quadrangle and mystic, columned temple; the Kingdom of the Future with its succession of oval arches painted in cerulean blue and the changing colors of ships and figures at the embarcation of the unborn children for their voyage to this world; the magic Garden filled with radiant blue birds, ceaselessly fluttering hither and thither, through the instrumentality of the wonder-working biograph; and the austere dignity of the Forest, with its gnarled, primeval, dense-packed trees. Children sat speechless and spellbound in unsophisticated contemplation of this youthful, modern quest of a new Holy Grail, while men and women read therein the meanings vouchsafed them by their own life-quests. The pretty fantasy with its individualized figures, whether of abstraction or beast or inanimate object, its eager, earnest children, its easy dialogue, its simple allegory and symbolism, its light hints of a secondary intention, its poetic imaginativeness and above all its delicate and playful humor, reveal a Maeterlinck who at once endears himself to all who love children and to all who have ever engaged in a perhaps not wholly fruitless quest for that elusive and evanescent thing we call Happiness.

In *Mary Magdalene,* one divines another illustration of that ethereal mimetic instinct which haunts Maeterlinck in some of the higher flights of his dramatic fancy. In this effort to clothe reality in the garb of mysticism, there is something at once thin, high and remote. As Maeterlinck has successively laid Dante, Shakspere, Browning, Strindberg and Barrie under contribution, so now he turns to Paul Heyse, great German poet, the profound creator of *Maria von Magdala.* Heyse's complex tissue of emotion and conversion is a work of true greatness; the interpretation, by Minnie Maddern Fiske, of the great-souled Mary, swayed, overborne, transfigured under the magic, pure spell of the Master, I recall as a noble achievement of histrionic art.

Actuated by feelings natural if not quite generous, Heyse forbade the utilization by Maeterlinck of motives employed in *Maria von Magdala.* Maeterlinck nevertheless not only felt that the words of Christ were available for all artists; he himself had already imagined the crucial theme of the play in his *Joyzelle,* written before he had ever seen *Maria von Magdala.* Maeterlinck's *Mary Magdalene,* despite its apparent imitativeness, stands fully justified in view of its strange beauty and authentic artistic worth.

In several of Maeterlinck's most remarkable works for the stage, the problem which inspires his muse is the feminine sacrifice of virginity for ends transcending the conventional and the personal. Vanna will surrender herself—"nude beneath her mantle"—to the barbarian conqueror. To save the life of her lover, Joyzelle will yield herself to Merlin — selfless in the transcendent sacrifice of love. Now again, in *Mary Magdalene,* Maeterlinck once more concerns himself with this disquieting problem.

In Bethany, Appius, Lucius Verus, a military tribune, and *Mary Magdalene* gather at the villa of Annoeus Silanus, where they discuss the teachings of Jesus, the itinerant preacher. The teachings of Longinus are advanced in opposition to those of Jesus; but it is Mary, with feminine intuition, who perceives that the reasoning of Longinus neither dispels sorrow nor heals the mortal wounds of the heart. Across their discussions sounds the clear, sweet, penetrating voice of Jesus, addressing a great crowd nearby. Transfixed with an emotion of which she can give no account, Mary moves as in a trance towards Jesus. She must see that face, drown her senses in the deeper meanings of those strangely healing words. The crowd, with the cry "The adulteress!" would stone her; but Jesus stills the tumult. "He that is without sin among you, let him cast the first stone at her!"

The miracle begins to work in Mary. The spirit of Christ has touched her spirit. To the suit of the enamored Verus, Mary is withheld from yielding by a new, strange reluctance of which she is but half conscious. Gathered at the villa of Mary, the friends discuss the marvel of the raising of Lazarus and invoke Roman and Greek philosophy to its depths, in a spirit of defiant opposition. Suddenly, without warning, the resurrected Lazarus appears in their midst and addresses Mary: "The Master calls you." Verus endeavors to hector Lazarus, to free Mary from this new obsession. Moving as if in a dream, and deaf to the impassioned entreaties of Verus, Mary follows Lazarus amid awe-stricken silence.

At the house of Joseph of Arimathæa now gather many followers of Christ — Nicodemus, Lazarus, Cleophas, Zaccheus; Mary, Salome, Martha, the sister of Lazarus, and others. As they discuss plans for the rescue of the Christ, who has been arrested and led away under the lash of his Roman captors, comes Mary Magdalene, dishevelled, barefoot — to plan a rescue, to arouse the broken spirit of Christ's followers, who shrink from the thought of consequences. Joseph of Arimathæa asserts that Christ has made known his will and desires no rescue — against which Mary passionately protests. "We save those whom we love; we listen to them afterwards!" Hither comes Verus with the miracle wrought — for Pilate, eager to evade responsibility, has consented to surrender Christ to Verus; Christ will be permitted to escape, for which Verus will suffer exile. To a Roman, death is sweet compared to exile; but to win Mary, he suffers even exile. The Christians plead with

Mary to yield to Verus; but in the moment of spiritual crisis, she seems endowed with heavenly clairvoyance. "If I bought his life at the price which you offer, all that He wished, all that He loved, would be dead! I should be destroying him altogether, destroying more than himself, to gain for him days that would destroy everything. . . ." As Jesus passes beneath the window, to the bloodthirsty shouts of the mob, "Crucify him! Crucify him!" the Magdalene stands motionless — not bowed down with grief unutterable — but transfixed, as if in ecstasy, illumined with the light of eternity.

In that sweet, sad vision of *Soeur Béatrice*, the Maeterlinck, who once said that by the side of women "one has at times a momentary but distinct presentiment of a life that does not seem always to run parallel with the life of appearances," revealed a rare power of emotive, intuitive subtlety. In *Mary Magdalene* that power has been elevated to an even higher plane of serenity and wisdom. The Magdalene knows the secret of truth — she has become "the master of reality." Hers is the spiritual divination to see that it profiteth not to gain the whole world, even the salvation of the life of the Master, and lose one's own soul.

The plays which Maeterlinck has produced since the Great War, while marked with many of the characteristics of his individual style, are, with the exception of *The Betrothal*, lacking in the peculiar quality we have come to associate with his name. *The Betrothal*, a sort of sequel to *The Blue Bird*, is a Christmas pantomime play—a play for children, with just enough of elementary symbolism to interest the adult mind. The three other plays are tentatives at the contemporary drama—plays with a geography and a period, the present. An interest, chiefly historical, will continue to attach to *The Burgomaster of Stilemonde*. It paints in primary colors a tragedy of the German invasion of Belgium: the shooting to death of the Burgomaster by the German commander for a technical violation of an inhuman order; and the consequent alienation of the Burgomaster's daughter and her lover, a German officer. The contrast in ideas produces a tragic conflict which has an inevitable result. *The Cloud That Lifted* is a play of complex emotions on the theme of the eternal triangle; but it is lacking in any strong dramatic quality. The characters are melodramatic; the emotions overdrawn and ineffectively expressed. *The Power of the Dead*, a modern miracle play, with elaborate setting and well-chosen titles, might prove a success on the film, but the familiar device of the dream is quite outworn for the stage.

Maeterlinck will always hold a place in the history of the stage. But it will not be for plays in this new, unhappy manner. The Maeterlinck we shall cherish is the author of the plays of mystery, pity, and terror, the creative artist who made something new, unique, and strange in the history of dramatic art.

OSCAR WILDE

"I had genius, a distinguished name, high social position, brilliancy, intellectual daring; I made art a philosophy and philosophy an art: I altered the minds of men and the colours of things: there was nothing I said or did that did not make people wonder. I took the drama, the most objective form known to art, and made of it as personal a mode of expression as the lyric or the sonnet; at the same time I widened its range and enriched its characterization. Drama, novel, poem in prose, poem in rhyme, subtle or fantastic dialogue, whatever I touched, I made beautiful in a new mode of beauty: to truth itself I gave what is false no less than what is true as its rightful province, and showed that the false and the true are merely forms of intellectual existence. I treated art as the supreme reality and life as a mere mode of fiction...I awoke the imagination of my century so that it created myth and legend around me. I summed up all systems in a phrase and all existence in an epigram."

De Profundis.
Wilde's Works. Authorized Edition.
Vol. XI., pp. 45-46.

OSCAR WILDE

In this age of topsy-turvydom — the age of Nietzsche, Shaw, Wilde, Chesterton — criticism masquerades in the garb of iconoclasm; and fancy, fantasy, caprice and paradox usurp the rôles of scholarship, realistic valuation, and the historic sense. The ancient and honorable authority of the critic is undermined by the complacent scepticism of the period. And the gentle art of appreciation is only the individual filtration of art through a temperament. The mania for certitude died with Renan, confidence had its last leader in Carlyle, and authority relinquishes its last and greatest adherent in the death of Brunetière. The ease of blasphemy and the commercialization of audacity are accepted facts; we have lost the courage and simplicity for the expression of the truth unvarnished and unadorned. "We know we are brilliant and distinguished, but we do not know that we are right. We swagger in fantastic artistic costumes; we praise ourselves; we fling epigrams right and left; we have the courage to play the egotist, and the courage to play the fool, but we have not the courage to preach." The symbol of art is no longer a noble muse, but only a tricksy jade. Criticism, once the art of imaginative interpretation, is now mere self-expression — as Anatole France puts it, "the adventures of a soul among masterpieces." We are expected to believe that the greatest pictures are those in which there is more of the artist than the sitter. The defects of current criticism are well expressed by a brilliant Frenchman — Charles Nodier, was it not? — in the opinion that if one stops to inquire into the probabilities, he will never arrive at the truth!

The world has never seen an age in which there was more excuse for questioning the validity of contemporary judgment. It would be the height of folly to expect posterity to authenticate the vaporings of an appreciation which, in shifting its stress from the universal to the *personnel,* has changed from criticism into colloquy, from clinic into *causerie.* Indeed, it is nothing less than a truism that the experience of the artist in all ages, according to the verdict of history, is identical with itself. In the words of Sidney Lanier: " . . . the artist shall put forth, humbly and lovingly, the very best and highest that is within him, utterly regardless of contemporary criticism. What possible claim can contemporary criticism set up to respect — that criticism which crucified Jesus Christ, stoned Stephen, hooted Paul for a madman, tried Luther for a criminal, tortured Galileo, bound Columbus in chains, drove Dante into exile, made Shakspere write the sonnet,

'When in disgrace with fortune and men's eyes,' gave Milton five pounds for 'Paradise Lost,' kept Samuel Johnson cooling his heels on Lord Chesterfield's doorstep, reviled Shelley as an unclean dog, killed Keats, cracked jokes on Gluck, Schubert, Beethoven, Berlioz and Wagner, and committed so many other impious follies and stupidities that a thousand letters like this could not suffice even to catalogue them?" The verdict of the *intellectuels* has always been a veritable stumbling block in the path of genius.

"It is from men of established literary reputation," asserts Bernard Shaw, "that we learn that William Blake was mad; that Shelley was spoiled by living in a low set; that Robert Owen was a man who did not know the world; that Ruskin is incapable of comprehending political economy; that Zola is a mere blackguard, and Ibsen is Zola with a wooden leg. The great musician accepted by his unskilled listener, is vilified by his fellow musician. It was the musical culture of Europe which pronounced Wagner the inferior of Mendelssohn and Meyerbeer."

It is not enough to say, with the brilliant author of *Contemporains,* that contemporary criticism is mere conversation; it is often little more than mere gossip. One is often inclined to question, with Lowell, whether the powers that be, in criticism, are really the powers that ought to be. Especially is this true of a time uniquely characterized by its tendency to relentless rehabilitation. The immoral iconoclast of a former age becomes the saintly anarch of this. The jar of lampblack is exchanged for a bucket of whitewash; and in this era of renovation the soiled linen of literary sinners emerges translucent and immaculate from the presses of the critical laundry. We are darkly and irretrievably given over into the hands of those whom Mr. Robert W. Chambers has aptly termed " repairers of reputations."

In view of the premises, it may appear at once paradoxical and perverse to attempt any criticism at all, especially of the works of a man like Oscar Wilde, whose mere name to many is a synonym for the appalling degeneracy of an age lashed by the polemics of Ibsen, the objurgations of Tolstoi, the satire of Shaw, and the invective of Nordau. All that pertains to Wilde has for long been *res tacenda* in English society; and he himself, to use his own phrase, has passed from a sort of eternity of fame to a sort of eternity of infamy. In many instances, the critical works dealing with Wilde have been marred by wrong-headed judgment, unhealthy defence, and attempted justification. The fatal flaw of contemporary criticism, as Brunetière says, is that we do not see our contemporaries from a sufficient height and distance. That we are unable to profit by what Nietzsche terms " the pathos of distance," is a deficiency that cannot be remedied. But at least it is the prerogative of art, peculiarly of the art of criticism, to make the attempt, if not to fix the position, certainly to express judgment upon the work of contemporaries. Irresistibly there arises the conscientious proposition of the question whether the work of Wilde is worthy of genuine critical study. In speaking of Sainte Beuve, self-styled the "naturalist of the human heart," Emile Faguet once remarked that men are, without being entirely right, at least not entirely wrong in ignoring many faults in the man who possesses the virtue proper to his own profession. People are accustomed to overlook dissipation in the brave soldier, intolerance in the compassionate priest, harshness in the successful ruler. One might even instance that frail woman, mentioned in Holy Scripture, who was forgiven because she loved much. The point of departure for an estimate of Wilde is to be found, neither in a sense of outrage against society nor in a groping for hopeless excuse behind the imperfect researches of pathological criminology. The reason for any future study of Wilde is to be found either in the palliative charm of his personality as friend and temperament as artist, or in the orchidaceous modernity and brilliant exoticism of his spoken and written art. In art, as in life, much virtue inheres in the professional conscience; and the peccable artist in all ages has been granted a hearing on account of his unfaltering love of art. "If one loves art at all," Wilde once wrote, "one must love it beyond all other things in the world, and against such love the reason, if one listened to it, would cry out. There is nothing sane about the worship of beauty. It is something entirely too splendid to be sane. Those of whose lives it forms the dominant note will always seem to the world to be pure visionaries." And with all his affectation of singularity, his assumption of the dangerous and delightful distinction of being different from others, his joyous treading of the primrose path of self-exploitation, his æsthetic posturing, charlatanry, and *blague* — Oscar Wilde was assuredly a personality of whose life art formed the dominant note.

The biography of such souls as D'Annunzio, Verlaine, Dowson, or Wilde connotes the infinitely delicate and complex task of tracing that thin demarcative line which divides the famous from the infamous. Nor is the contemplation of the personal failure of a brilliant artist like Wilde — drifting derelict upon the tumultuous sea of passion — either congenial or edifying. There is no more tragic spectacle than that of a man of genius who is not a man of honor. And yet, until vaster and more definitive studies of the problems of homosexuality, of degeneracy, and of criminal pathology shall have been completed, Wilde will continue to be what Byron has been aptly termed: "a fascinating trouble." There is a sort of melancholy fascination inherent in the determination of the causes underlying discrepancy between purpose and performance, between art and morality. The spirit warreth against the flesh, the flesh against the spirit. The selfsame soul which joyfully mounts to the shining summits of art cries forth its despairing *Mea Culpa* from the depths of life. In the heart of every man is lodged not only a *Paradiso,* but a *Purgatorio.* As artist and man, Oscar Wilde might truly have said with Omar Khayyam: "I myself am Heaven and Hell."

There exists no more salient exemplification of the reality of the identity between destiny and human character than is to be discovered in the case of Oscar Wilde. The *crux* of his mania was blindness to the truth that the man who is the lackey of his passion can never be the master of his fate. The secret of his downfall is found in the fact that this leader in the ranks of individualism was not the captain of his own soul. "Not even the most insignificant actions," says one of Echegaray's characters in *El Gran Galeoto,* "are in themselves insignificant or lost for good or evil. For, concentrated by the mysterious influences of modern life, they may reach to immense effects." Wilde's life signally exemplifies, in Amiel's words, "the fatality of the consequences incident to human acts." It was Wilde's tragedy to drink to the dregs "the bitter tonic draught of experience," and to realize, in infinite wretchedness and isolation, the truth of George Eliot's dictum that consequences are unpitying. In his own words, "I forgot that every little action of the common day makes or unmakes character, and that therefore what one has done in the secret chamber one has some day to cry aloud on the housetop." What strange and pathetic prophecy in his eery poem, *Hélas!*

> To drift with every passion till my soul
> Is a stringèd lute on which all winds can play,
> Is it for this that I have given away
> Mine ancient wisdom, and austere control?
> Methinks my life is a twice-written scroll
> Scrawled over on some boyish holiday
> With idle songs for pipe and virelay,
> Which do but mar the secret of the whole.
>
> Surely there was a time I might have trod
> The sunlit heights, and from life's dissonance
> Struck one clear chord to reach the ears of God.
> Is that time dead? Lo! with a little rod
> I did but touch the honey of romance —
> And must I lose a soul's inheritance?

No one would deny to Wilde the title of a Prince of Paradoxers. And yet this acolyte of the obverse, to whom perversity was a passion, never created so puzzling a paradox as the paradox of his own life. He to whom humanity was always a disquieting problem has bequeathed himself as a far more disquieting problem to humanity. Irony incarnate, yet unconscious, lay in his reiterated injunction that it is not so much what we say, nor even what we do, but what we *are* that eternally matters. He yearned to live and to live more abundantly—"to be, to know, to feel . . . to go through everything, to turn every page, to experience all that can be experienced upon the earth." He early confessed that he "wanted to eat of the fruit of all the trees in the garden of the world"; and he went forth into the world with that passion in his soul. But he ate only the bitter-sweet fruit of the trees of pleasure; and it turned to ashes upon his tongue. If he ate of the fruit of the tree of knowledge, it was knowledge of evil, not of good. This master of the half-truth is condemned in the very phrase; it was the fate of his character not simply to know, but to wish to know, only the half of the truth, of the meaning of life.

"Virtue," says Bernard Shaw, "consists, not in abstaining from vice, but in not desiring it." Judging by the criterion of this post-Nietzschean valuation of virtue, Wilde was, constitutionally and congenitally, one of the most vicious of men. If Wilde could be termed virtuous in any sense, it was in no other than the professional sense. In his life as artist, it was his sincerity to be insincere. The final verity about the man is that, through the refractory lens of his temperament, all truth appeared encased in a paradox. Far from being universal or fundamental, truth to Wilde was so individual, so personal a thing that the moment it became the property of more than one person, it became a falsehood. If his art ever ceased to live for its own sake, it was because it lived for Wilde's sake. Indeed Wilde was of his essence what the French call *personnel;* and a work of art, as he phrased it, is always the unique result of an unique temperament. To Ibsen, creation in art consisted in holding judgment-day over oneself. To Wilde, creation in art consisted in the celebration of a holiday of mentality. In the guise of interpreter of the modern spirit, he was always happening upon the discovery of a great, an unique truth; and this he flippantly and condescendingly consented to communicate to that boorish monster, the public. Art was an ivory tower in which dwelt the long-haired seraph of the sunflower. The drama was merely a platform for the *flair* of the *flaneur.* All the world was a stage for the wearer of the green carnation.

It has ceased to be a paradox to attribute an exalted, if extravagant sense of virtue, sanity, and morality to Walt Whitman, to Elisée Reclus, to Bernard Shaw. Their notions of right, of justice, and of morality differ from those of the average man — Zola's *l'homme moyen sensual* — in that they sharply diverge from, and not infrequently transcend, the conventional standards, the perfunctory concepts of right living and just conduct. If Wilde could be said to have any morals, it was a faith in the artistic validity of poetic justice. If he could be said to have any conscience, it was the professional conscience of the impeccable artist — of Poe, of Pater, of Sainte Beuve. If he could be said to have a sense of right, it was a sense of the right of the artist to live his own untrammelled life.

Nothing is easier than acquiescence in Wilde's dictum that the drama is the meeting place of art and life. And yet nowhere more clearly than in Wilde's own plays do we find the purposed divorce of art from life. It was his fundamental distinction, in the rôle of critic as artist, to trace with admirable clarity the line of demarcation between unimaginative realism and imaginative reality. The methods of Zola and the Naturalistic school always drew Wilde's keenest critical thrusts. The greatest heresy, in his opinion, was the doctrine that art consists in holding up the camera to nature. He was even so reactionary as to assert that the only real people are the people who never exist. The view of Stendhal, that fiction is *un miroir qui se promène sur la grande route,* found as little favor in his eyes as the doctrine of Pinero that the dramatists are the brief and abstract chronometers of the time. The function of the artist, in Wilde's view, is to invent, not to chronicle; and he even goes so far as to say that if a novelist is base enough to go to life for his personages, he should at least pretend that they are creations, and not boast of them as copies. To the charge that the people in his stories are "mere catchpenny revelations of the non-existent," he unblushingly retorted: "Life by its realism is always spoiling the subject-matter of art. The supreme pleasure in literature is to realize the non-existent."

II

One year before Arthur Pinero and two years before Bernard Shaw, Oscar Fingal O'Flahertie Wills Wilde was born at No. 1 Merrion Square, Dublin, on October 16, 1854. His parents, both brilliant and distinguished figures, took a leading part in the life of their age; and certain of the distinctive traits of each find striking reproduction in their unhappy son. Mr., afterwards Sir, William Wilde, Oscar's father, early distinguished himself in the field of letters; but the logical bent of his mind was toward medical study, which he pursued in London, Berlin and Vienna. He devoted his first year's fees as a physician, indeed, more, the first thousand pounds of his professional earnings, to the founding of St. Mark's Ophthalmic Hospital where the poor could be treated for eye and ear diseases; and his distinction as a physician won him the title of "the father of modern otology." He received many honors, including knighthood, during his lifetime; but it was Oscar Wilde's misfortune to inherit from his father, not his talents as a scientific specialist, but his vicious traits as immoralist and libertine. Just as Bernard Shaw derived his musical bent from his mother, so Oscar Wilde derived his literary sense, in great measure, from his brilliant mother — Jane Francesca Elgee. Signing her verses "Speranza" and her letters "John Fanshaw Ellis," this woman of genius, as Sir Charles Gavan Duffy called her, contributed frequently to *The Nation,* of Dublin, from 1847 on; and her celebrated Nationalist manifesto, *Jacta Alea Est,* inspired by Williams' *The Spirit of the Nation,* gave her a notoriety little short of treasonable. In *savoir faire,* in all the arts of the *salon,* Lady Wilde was unexcelled; and it was the testimony of all who met her that she was a personage. In her son are reproduced certain marked characteristics: indifference to practical affairs of life, brilliancy in the art of social converse, profound aversion to "the miasma of the commonplace," and a moral laxity of tone in conversation which, in her case, found no counterpart in her actual life.

"Under 'direct inheritance' or 'transmission by blood,'" records one of Wilde's recent biographers, "may, perhaps, be classed his literary capacity, his gifts of poetry, languages, of ready mastery of difficult studies, his love of the beautiful, the sound common-sense of his normal periods, his family and personal pride, and his moral courage in the face of danger, but also an indifference to the dangers of alcoholism, an aversion from failure, physical, social and mental, an exaggerated esteem, on the other hand, for wealth, titles and social success, a tolerance for moral laxness."

As a very small lad, Oscar was spoken of by his mother as "wonderful," as a child of phenomenal versatility. His fondness for mystery and romance was born through his tours with his father in quest of archæological treasures; and his natural wit was sharpened by listening to Ireland's thought and wit in the *salon* of his mother. It was at his father's dinner-table and in his mother's drawing-room, as has been justly said, that the best of his early education was obtained; but he doubtless gained not a little from his schooling at the Portora Royal School. He had no aptitude for mathematics, nor was his talent for composition at this time in evidence; but he had a marvellous faculty of intellectual absorption, mastering the contents of a book in an incredibly short space of time. He kept aloof from his companions, practised his wit in bestowing nicknames upon them, and enjoyed nothing more than leading his teachers into long discussions of some point which "intrigued his fancy." His brilliancy in reading and interpreting the classics was proven at the time of his entrance to Trinity College, Dublin — October, 1871. Like his great-uncle Ralph, Oscar won the Berkeley Gold Medal at Trinity, as well as a scholarship; but he never held his scholarship, preferring to seek better things at Oxford.

"I want to get to the point," Oscar Wilde says in *De Profundis,* "where I shall be able to say quite simply, and without affectation, that the two great turning-points in my life were when my father sent me to Oxford and when society sent me to prison." Certain it is that at Oxford he first began to exhibit that devotion to art, that attachment to literature, and that passion for beauty which were the foundations for whatsoever of value is to be found in his writings. Here he sat under Ruskin; and there is little reason to doubt that the artistic and personal influence of Ruskin upon Wilde was far from inconsiderable. "The influence of Ruskin was so great," we read in a biographical notice of Wilde, "that Mr. Wilde, though holding games in abomination, and detesting violent exercise, might have been seen of grey November mornings breaking stones on the roadside — not unbribed, however; 'he had the honour of filling Mr. Ruskin's especial wheelbarrow,' and it was the great author of 'Modern Painters' himself who taught him how to trundle it." There is, however, little reason to believe, in spite of the evidence of *The Soul of Man Under Socialism,* that in Wilde's mind were sown any of the seeds of that "practical interest in social questions which is the 'Oxford Movement of to-day.'" Ruskin's influence upon Wilde is chiefly exhibited in the growth of the latter's artistic tastes; for Wilde's rooms at Oxford were noted for their beautiful decoration and for the display of collections of "objects of *vertu*." Recall his well-known remark: "Oh, would that I could live up to my blue china!" In his early Oxford days he began to contribute both prose and verse to magazines published in Dublin, notably to *Kottabos* and *The Irish Monthly*. About this time he visited Italy; and although inclined, through the spiritual element in art, to Roman Catholicism,— even writing notable poems such as *Rome Unvisited*, which won high praise from Cardinal Newman,— his faltering faith lacked the strength of ultimate conviction.

Wilde's journey in Greece with the party which accompanied John Pentland Mahaffy was the profoundest determinative influence which had yet come into his life. And if it did not make of him a "healthy Pagan," certainly it was a confirmation of all his dreams and visions of beauty undreamed and unimaginable. In his own words, in regard to this experience, "the worship of sorrow gave place again to the worship of beauty." For a time he dreamed of the beauty of religion; for all time afterwards he devoted himself in art to the religion of beauty. It has been suggested that Wilde's classical studies at Oxford so familiarized him with certain pathological manifestations that he really failed to realize their horror; and the brilliant French symbolist,

Henri de Régnier, does not hesitate to attribute his downfall to the fact that he had so steeped himself in the life of by-gone days that he did not realize the world in which he was actually living. Oscar Wilde believed that "he lived in Italy at the time of the Renaissance or in Greece at the time of Socrates. He was punished for a chronological error. . . ."

During his stay at Oxford, he acquitted himself very ably in his classes; and possibly through the happy chance that Ravenna, which he had recently visited, was announced as the topic for the Newdigate competition, he won the Newdigate prize for English Verse in 1878. This poem exhibits a great advance on his previous work, and in many respects, despite its lack of a controlling central thought, deserves high praise. On leaving Oxford, he went up to London in the rôle of a "Professor of Æsthetics and Art critic," according to Foster's statement in the *Alumni Oxoniensis*. Now he began to assume that "affectation of singularity" which so distinctively marked the author of *Melmoth the Wanderer* — that eccentric genius, the toast of Baudelaire and Balzac — Oscar Wilde's great-uncle, Charles Maturin. Like Zola, like Shaw, Wilde realized that this is an age of push and advertisement. He saw years of neglect at the hands of the public stretching out drearily before him if he did not force himself, by sensational methods, upon its attention. When the treasures of his mentality went for naught, he unhesitatingly focussed the public gaze upon the eccentricities of his personality. Like Thomas Griffiths Wainewright, he assumed the "dangerous and delightful distinction of being different from others." Prior to this time, his garb was characterized by no marks of affectation or preciosity; but he now hit upon the spectacular device of *outré* and *bizarre* costume. Celebrities often exhibit a harmless and pardonable penchant for peculiarity of dress — the scarlet waistcoat of Gautier, the monk's cowl of Balzac, the *vaquero* costume of Joaquin Miller. In his rôle of æsthete, Wilde wore a "velvet coat, knee-breeches, a loose shirt with a turn-down collar, and a floating tie of some unusual shade, fastened in a Lavallière knot, and he not infrequently appeared in public carrying in his hand a lily or a sunflower, which he used to contemplate with an expression of the greatest admiration!" It was Wilde's pompous pose, as the high priest of Æstheticism, to plume himself upon the discovery of whatsoever of real beauty exists in nature and art; by inference, those whose eyes were not thus opened to the miracles of the common day were "hopelessly private persons" — termed Philistines. Wilde and his cult were shining marks for the wit, satire and caricature of Du Maurier and Burnand; W. S. Gilbert caricatured Wilde in "Patience," and *Punch* overflowed with

Copyright by Elliott & Fry, Ltd.

OSCAR WILDE

cartoons and skits of which the following is a typical example:

> "Æsthete of Æsthetes!
>   What's in a name?
> The poet is WILDE
>   But his poetry's tame."

Wilde's notoriety was enhanced by a pseudo social lionization; but in spite of a certain sort of superficial lustre attaching to him, he was regarded with suspicion — the suspicion that at any time his lion's skin, as in the fable, might fall to the ground and reveal only a braying ass. Thus he began his career under the cloud of a not unjustifiable suspicion of *réclame*, quackery, and imposture; and it is a suspicion that not only his life, but even his death, have been inadequate to allay. At any rate his notoriety, though won by questionable and unworthy means, enabled him to secure a publisher for his first volume of verse; and won him an invitation to lecture in the United States. He was encouraged to visit America not as the author of a book of poems which had been most widely read in America, but as the much-discussed leader of the "Æsthetic Movement and School." Some verses in the *World*, in which Wilde is labelled "Ego Upto Snuffibus Poeta" appeared just before his departure for New York; they sound the dominant note of public opinion:

"Albeit nurtured in Democracy,
And liking best that state Bohemian
Where each man borrows sixpence and no man
Has aught but paper collars; yet I see
Exactly where to take a liberty.

"Better to be thought one, whom most abuse
For speech of donkey and for look of goose,
Than that the world should pass in silence by.
Wherefore I wear a sunflower in my coat,
Cover my shoulders with my flowing hair,
Tie verdant satin round my open throat,
Culture and love I cry, and ladies smile,
And seedy critics overflow with bile,
While with my Prince long Sykes's meal I share."

Wilde paid to the full the penalty for making himself a "motley to the view." Never afterwards was he allowed to forget that the way of the *blagueur* is hard.

In America he was greeted with amused incredulity, treated as a diverting sort of literary curiosity, ridiculed, satirized, caricatured. His intellectual arrogance gave tone to his remark at the New York Customs House: "I have nothing to declare but my genius." He was violently attacked in many quarters, and few cared to face the ridicule inevitably consequent to any defence of his theories and practice. Not a few personages of distinction, nevertheless, showed him courtesy and hospitality, among whom may be mentioned John Boyle O'Reilly, Julia Ward Howe, Oliver Wendell Holmes, Clara Morris, Henry Wadsworth Longfellow, Joaquin Miller, General Grant and the Rev. Henry Ward Beecher. Although Wilde, as one of his friends records, suffered poignantly from the attacks directed against him, he cannot be absolved from the charge of occasionally provoking them. "I am not exactly pleased with the Atlantic. It is not so majestic as I expected," gave rise to an infinitude of humorous verse; and his oft-quoted remark about Niagara was nothing more nor less than a clever bait thrown out to the press: "I was disappointed with Niagara. Most people must be disappointed with Niagara. Every American bride is taken there, and the sight of the stupendous waterfall must be one of the earliest if not the keenest disappointments in American married life." Such provoking pleasantries inevitably excited amused comment — notably his description of American girls as "little oases of pretty unreasonableness in a vast desert of practical common-sense." Most people attended his lectures out of vulgar curiosity to see and to laugh at this licensed buffoon; it did not seem to occur to them, as we read in a contemporary review in the *Sun,* that his lecture was "not a performance so trifling as to insult the intelligence of the audience, but a carefully prepared essay which proves its author to be a man of cultivation, taste, imagination, education and refinement." One of his lectures was described to me, by one who heard it, as a weak solution of Ruskin; and this is a fair indication of the contemporary valuation. The truth of the matter is that his lecture on the English Renaissance was a very artistic and capable, if somewhat paradoxical and precious appreciation of the significance of that movement. And his *Decorative Art in America* was a simple and straightforward expression of many sane, practical truths which the utilitarian thrust of modern art has amply substantiated. Not by any means is it to be understood that Wilde originated all the ideas he gracefully presented; he simply gave concrete expression to much that was in the air in the art criticism of the day. "As a plea for the encouragement of the handicraftsman," writes Mr. Glaenzer in regard to *Decorative Art in America;* "for the rejection of the hideously naturalistic tendency in house-furnishing; for the establishment of museums, enriched by the finest examples from the finest periods of decorative art; for their beautiful surroundings for children, and for schools in which these children might develop their artistic proclivities under the guidance of artists and capable artisans — as a *plea* for all that is beautiful, noble and sane in art, this lecture falls little short of being a masterpiece."

Now that his "apostolic task," to his secret relief, was concluded, Wilde lightly disclaimed any intention of continued charlatanry. Of his connection with the Æsthetic Movement, he said in 1883: "That was the Oscar Wilde of the second period. I am now in my third period." He settled in Paris in the Hotel Voltaire, and soon made himself known, through presentation copies of his *Poems,* to a number of the leading figures in the world of art and letters in Paris. Well received in many quarters, Wilde numbered among his acquaintances Victor Hugo, Edmond de Goncourt, Paul Bourget, Alphonse Daudet, Sarah Bernhardt, and many of the leaders of the impressionist school of painters. His success in Parisian circles would have been greater if he had only possessed the necessary reserve and tact. His desire to "astonish the natives," to indulge in affectations and extravagances of dress, and to talk paradoxical stuff about art and letters, rather rubbed the Parisians the wrong way. He took Balzac for his model, wore the Balzacian cowl whenever he was at work, and carried on the street a replica of that celebrated *Canne de Monsieur Balzac* perpetuated in the novel of Delphine Gay. His imitation of Balzac took one good direction: he began to take infinite pains with his art. During this period Wilde wrote *The Duchess of Padua,* a five-act drama in the Elizabethan style. Under the influence of Poe, through Baudelaire, whose *Fleurs de Mal* made a profound impression upon Wilde, he wrote a strangely pagan and sensual poem *The*

Sphinx — an excellent type of the derivative poem, of the art which is not spontaneous. But all his diligent application temporarily went for naught. *The Duchess of Padua* was refused by Mary Anderson for whom it was written; and the proceeds of the sale of Wilde's property in Ireland could not long survive the onslaughts made upon it by his extravagant mode of life; his literary work brought him nothing. And so, in the summer of 1883, he returned to London to try a hazard of new fortunes. There he was conspicuously dedicated to oblivion by a prominent journal in an article entitled "Exit Oscar." To which Wilde buoyantly replied: "If it took Labouchere three columns to prove that I was forgotten, then there is no difference between fame and obscurity."

During the years from 1883 to 1891, the output of Wilde was quite small — he gave himself up to the art of living rather than to the art of writing. For a time, at first, he was compelled once more to take the lecture platform, this time in England; but he resolutely refused to make capital out of the eccentricities of his personal appearance and costume. During one of his lecture tours, he met in Dublin the lovely Constance Lloyd, who became his wife on May 29, 1884. Mrs. Wilde's dowry enabled the young couple to lease a house in Tite Street, decorated under the direction of Whistler, who became a close acquaintance of Wilde. Garbed in a charming " æsthetic " costume of the period, Constance Wilde was a beautiful picture in the artistic Tite Street setting with her chestnut hair touched with gold, blue-green eyes, brunette skin with vivid cheeks and lips. Decoration not entertainment was her rôle; for while bright in manner and conversation, she paled into insignificance in face of the conversational dazzle of her husband. This couple for a time were the cynosure of fashionable London. Wilde's *mots* were repeated everywhere; and Mrs. Wilde's sartorial taste set the fashion. Even the slightest details of the Wilde household were chronicled as matters of interest in the social and artistic world. For several years Wilde wrote various signed and unsigned articles for the press, purely ephemeral in character, and a number of those beautiful modern fairy tales which combine a delicacy of fancy with a touch of social philosophy, rarely charming and arresting. But it became increasingly difficult for Wilde to earn a living; and even Whistler — in *The Gentle Art of Making Enemies* — took a hand in facilitating his downhill progress. When Messrs. Cassell and Company offered him the editorship of *The Woman's World* in 1887, he was in no position to refuse; and his connection with that magazine lasted from October, 1887, to September, 1889. If he was not precisely a success as an editor, though conscientious and industrious at this period, it was because his taste was too refined, too artistic and subtle for the clientèle of his magazine. It is the verdict of his greatest admirers, especially among foreign critics, that the works which he wrote between the time of his marriage and the year 1892 entitle him to an exalted place in English literature, and give him rank as a philosopher of acute penetration and delicate insight. There were *The Happy Prince* and *The House of Pomegranates* — fanciful *Märchen* shot through with a sensitive and beautiful social pity, like embroidered, jewelled fabrics firmly filiated with a crimson thread. There was *The Picture of Dorian Gray,* reminiscent of Balzac's *Peau de Chagrin,* rich in opulent fancy, in subtle mystery, and in the strangely ominous prevision of its author's own coming fate. And there, too, was *The Soul of Man Under Socialism,* that brilliant and paradoxical revelation of Wilde's temperament — a brochure which has gone triumphantly forth to the very ends of the earth. Last, and highest, was *Intentions,* that miraculous masterpiece of connected writings, with its inverted truisms and forthright paradoxes, its fanciful reasoning and reasonable fancy — quintessence of style, of form, of taste in art.

During the years from 1892 to 1895, Wilde attained to remarkable success as a playwright; and at last the rewards of literature flowed without cessation into the pockets of this lavish spendthrift. *Lady Windermere's Fan, A Woman of No Impor-*

tance, An Ideal Husband, and *The Importance of Being Earnest,* were phenomenal successes; and at one time three of Wilde's plays could have been witnessed on a single night in London. But in March, 1895, the downfall came; and the information for criminal libel which Wilde, in a state verging upon intoxication, laid against the Marquess of Queensberry, was the beginning of his undoing. Wilde at last was hoist by his own petard. The history of the two trials, Wilde's condemnation and disgrace, his two years of poignant anguish and physical suffering in prison, his subsequent piteous descent to disaster and death — the harrowing details may be learned elsewhere. Suffice it to say that his predisposition to vice through inheritance, the fearful effect upon him of intoxicants which seemed to lash his brain to madness, and the indulgence in ultra-stimulative food and drink in the two or three years immediately preceding his disgrace serve, in the eyes of the specialist in pathology and degeneracy, as indicative causes of his downfall and ruin. There survive from the days of imprisonment his greatest poem *The Ballad of Reading Gaol,* and that soul autobiography *De Profundis* — morbid, pitiable, yet wonderful mixture of confession and palliation, penance and defiance, self-incrimination and exculpation. Wonderful document — true confession or disingenuous plea, soul creed or soul blasphemy!

"Man is least himself when he talks in his own

person. Give him a mask and he will tell you the truth." There is no means, to be sure, of escaping the everlasting return of life upon art — art, the mirror which the Narcissus of artists holds up to himself. Let us, however, remember with Novalis that he who is of power higher than the first is a genius. Nietzsche says, "All that is profound loves a mask." And even if, occasionally and unwittingly, we traverse the circuit from art to life, at least we may have the satisfaction of making the attempt to dissociate the merits of the dramatist from the demerits of the man.

III

In 1882, Wilde wrote to Mr. R. D'Oyly Carte, manager of the Savoy Theatre, London, that his play *Vera; or The Nihilists* was meant not to be read, but to be acted. This opinion has never received any support from either critic or public. Written when Wilde was only twenty-two years old (*The New York World*, August 12, 1883), this play early enrolled him under that *drapeau romantique des jeunes guerriers* of which Théophile Gautier speaks; yet the time doubtless came when Wilde regarded *Vera,* as he certainly regarded his first volume of poems, merely in the light of a youthful indiscretion. Unlike Ibsen, Pinero or Phillips, Wilde was fortified by experience neither as actor nor manager; there is no record that he ever, like Bernard Shaw, acted even in amateur theatricals. A cousin in near degree to W. G. Wills, the dramatist, painter and poet, Wilde may have derived his dramaturgic talent in some measure from the same source. In youth he learned the graceful arts of conversation in the brilliant salon of his mother, Lady Wilde; and his predilection for the dialogue form early revealed itself in certain of his critical essays.

The play *Vera* ushers us into the *milieu* of Henry Seton Merriman's *The Sowers*, but it bears all the fantastic earmarks of the yellow-backed fustian of the melodramatic yarn-spinner, Marchmont. One might easily imagine it to be the boyish effusion of a romantic youth in the more recent day of Von Plehve, Gorki, and the Douma. "As regards the play itself," wrote Wilde to the American actress, Marie Prescott, in July, 1883, "I have tried in it to express within the limits of art that Titan cry of the people for liberty which, in the Europe of our day, is threatening thrones and making Governments unstable from Spain to Russia, and from north to southern seas. But it is a play, not of politics, but of passion. It deals with no theories of Government, but with men and women simply; and modern Nihilistic Russia, with all the terror of its tyranny and the marvel of its martyrdoms, is merely the fiery and fervent background in front of which the persons of my dream live and love.

With this feeling was the play written, and with this aim should the play be acted." Despite these lofty and promising words, the play warrants no serious consideration — even though it won the admiration of the great American actor, Lawrence Barrett.

A pseudo-*Volksdrama, Vera* images the conflict between despotism and nihilism, between a vacillating, terror-obsessed Czar and a Russian Charlotte Corday. The " love interest " inheres in the struggle of the Czarevitch, who is in sympathy with the people, between his duty to the Empire and his love for the people's champion, the Nihiliste Vera. The theme is one that well might fire to splendid efforts; but instead of creatures of flesh and blood, looming solid in a large humanity, we see only thin cardboard profiles — bloodless puppets shifted hither and thither, as with Sardou, at the bidding of the mechanical showman. One-sided in the possession of only one feminine rôle, the play is largely taken up with interminable passages of pointless persiflage between superfluous characters. To one who knows the later Wilde, *Vera* seems less like a predecessor of the comedies than a contemporary parody; this Wilde has acquired no mastery of the arts of epigram, paradox and repartee. In the *dénouement, Vera,* chosen by lot to assassinate her lover the Czarevitch, now become Czar, turns upon her own breast the dagger meant for him, and then tosses it over the balcony to the ravening conspirators below with the cry, "I have saved Russia!"—this is the very acme of the "theatric" in the worst sense, the very quintessence of Adelphi melodrama. Not inapposite, perhaps, was the characteristic paragraph in *Punch* (December 10, 1881) under *Impressions du Théâtre:*—

The production of Mr. Oscar Wilde's play "Vera" is deferred. Naturally no one would expect a Veerer to be at all certain; it must be, like a pretendedly infallible forecast, so very weather-cocky. "Vera" is about Nihilism; this looks as if there was nothing in it. But why did Mr. O. Wilde select the Adelphi for his first appearance as a dramatic author, in which career we wish him all the success he may deserve? Why did he not select the Savoy? Surely where there's a donkey cart—we should say D'Oyly Carte—there ought to be an opportunity for an 'Os-car?

In the Wilde of the "third period," as he described himself in 1883, is revealed a strangely different man from the apostle of æstheticism. If he has not learned to scorn delights, at least he has learned to live laborious days. He takes up his quarters at the Hotel Voltaire in Paris, and though still guilty of affectation in his assumption of the cane and cowl of Balzac, yet he takes the great French master for his model and disciplines himself to that unremitting labor which, in Balzac's view, is the *sine qua non*, the law, of art. Recall the precious anecdote of Wilde's day's work upon his manuscript — deleting a comma in the forenoon and re-inserting it in the afternoon! In these days of the theatrical "star," for whom "parts" are especially written — Cyrano for Coquelin, Vanna for Mme. Maeterlinck, the Sorceress for Bernhardt, Ulysses for Tree, Lady Cicely Waynflete for Terry, and so on — Wilde thought to play his part in writing *The Duchess of Padua* for Mary Anderson, the distinguished actress, now Mrs. de Navarro.

In a letter to *The Times,* London, March 3, 1893, Wilde affirmed: "I have never written a play for any actor or actress, nor shall I ever do so. Such work is for the artisan in literature, not for the artist." This affirmation is both illogical and disingenuous; and is belied by the account of his biographer.

The Duchess of Padua, with its Websterian title, is a play laid in the sixteenth century — century of tears and terror, of poetry and passion, of madness and blood. While lounging in his cowl, in imitation of Balzac, Wilde was evidently studying Victor Hugo instead; and in *The Duchess of Padua* there is not a little besides of the bombast, fustian and balderdash of Webster and Tourneur. In reality, *The Duchess of Padua* is an almost lyrical echo of the Shaksperean strain — positively rapturous in imitativeness. If Lady Macbeth, after the murder, say that "A little water clears us of this deed," and, later, "Who would have thought the old man to have had so much blood in him," Wilde's Duchess, after killing her husband, voices the juvenile plagiarism:

"I did not think he would have bled so much, but I can wash my hands in water after."

If Dogberry voices the opinion that "they that touch pitch will be defiled," Wilde's dispenser of comic relief can cap it only with such feeble repetition as, "if one meddles with wicked people one is like to be tainted with their wickedness." Unable to catch the magic sheen and heroic gleam of his original, Wilde gives us not an original creation but an appreciative commentary marred by its false rhetoric, exaggerativeness, and toploftical strain. Wilde was only too ready to employ the "strong" curtain, after the fashion set by Hugo, as a concession to modern taste; in every other respect, this play, in pure externals, is so faithful in its reproduction of the Elizabethan style as to seem but one remove from refined caricature.

And yet the play possesses real interest and charm, not perhaps for its subject but because of its spiritual and emotional content — the violently transitional moods of romantic passion. It is a tale, in five acts, of the love of the gentle Beatrice, Duchess of Padua, and of the young Guido Ferranti, sworn to avenge the inhuman murder of his noble father at the hands of the old and heartless Duke, the husband of Beatrice. Ferranti and Beatrice have just confessed their love for each other, when the pre-arranged message reaches Ferranti that the hour to strike down the Duke is come. He tears himself away from Beatrice in definitive farewell, with poignant agony, crying out that a certain insurmountable obstacle stands in the way of their love. That night, as he pauses outside the Duke's chamber meditating upon assassination, there comes to Ferranti the belated recognition not only that he can never approach Beatrice again with the blood of the murdered Duke upon his hands, but that such a revenge is deeply unworthy of the memory of his noble father. But as Anael comes forth from the murder of the Prefect to her Djabal, comes forth Beatrice to her Guido. For under the tyranny of her love for Guido, she has slain him to whom she was ever but a worthless chattel — the Duke, the sole obstacle to the fulfilment of her passion. Guido recoils from her upon whose hands is the blood which he himself had solemnly — but suddenly! — refused to shed. And though Beatrice, like Juliet, is transformed into a very "Von Moltke of love," she cannot, with all the mustered array of her forces, storm the bastion of Guido's soul. So sudden and so supreme is her own revulsion of feeling that she finds herself passionately denouncing Ferranti to the passers-by as the assassin of her husband. Follows the trial of Ferranti for his life — a scene quite memorable for its undulation of emotional process, the conflicting fears and hopes of the heart-wrung Duchess, and the crisis: Ferranti's false confession that the murderer is none other than himself. Visiting the condemned Ferranti in his cell, the heartbroken Duchess, in the excess of her spiritual agony, takes poison; and Guido, realizing at last the inner, essential nobility of her character, avows for her his undying love, and dies upon the point of his dagger.

The Duchess of Padua is noteworthy for its tender lyrism, the delicate beauty of its imagery, and its glow of youthful fire; and despite its mimetic stamp, displays real power in instrumentation of feeling and in the temperamental and passional shades of its mood. The play links itself to Hardy and to Whitman, rather than to Shakspere, in its intimation of purity of purpose as the sole criterion of deed. For here Wilde, concerned less with the primitive basis of individuality than with the fundamental impulses of instinctive temperament, reveals life as fluid and evolutional. "In every creature," writes Hedwig Lachmann, the critic of Wilde, "lurks the readiness for desperate deeds. But when all is over, man remains unchanged. His nature does not change, because for a moment he has been torn from his moorings. After the stormy waters which forced its overflow have run their course, the river once more glides back into its bed." Like Maeterlinck's Joyzelle, Beatrice is forgiven, not because "Who sins for love sins not," but because she has loved much. In Wilde's own startling words — in *The Soul of Man under Socialism,* written some eight years later —: "A can cannot always be estimated by what he does. He may keep the law and yet be worthless. He may break the law and yet be fine. He may be bad without ever doing anything bad. He may commit a sin against society, and yet realize through that sin his true perfection." Maeterlinck maintains that justice is a very mysterious thing, residing not in nature or in anything external, but, like truth, in ourselves. It is in this play, as Mr William Archer has said, that Wilde reveals himself a poet of very high rank. Nothing is easier, and therefore possibly more misleading, than to say that *The Duchess of Padua* is not *du théâtre;* for the tests of its suitability for the stage have been inconclusive. To Wilde's intense disappointment, it was refused by Mary Anderson; but it was afterwards produced in the United States by Lawrence Barrett with moderate success. Although announced as in preparation in the *Publishers' List* for 1894, *The Duchess of Padua* was actually not published until ten years later — in the fine translation of Dr. Max Meyerfeld of Berlin. An unauthorized *prose* re-translation from Meyerfeld's German version was first published in English. The original manuscript of the play, stolen from Wilde's house in 1895, has never come to light; the best version, based on a prompt copy used by Wilde and containing his own corrections, is found in the authorized edition of his works, edited by Robert Ross. In addition to its production in America with Lawrence Barrett and Mina Gale in the leading rôles, there have been at least two productions on the continent. At Hamburg, Germany, in December, 1904, where it was produced under the most adverse circumstances, the play proved a failure, being withdrawn after three nights. And when it was produced in Berlin early in 1906 it was killed by the critics, resulting in a heavy loss for its champion, Dr. Meyerfeld. The play is "theatrical" in the proper sense, and, despite its reverses, might, I think, afford a suitable medium for the talent of a Julia Marlowe or an Ellen Terry under favoring conditions. It is interesting to note that Wilde at the end of his life acknowledged, according to Mr. Robert Ross, that *The Duchess of Padua* artistically was of minor importance.

It was Wilde's pleasure, during his frequent visits to Paris, to delight the French world of art and letters with brilliant *causeries.* The masterly ease and exquisite purity of his French were a marvel to all who heard him. And Wilde once explained (*Pall Mall Gazette,* June 29, 1892) the idea he had in mind in writing the play of *Salomé* in French:—"I have one instrument that I know I can command, and that is the English language.

There was another instrument to which I had listened all my life, and I wanted once to touch this new instrument to see whether I could make any beautiful thing out of it. . . . Of course, there are modes of expression that a Frenchman of letters would not have used, but they give a certain relief or color to the play. A great deal of the curious effect that Maeterlinck produces comes from the fact that he, a Flamand by grace, writes in an alien language. The same thing is true of Rossetti, who, though he wrote in English, was essentially Latin in temperament." In this connection, "Leonard Cresswell Ingleby" pertinently quotes Max Beerbohm's remark that Walter Pater wrote English as though it were a dead language. Although Wilde's *Salomé* was revised by Marcel Schwob, it still bore after the revision, slight as it must have been, the trail of the foreigner. The English version, by Lord Alfred Douglas, is a marvellously sympathetic and poetic rendition.

In writing his *Salomé,* Wilde was strongly influenced by *Hérodias,* one of Gustave Flaubert's *Trois Contes,* though in Flaubert's tale it is at the instigation of Herodias that Salome dances for the head of the prophet. Gomez Carrillo, the Spanish translator of *Salomé,* records that Wilde said to him at the time he was writing the play: "If for no other reason, I have always longed to go to Spain that I might see in the Prado Titian's Salome, of which Tintoretto once exclaimed: 'Here at last is a man who paints the very quivering flesh!'" And Carrillo mentions that only Gustave Moreau's picture, immortalized by Huysmans, unveiled for Wilde the "soul of the dancing princess of his dreams." Whilst Wilde has twisted the Biblical story to his individual ends, his interpretation is said to follow a fairly widespread tradition — as hinted at, for instance, in Renan's *Life of Jesus.* In both Sudermann's *Johannes* and Massenet's opera of *Herodiade,* Salome is the object of Herod's infatuation. Wilde has given the Biblical story an interpretation fundamentally dramatic in its abnormality. As a reconstitution of classic antiquity, *Salomé* belongs erotically to the school of Pierre Louys' *Aphrodite* and Anatole France's *Thais.* Like Poe, like Baudelaire, like Maeterlinck, Wilde has revealed with masterful if meretricious artistry, the beautiful in the horrible.

Salomé is a fevered dream, a poignant picture — it is like one of those excursions into the *macabre* with which Wilde succeeded in fascinating the Parisians. In it one discerns the revolting decadence of an age when vice was no prejudice and sensuality no shame; we hear the resonance of lawless passion, and the reverberations of obscure, half-divined emotions. The characters stand forth in chiselled completeness from the rich Galilean background like the embossed figures upon a Grecian urn. The insatiable, sensual Herodias, symbolic figure of the malady of that age; and Herod, the Tetrarch, obsessed with profoundly disquieting inclinations to unlawful passion, ultimately cutting at a single blow the Gordian knot of his problem, for the untying of which he lacks both courage and conscience. Like Hebbel's Daniel, Jokanaan is a wonderfully realized figure — the incarnation of a primitive, intolerant prophet, the voice crying in the wilderness — commanding rapt attention far less by what he says than by what he is. There is Salome — "she is like a dove that has strayed . . . she is like a narcissus trembling in the wind . . . she is like a silver flower. . . . Her little white hands are fluttering like white butterflies." She is unmoved at first by any strangely perverse, nameless passion for the forbidden. But as in a dream, a memory of forgotten, yet half-divined reality, erotic passion wakens under the spell of Jokanaan's presence; and his scorn, his anathemas, his objurgations rouse to life and to revolt within her the dormant instincts of an Herodias. She will sing the swan song of her soul in the pæan of the dance, and for the sake of revenge so ensnare the plastic Herod in the meshes of her perilous and dissolving beauty that he can refuse her nothing — even though it were the half of his kingdom. The world swims in a scarlet haze before her eyes; and though lust, scorn, revenge, and death meet in that terrible kiss of a woman scorned, the hour of her own fate has struck. Impressive, awful, imperial, Herod speaks the laconic words: "Kill that woman!" Salome, daughter of Herodias, Princess of Judea, is crushed beneath the shields of the soldiers, and her death sounds the death knell of a decadent and degenerate age. A new epoch of culture is at hand.

In *Salomé*, Wilde depicts a crystallized embodiment of the age, rather than the age itself. To the naturalism of sensation is super-added stylistic symmetry and, in places, what Baudelaire termed supreme literary grace. The influence of Maeterlinck is inescapable in the simplicity of the dialogue in places, the iterations and reverberations of the leading motives, the evocation of the atmosphere and imminence of doom. Nature symbolically cooperates in intensifying the feeling of dread; and we dimly entertain the presentiment of vast and fateful figures lurking in the wings. In such passages as the long protests of Herod, there is all the decorative opulence of Flaubert; and in the mouth of Salome the poetic phrasing holds at times a moonlit radiance. With all its verbal jewellery, the dialogue is at times momentously laconic; as in the words of Salome in explanation of Herod's passion: "Why does the Tetrarch look at me all the while with his mole's eyes under his shaking eyelids? It is strange that the husband of my mother looks at me like that. I know not what it means. Of a truth I know it too well." Wilde declared that *Salomé* was a piece of music — with its progressive crescendo, emotional pæan and tragic finale. And Richard Strauss justified Wilde's dictum in his opera *Salomé* of far-flung notoriety, asymmetric in its form, barbaric in its passion, most arresting at the emotional climax of Salome's erotomania. It is significant that this, the one play of Wilde's not primarily written for the stage, is a true drama in the most real sense, bearing the stamp of the conviction of the real artist. No credence need be given the statement of Gomez Carrillo, in his *El Origèn de la Salomé de Wilde,* that this play was written for Sarah Bernhardt. The play was written in Paris at the turn of the year 1891-2; and Wilde himself said to an interviewer (June, 1892), a statement supported by Mr. St. John Hankin: "A few weeks ago I met Madame Sarah Bernhardt at Sir Henry Irving's. She had heard of my play, and asked me to read it to her. I did so, and she at once expressed a wish to play the title-rôle." It is lamentable that *Salomé* focusses attention upon abnormal and lascivious states of feeling, indicative of Wilde's own degeneracy. When I last heard Strauss' opera at the Royal Opera House in Berlin, this impression was deepened and intensified by the "argument of the flesh," and the potent instrumentality of the temperamentally intense music. And yet, withal,

Copyright by Underwood & Underwood

JOHN GALSWORTHY

Salomé is Wilde's one dramatic achievement of real genius, an individual and unique literary creation.

Since Wilde's death, *The Duchess of Padua* has been printed in both German and English versions; of the unpublished plays, only *A Florentine Tragedy,* a fragment, was saved by Wilde's executor, Mr. Robert Ross, from the house at 16 Tite Street, Chelsea. The manuscript of *The Woman Covered with Jewels* is so fragmentary as to be negligible. Mr. Willard, the romantic actor, likewise possessed a copy of *A Florentine Tragedy,* agreeing in every particular with the one recovered by Mr. Ross; in each the opening scene was gone, showing that Wilde had never written it. "It was characteristic of the author," says Mr. Ross, "to have finished what he never began." It has since been published (Luce, Boston) with an introductory note by Mr. Ross; he also narrated the history of the play's recovery in the *Tribune* (London) in June, 1906. The opening act has been supplied by Mr. T. Sturge Moore, well known as the poet of *The Vinedresser and Other Poems, Absalom, The Centaur's Booty,* etc., and the critic of Dürer and Correggio. This bit of reconstruction in *A Forentine Tragedy* is remarkable, alike for catching Wilde's tone and for its individual charm. Though the play was originally written for Mr. George Alexander and afterwards submitted to Mr. Willard, it did not see the footlights in England until June 18, 1906, when it was produced together with *Salomé* by the Literary Theatre Club, at the King's Hall, Covent Garden. In Dr. Max Meyerfeld's translation, the play has been produced with moderate success in Germany (Leipzig, Hamburg and Berlin).

A Florentine Tragedy is a much slighter performance than *Salomé;* and acting both deep and subtle is required to vitalize the characters into real human semblance. It is the triangular affair — with a difference; and the *dénouement* is a startling climax. In the absence of the merchant Simone, his fair young wife Bianca is visited by the Florentine Prince, Guido Bardi, and courted in Young Lochinvar fashion:

> O, make no question, come!
> They waste their time who ponder o'er bad dreams.
> We will away to hills, red roses clothe,
> And though the persons who did haunt that dream
> Live on, they shall by distance dwindled, seem
> No bigger than the smallest ear of corn,
> That cowers at the passing of a bird;
> And silent shall they seem, out of earshot
> Those voices that could jar, while we gaze back
> From rosy caves upon the hill-brow open,
> And ask ourselves if what we see is not
> A picture merely — if dusty, dingy lives
> Continue there to choke themselves with malice.
> Wilt thou not come, Bianca? Wilt thou not?

Simone entering, interrupts the ardent courtship; and with Southern subtlety feigns the utmost regard for his guest. They chat, with an undercurrent of meaning in their words, while the old merchant displays his gorgeous wares. Interest quickens in the discovery that Simone is "playing" the egoistic Guido, cunningly drawing him by almost imperceptible gradations into a trial of skill — or shall it be a duel? Bianca holds aloft a torch to the struggle until Simone disarms Guido. As they close with each other, daggers drawn, Bianca dashes her torch to the floor,— only in the end to hear Guido die the death of a poltroon. With an exclamation "Now for the other!" Simone rises from his bloody work and gazes at his trembling wife. The splendid manhood of her husband has dazzled her; and in wonder and subjugation she goes towards him with arms outstretched, murmuring the words, "Why did you not tell me you were so strong?" Her tremendous revulsion of feeling is matched by one no less instantaneous or momentous than her own. And with the words, "Why did you not tell me you were so beautiful?", Simone takes Bianca in his arms and kisses her on the mouth. Strange lovers, stranger reconciliation!

IV

A new, a strikingly different Wilde, next makes his *début* in the society comedy. Wilde's earlier plays brought him nothing, scarcely even notoriety; for the British public could not be persuaded to believe that any work of poetic beauty or dramatic art could emanate from a licensed jester, angler before all for the public stare. Wilde had incontestibly established his reputation as a buffoon; and once a buffoon, always a buffoon! One may truly say of Wilde, as Brandes once said of Ibsen, that at this period of his life he had a lyrical Pegasus killed under him. Like Bernard Shaw, Wilde was forced to the conclusion that the brain had ceased to be a vital organ in English life. As he expressed it, the public used the classics as a means of checking the progress of Art, as bludgeons for preventing the free expression of Beauty in new forms. It was his aim to extend the subject-matter of art; and this was distasteful to the public since it was the expression of an individualism defiant of public opinion. And to Wilde, public opinion represented the will of the ignorant majority as opposed to that of the discerning few. Far from holding that the public is the patron of the artist, Wilde vigorously maintained that the artist is always the munificent patron of the public. The very bane of his existence was the popular, yet profoundly erroneous, maxim that "the drama's laws the drama's patrons give." The work of art, he rightly avers, is to dominate the spectator: the spectator is not to dominate the work of art. The drama must come into being, not for the sake of the theatre, but through the inner, vital necessity of the artist for self-expression. He scorned the field of popular novelism, not only because it was too ridiculously easy, but also because to meet the requirements of the sentimental public with its half-baked conceptions of art, the artist would have to " do violence to his temperament, would have to write, not for the artistic joy of writing, but for the amusement of half-educated people, and so would have to suppress his individualism, forget his culture, annihilate his style, and surrender everything that is valuable to him." In his search for lucrative employment for his individual talents, his eye fell upon the comic stage. It dawned upon him that Tom Robertson, H. G. Byron and W. S. Gilbert — to say nothing of Sheridan — were still living factors in the English drama, and that the style of Dumas *fils,* in the Scribishly " well-made " pattern, met the most important requirements of popular taste. While little scope was allowed the creator of the higher forms of dramatic art, in the field of burlesque and light, even farcical comedy, the artist was allowed very great freedom in England. It was under the pressure of such convictions that Wilde now sought a hazard of new fortunes.

The four society comedies which Wilde wrote in rapid succession, which immediately gained huge success in England, and have since been played to vastly appreciative audiences in Europe and the

United States, are so similar in style, treatment and appeal as almost to warrant discussion as a unique *genre*. Only *The Importance of Being Earnest* really differentiates itself, generically, from its predecessors.

Lady Windermere's Fan, perhaps the most celebrated of Wilde's comedies, is concerned with the hackneyed theme of the eternal triangle — the theme of *Odette*, *Le Supplice d'une Femme*, and countless other comedies of the French school. Only by means of the flashing dialogue is Wilde enabled to conceal the essential conventionality and threadbare melodrama of the plot. The characters are lacking in the ultimate stamp of reality, functioning primarily as social types in a situation, only secondarily as individuals working out their own salvation. And yet somehow he has managed to give them the "tone of their time," and to endow them with that air of social ease in a drawing-room which is the essential to comedy in an enlightened society. The following scene in which Mrs. Erlynne discovers the letter of farewell from Lady Windermere to her husband, is significant and dramatically impressive; but it seems obviously suggested by the incident in Ibsen's *Ghosts*, which inspired the title.

Parker. Her Ladyship has just gone out of the house.

Mrs. Erlynne. (*Starts, and looks at the servant with a puzzled expression on her face.*) Out of the house?

Parker. Yes, madam — her ladyship told me she had left a letter for his lordship on the table.

Mrs. Erlynne. A letter for Lord Windermere?

Parker. Yes, madam.

Mrs. Erlynne. Thank you. (*Exit Parker. The music in the ballroom stops.*) Gone out of her house! A letter addressed to her husband! (*Goes over to bureau and looks at letter. Takes it up and lays it down again with a shudder of fear.*) No, no! It would be impossible! Life doesn't repeat its tragedies like that! Oh, why does this horrible fancy come across me? Why do I remember now the moment of my life I most wish to forget? Does life repeat its tragedies? (*Tears open letter and reads it, then sinks down into a chair with a gesture of anguish.*) Oh, how terrible! The same words that twenty years ago I wrote to her father! and how bitterly I have been punished for it! No; my punishment, my real punishment is to-night, is now!

One other scene, that in which Mrs. Erlynne finally persuades Lady Windermere to return to her husband and child, is a situation of very nearly real seriousness on the stage; it is Wilde's mistake to put into the mouth of Mrs. Erlynne only the words the average spectator expects her to say, not the expression of the sentiments a woman who had passed through her devastating experience would inevitably feel.

In *A Woman of No Importance,* Wilde pretends to break a lance in behalf of even justice at the hands of society for men and women who have committed indiscretions. In his own words, this play is the embodiment of his conviction that there should not be "one law for men and another law for women." He was too much preoccupied with his thesis to make his characters real human beings; and the epigrammatic brilliance of the dialogue gives a sort of family resemblance to many of the "characters." Playing with great restraint, simplicity and *finesse,* Marion Terry as Mrs. Arbuthnot won the sympathy of her audience at a recent revival I attended at His Majesty's Theatre, London; but Beerbohm Tree could not accomplish the miracle of vitalizing Lord Illingworth. Hester Worsley argues with futility against a jury "packed" against her declamatory prudery; and Gerald is a brainless dolt. Lady Hunstanton and Lady Caroline Pontefract are delightful and naïve, comic admixtures of natural shrewdness, kindliness of heart, and surpassing British ignorance and insularity. The opening scene is something new in drama, the forerunner of *Don Juan in Hell* and *Getting Married;* indeed, Wilde declared that he wrote the first act of *A*

Woman of No Importance in answer to the complaint of the critics that *Lady Windermere's Fan* was lacking in action. " In the act in question," said Wilde, " there was absolutely no action at all. It was a perfect act! " Wilde once asked Ouida what she herself considered the chief feature in her work which won success. " I am the only living English writer," she replied, " who knows how two Dukes talk when they are by themselves! " It might, with truth, be said of Wilde that he was the only living English writer who knew how two Duchesses talk when they are by themselves.

An Ideal Husband is somewhat more compact and straightforward than either of the two previous comedies; the dialogue is more immediately germane to the action; the epigram is less frequently employed for the sake of covering deficiencies of plot or tiding over lapses in interest. Wilde was a curious mixture of the ultra-modern and the sentimental reactionary. The triteness of his technique was balanced by his facility in contriving " scenes," " situations," and " curtains." The modernity of his dialogue is matched by the mawkish conventionality of his moral *fond.* The long soliloquy at the beginning of the third act of *Lady Windermere's Fan* appears hopelessly antiquated as a theatrical device to a generation bred on Ibsen's rigorous technique; and yet Wilde imitated Ibsen in long stage directions, descriptive of the characters of his plays. Bernard Shaw himself could not have improved upon Wilde's thumb-nail sketch of Sir Robert Chiltern:

> A man of forty, but looking somewhat younger. Clean-shaven, with finely-cut features, dark-haired and dark-eyed. A personality of mark. Not popular — few personalities are. But intensely admired by the few, and deeply respected by the many. The note of his manner is that of perfect distinction, with a slight touch of pride. One feels that he is conscious of the success he has made in life. A nervous temperament, with a tired look. The finely-chiselled mouth and chin contrast strikingly with the romantic expression in the deepset eyes. The variance is suggestive of an almost complete separation of passion and intellect, as though thought and emotion were each isolated in its own sphere through some violence of will-power. There is no nervousness in the nostrils, and in the pale, thin, pointed hands. It would be inaccurate to call him picturesque. Picturesqueness cannot survive the House of Commons. But Vandyck would have liked to paint his head.

The real difference between the spirit of Wilde and the spirit of Ibsen is exhibited in the dénouement of *An Ideal Husband* as contrasted with that of *The Pillars of Society*. Ibsen's "hero" ultimately confesses his moral delinquency in the most public way, and the curtain falls upon a self-humiliated and repentant man ready to "begin over again" in order to work out his own salvation. Aside from a good scare, Sir Robert Chiltern is not only allowed to go scot-free, but is actually elevated to a vacant seat in the Cabinet! Wilde is reported to have said: "Nobody else's work gives me any suggestion. It is only by entire isolation from everything that one can do any work. Idleness gives one the mood, isolation the condition. Concentration on one's self recalls the new and wonderful world that one presents in the color and cadence of words in movement." It is matter for regret that not Ibsen, but Sardou and Dumas *fils* usually gave Wilde his suggestions. For with all his faults, he possessed in rich measure "the sense of the theatre." His plays ran so smoothly that the public was convinced that it was an easy task to write them. At the height of Wilde's fame, Bernard Shaw laconically remarked: "I am the only person in London who can't sit down and write an Oscar Wilde play at will!"

It was Wilde's characteristic contention that there never would be any real drama in England until it is recognized that a play is as personal and individual a form of self-expression as a poem or a picture. Here Wilde laid his finger upon his own fundamental error. By nature and by necessity, the drama is, of all the arts, the most impersonal: Victor Hugo said that dramatic art consists in being somebody else. So supreme an individual was Wilde that he lacked the dramatic faculty of intellectual self-detachment. Conversationally he could never be anybody but himself. To Bernard Shaw, Wilde appeared as, in a certain sense, the only thorough playwright in England — because he played with everything: with wit, philosophy, drama, actor and audience, the whole theatre. The critics thought that *An Ideal Husband* was a play about a bracelet; but Wilde maintained — and not without show of reason — that they missed its entire psychology: "The difference in the way in which a man loves a woman from that in which a woman loves a man; the passion that women have for making ideals (which is their weakness), and the weakness of a man who dares not show his imperfections to the thing he loves." They did not miss Wilde's besetting sin, however: manufacturing the great majority of his characters, as talkers, in the image and superscription of Wilde. It is little short of astounding that Wilde's comedies are resplendent by reason of qualities which have no intrinsic or organic relation to dramatic art.

The Importance of Being Earnest is Wilde's nearest approach to the creation of an unique *genre*. It is characteristic of Wilde that his most important comedy was cast in the most frivolous form. Perhaps additional testimony to its value and essential novelty is found in the fact that German critics, deceived by its extravagant plot, branded it as of no value! Its point of departure is the titular pun; but its real purpose could not have been better expressed than in the sub-title: "A Trivial Comedy for Serious People." Though Wilde, rather suggestively, chose to designate it on one occasion as a "rose-coloured comedy," the truth is that it is an epigrammatic extravaganza, cast in the form of farce. Meredith's "oblique ray" floods it throughout, and the action proceeds to the humanely malign accompaniment of "volleys of silvery laughter." Based on the absurd complications arising from the endless employment of *aliases* and written in the light, French style, this play is actually social satire on the fantastic plane. I recall the strong sense of the genuinely comic with which I was affected on once seeing in London Sir George Alexander as Worthing, in that devastating entry in deep mourning for the loss of the brother he had glibly invented — only to happen upon his friend who is at that moment personating the fictitious brother! Like Shaw's *You Never Can Tell,* it is psychological farce; and the characters, to borrow a phrase of Mr. Huneker's, indulge in "psychical antics." Its congeners are St. John Hankin's *The Charity that Begins at Home,* Shaw's *The Philanderer,* and Barrie's *The Admirable Crichton.* Mr. St. John Hankin has pertinently remarked that the type of play Wilde struck out in *The Importance of Being Earnest* was the only quite original thing he contributed to the English stage — in which view he has been supported by the clever German, Alfred Kerr. Among

German critics, Hermann Bahr is noteworthy in refusing to consider Wilde as fundamentally frivolous, maintaining that his paradoxes rest upon a profound insight into humanity. "Wilde says serious and often sad things that convulse us with merriment, not because he is not 'deep,' but precisely because he is deeper than seriousness and sadness, and has recognized their nullity." Wilde always affirmed that he respected life too deeply ever to discuss it seriously. Illuminating — almost prophetic! — is Shaw's characterization of Wilde, evoked by this play on its original production:

"Ireland is, of all countries, the most foreign to England, and to the Irishman (and Mr. Wilde is almost as acutely Irish as the Iron Duke of Wellington) there is nothing in the world quite so exquisitely comic as an Englishman's seriousness. It becomes tragic, perhaps, when the Englishman acts on it; but that occurs too seldom to be taken into account, a fact which intensifies the humour of the situation, the total result being the Englishman utterly unconscious of his real self, Mr. Wilde keenly observant of it, and playing on the self-unconsciousness with irresistible humour, and finally, of course, the Englishman annoyed with himself for being amused at his own expense, and for being unable to convict Mr. Wilde of what seems an obvious misunderstanding of human nature. He is shocked, too, at the danger to the foundations of society when seriousness is publicly laughed at. And to complete the oddity of the situation, Mr. Wilde, touching what he himself reverences, is absolutely the most sentimental dramatist of the day."

V

The comedies of Oscar Wilde stem not from the Ibsen of *Love's Comedy,* but from the Dumas *fils* of *Francillon,* the Sardou of *Divorçons,* and the Sheridan of *The School for Scandal.* Nor are they lacking in that *grain de folie* which was the sign manual of Meilhac and Halévy, of Gilbert and Sullivan. In verve, *esprit* and brilliance Wilde is close akin to his compatriot and fellow townsman, Bernard Shaw; in both we find a defiant individualism, a genius for epigrammatic formulation of the truth, and a vein of piquant and social satire. Inferior to Shaw in most respects, Wilde surpasses him in two features: the sensitiveness of his taste, and the remarkable social ease of his dialogue. As an artist Wilde was generously endowed with the discretion which Henry James aptly terms the "conscience of taste"; and, unlike Shaw, he was far more intent upon amusement than upon instruction. To attempt analysis of Wilde's comedies were as profitless as to inquire into the composition of a *soufflée* or the ingredients of a Roman Candle. It is enough that he translates us into *le monde ou l'on ne s'ennuie pas.* Why carp because Wilde's theatric devices are as superficial as those of Scribe, his sentimentality as mawkish as that of Sydney Grundy, and his moralizing as ghastly a misfit as the *Mea Culpa* of a Dowson or the confessional of a Verlaine!

The phenomenal popularity of Wilde's comedies in an epoch of culture associated with naturalism in art is significant testimony to his rare quality as a purveyor of intellectual pleasure. In the category of the great drama of the day considered as drama — Ibsen, Hauptmann, Sudermann, Hervieu, Strindberg — they have no place, in that in no ultimate sense are they conditioned by the fundamental laws of the drama. They are deficient in final portraiture of character, the play and interplay of really vital emotions, and the indispensable conflict of wills and passions without which drama is mere sound and fury signifying nothing. Bernard Shaw pronounced Wilde the arch-artist: he was so colossally lazy. An æsthetic and luxurious idler, Wilde was incapable of sustained and laborious pre-occupation with his art work. It has been told of Wilde that he filled notebooks with the casual inspirations of his own conversation and made his plays out of these notebooks. It was true, though sounding like the vainest of poses, that even when his life was most free from business cares he never had, as he put it, either the time or the leisure for his art. In the deepest sense, he lacked what Walter Pater called the responsibility of the artist to his material; although this is not to say that he failed to recognize, from the standpoint of *style,* the beauty of the material he employed, and to use that beauty as a factor in producing the æsthetic effect. Like Thomas Griffiths Wainewright, he sought to put into practice the theory that "life itself is an art, and has its modes of style no less than the arts that seek to express it." And the great drama of his life, as he confessed to André Gîde, was that he had given his genius to his life, to his work only his talent.

There is no term which so perfectly expresses the tone of Wilde's comedies as *nonchalance.* The astounding thing is that, in his sincere effort to amuse the public, he best succeeded with the public by holding it up to scorn and ridicule with the lightest satire. "If we are to deliver a philosophy," says Mr. Chesterton, in speaking of contemporary life, "it must be in the manner of the late Mr. Whistler and the *ridentem dicere verum.* If our heart is to be aimed at, it must be with the rapier of Stevenson, which runs through without either pain or puncture." If our brain is to be aroused, he might have added, it must be with the paradox and epigram of Oscar Wilde. Horace Walpole once said that the world is a comedy for the man of thought, a tragedy for the man of feeling. He forgot to say that it is a farce for the man of wit. It was Wilde's creed that ironic imitation of the contrasts, absurdities, and inconsistencies of life, its fads and fancies, its quips and cranks, its follies and foibles, give far more pleasure and amusement than faithful portraiture of the dignity of life, its seriousness and profundity, its tragedy, pity, and terror. His comedies are marked, not by consistency in the characters, continuity of purpose, or unity of action, but only by persistence of the satiric vein and prevalence of the comic mood. Like Flaubert, Wilde gloried in demoralizing the public, and he denied with his every breath Sidney Lanier's dictum that art has no enemy so unrelenting as cleverness. His whole literary career was one long, defiant challenge to Zola's pronunciamento: *l'homme de génie n'a jamais d'esprit.*

While the dialogue of Wilde's comedies, as the brilliant Hermann Bahr has said, contains more verve and *esprit* than all the French, German, and Italian comedies of to-day put together, nevertheless our taste is outraged because Wilde lacks a developed sense for character, and employs a conventional and time-worn technique. Wilde's figures are lacking in vitality and humanity; it is impossible to believe in their existence. Put Wilde's cleverest sayings into the mouths of characters other than those that utter them — and the play remains essentially unaltered. The characters are mere mouthpieces for the diverting ratiocinations of their author, often appearing less as personalities than as personified customs, embodied prejudices and conventions of English social life. By means of these pallid figures, Wilde has at least admirably succeeded in interpreting certain sides of the English national character. The form of his comedies approximates to that of the best French farces, but his humor has the genuine British note. There is no escaping the impression, however, that his characters are automatons and puppets — masks which barely suffice to conceal the lineaments of Wilde. Here we see the *raisonneur,* the commentator, much as we find him in Dumas *fils,* or in Sudermann. It is in this way that Wilde itentifies his characters, not with their prototypes in actual life, but with himself.

As Bernard Shaw may be said to have invented the drama of dialectic, so Oscar Wilde may be said to have invented the drama of conversation.

In 1891 Walter Pater wrote: "There is always something of an excellent talker about the writings of Mr. Oscar Wilde; and in his hands, as happens so rarely with those who practise it, the form of dialogue is justified by its being really alive. His genial laughter-loving sense of life and its enjoyable intercourse goes far to obviate any crudity that may be in the paradox, with which, as with the bright and shining truth which often underlies it, Mr. Wilde startling his 'countrymen' carries on, more perhaps than any other, the brilliant critical work of Matthew Arnold." This characterization is the very truth itself. It is interesting to recall Wilde's confession that Keats, Flaubert, and Walter Pater were the only writers who had influenced him.

Jean-Joseph Renaud and Henri de Régnier have paid eloquent tributes to Wilde as a master of the *causerie*. A great lady once fantastically said of him: "When he is speaking, I see round his head a luminous aureole." The mere exaggeration of the phrase is testimony to Wilde's mastery in utterance of golden words. "He was," says W. B. Yeats, "incomparably the finest talker of his epoch. It was, perhaps, because I admired his conversation so much that I never fully appreciate his books. They remind me of something else, incomparably more spontaneous. Both he and George Moore seemed to me like Tennyson's Launcelot, who, by sheer vehemence of nature, all but saw the Grail — but the full vision was only for the meek Galahad." Wilde's inventive and imaginative faculty was inexhaustible; and for hours at a time he could recite poems in prose, indulge in a riot of paradox and epigram, or descant with miraculous and exquisite eloquence upon painting, literature, art, and — above all — upon life. The beauty of his sentences was the beauty of the arabesque; his eloquence was the eloquence of the rhythmical. In it all lurked the defect of the florid, the gaudy, the over-elaborated. Like the Japanese painters, Hokusai and Hokkei, Wilde was an artist in the little; and his art found room for expansion only in the microcosm. He was a slave to the Scheherazade of his fancy, and unsparingly lavish in the largess of his wit. He realized that he was a past-master in the gentle art of making conversation, and he nonchalantly ignored Goethe's precept: "Bilde, Kunstler, rede nicht!" The result is, that he does not construct, he only sets off a mine. His art is the expression of his enjoyment of verbal pyrotechnics. The height of his pleasure was to shock the average intelligence. The result in his comedies, while vastly diverting, is deplorable from the standpoint of dramatic art. For the conversations are disjointed, and, in the dramatic sense, incoherent, in that they live only for the moment, and not at all for the sake of elucidation and propulsion of the dramatic process. The comparison with Shaw in this particular immediately suggests itself; but the fundamental distinction consists in the fact that whereas in Shaw's comedies the conversation, witty and epigrammatic to a degree, is strictly germane to the action, with Wilde the conversation, with all its sparkling brilliancy, is in fact subsidiary and beside the mark. As Hagemann has said, in Wilde's comedies the accent and stress is thrown wholly upon the epigrammatic content of the dialogue.

At bottom and in essence, Wilde is a master in the art of selection. He is eminently successful in giving the most diverting character to our moments as they pass. His art is the apotheosis of the moment. "What may not be said," he once asked, "for the moment and the moment's monument"? Art itself, he averred, is "really a form of exaggeration, and selection, which is the very spirit of art, is nothing more than an intensified ode of over-emphasis." Wilde was a painter, a Neo-Impressionist. From the palette of his observation, which bore all the radiant shades and colors of his temperament, he selected and laid upon the canvas many brilliant yet distinct points of color. Seen in the proper light and from the just distance, the canvas takes on the appearance of a complete picture — quaint, unique, marvellous. It is only by taking precisely Wilde's point of view that the spectator is enabled to synthesize the isolated brilliant points into a harmonious whole. Oscar Wilde is a Pointilliste.

There is no room for doubt that Oscar Wilde was, as Nordau classed him, a pervert and a degenerate. And yet his case warrants distrust of the dictum that an artist's work and life are fundamentally indissociable. Wilde was a man, not only of multiple personality, but of manifest and disparate achievement. The style is not always the man; and the history of art and literature reveals not a few geniuses whose private life could not justly be cited in condemnation of their pictures, their poetry, or their prose. It is indubitable that Wilde, with his frequently avowed doctrine of irresponsible individualism and Pagan insistence upon the untrammelled expansion of the Ego, gave suicidal counsel to the younger generation. He based his apostolate upon the paradox; and as he himself asserts, the paradox is always dangerous. In his search for the elusive, the evanescent, the imaginative, he found certain exquisite truths; but they were only very partial and obscure truths, embedded in a mass of charmingly phrased, yet damnably perverse, falsehood. Much of his verse — flagrant output of what Robert Buchanan maliciously crystallized in the damning phrase, "The Fleshly School of Poetry"— is a faithful reflex of his personality and feeling, with its morbid and sensuous daydreams, its vain regrets for "barren gain and bitter loss," its unhealthy and myopic vision, its obsession with the wanton and the *macabre*. And yet, in spite not only of these things but also of the persistent reminder of alien influences, certain of his poems are lit with the divine spark and fitfully flame out with startling and disturbing lustre.

As an artist in words, as prose stylist, Wilde was possessed of real gifts. To read his confession is to realize that art was the passion of his life: "To give form to one's dreams, to give shape to one's fancy, to change one's ideas into images, to express one's self through a material that one makes lovely by mere treatment, to realize in this material the immaterial ideal of beauty — this is the pleasure of the artist. It is the most sensuous and most intellectual pleasure in the whole world." The social ease of his paradoxes, the opulence of his imaginative style, the union of simplicity and beauty of phraseology with vague and sometimes almost meaningless gradations and shades of thought, his insight into the real meaning of art, his understanding of the "thing as in itself it really is," and his rapt glimpses of art's holy of holies — all these things, at times and in intervals, were his. His faculty of imitation was caricature refined and sublimated to an infinite degree; and, with less real comprehension of the *arcana* of art, Wilde might have been the author of a transcendent *Borrowed Plumes*. And if he himself did not actually and literally masquerade in the literary garments of other men, certainly he possessed that rare faculty, now almost a lost art, of creeping into another's personality, temporarily shedding the husk of self, and looking out upon the world with new and alien eyes. There lies, it would seem, the secret of his genius — the faculty of creative and imaginative interpretation in its ultimate refinement. He was ever the critic as artist, never the creator in the fine frenzy of creation. It has been said of him that he knew everything; but in the last analysis his supreme fault, both as man and artist, was his arrogance and his overweening sense of superiority. Breaks down in Wilde's case — as does many another truism — the maxim: *Tout comprendre c'est tout pardonner.*

"To be free," wrote a celebrity, "one must not conform." Wilde secured a certain sort of freedom in the drama through his refusal to conform to the laws of dramatic art. He claimed the privileges without shouldering the responsibilities of the dramatist. He imported the methods of the *causerie* into the domain of the drama, and turned the theatre into a house of mirth. Whether or no his destination was the palace of truth, certain it is that he always stopped at the half-way house. Art was the dominant note of his literary life; but it was the art of conversation, not the art of drama. His comedies, as dramas, were cheap sacrifices to the god of success. He made many delightful, many pertinent and impertinent observations upon English life, and upon life in general; but they had no special relation to the dramatic theme he happened for the moment to have in mind. His plays neither enlarge the mental horizon nor dilate the heart. Wilde was too self-centred an egoist ever to come into any real or vital relation with life. It was his primal distinction as artist to be consumed with a passionate love of art. It was his primal deficiency as artist to have no genuine sympathy with humanity. And although he imaged life with clearness, grace, and distinction, certain it is that he never saw life steadily, nor ever saw it whole.

Wilde called one of his plays *The Importance*

of Being Earnest. In his inverted way, he aimed at teaching the world the importance of being frivolous. Only from this standpoint is it possible to appreciate, in any real sense, Wilde, the comic dramatist. Wilde is the arch enemy of boredom and ennui; we can always enjoy him as a purveyor of amusement and a killer of time. We are warned by his own confession against taking Wilde, as dramatist, too seriously. Nor should we take Wilde's own deliverances too seriously. "The plays are not great," he once confessed to André Gîde. "I think nothing of them — but if you only knew how amusing they are!" And the author of *The Decay of Lying* added: "Most of them are the results of bets!"

BERNARD SHAW

"It was easy for Ruskin to lay down the rule of dying rather than doing unjustly; but death is a plain thing: justice a very obscure thing. How is an ordinary man to draw the line between right and wrong otherwise than by accepting public opinion on the subject; and what more conclusive expression of sincere public opinion can there be than market demand? Even when we repudiate that and fall back on our private judgment, the matter gathers doubt instead of clearness. The popular notion of morality and piety is to simply beg all the most important questions in life for other people; but when those questions come home to ourselves, we suddenly discover that the devil's advocate has a stronger case than we thought: we remember that the way of righteousness or death was the way of the Inquisition; that hell is paved, not with bad intentions, but with good ones . . ."

Note on Modern Prizefighting, appended to *Cashel Byron's Profession* (authorized edition), H. S. Stone & Co., Chicago, 1901.

BERNARD SHAW

That modern Samuel Johnson, the late Benjamin Jowett, once spoke of Benjamin Disraeli as " a combination of the Arch-Priest of Humbug and a great man." Not otherwise has Bernard Shaw been freely characterized in this day and generation. The world-famed American showman, P. T. Barnum, built up a fortune upon the sweet and simple faith that the American people love to be " humbugged." In the minds of many, Bernard Shaw has become a world-author through the possession of a similar faith: that not America alone, but the whole world loves to be humbugged. " The public imagination demands a best man everywhere," Shaw once said; " and if Nature does not supply him the public invents him. The art of humbug is the art of getting invented in this way." According to the pontiffs of literature, a large part of Shaw's stock in trade consists in making himself " a motley to the view." Interrogated once as to the reason for his eccentric conduct, Charles Baudelaire complacently replied, *" Pour étonner les sôts."* Were Bernard Shaw challenged for the reasons for his eccentricity, he would doubtless reply, " To astonish the wise."

In a very literal sense does he subscribe to the Shaksperean view: "All the world's a stage, and men and women only players." In this day of persistent self-puffery, Bernard Shaw has deliberately chosen to stand in the limelight, to occupy the focus of the stage of the world. "In England as elsewhere the spontaneous recognition of really original work begins with a mere handful of people," he once said, "and propagates itself so slowly that it has become a commonplace to say that genius, demanding bread, is given a stone after its possessor's death. The remedy for this is sedulous advertisement. Accordingly, I have advertised myself so well that I find myself, while still in middle life, almost as legendary a person as the Flying Dutchman."

I

Even at the beginning of the twentieth century, much virtue still inheres in the statement that life has its realities behind its shows. Whoever would write the natural history of a literary phenomenon like Bernard Shaw must first disabuse his mind of the popular fantastic notions in regard to his life and personality. The legend of Saint Bernard fades into thin air before the plain recital of the life of Mr. Shaw. The year 1856, which witnessed the demise of the "first man of his century," Heinrich Heine, likewise witnessed the birth of the "laughing Ibsen," Bernard Shaw, in Dublin, Ireland, on

July 26th. Cursed with an impecunious father, he was early apprenticed to a land agent in Dublin to be taught the meaning of thrift. Blessed with a mother of rare talent for music, he unconsciously acquired a knowledge and appreciation of music which was to play no insignificant rôle in his later life. Revolted by the social pretensions and prejudices of his family, who "revolved impecuniously in a sort of vague second-cousinship round a baronetcy," he soon became animated with a Carlylean contempt for that type of snobbery denominated "respectability in its thousand gigs." He boasts of the fact that as a schoolboy he was incorrigibly idle and worthless, since the training of four schools he successively attended did him a great deal of harm and no good whatever. But it must not be supposed that his youthful years were barren in educative influence. Parrot-like, he would whistle the oratorios and operatic scores he heard repeatedly practised at home by the musical society of which his mother was a leading figure — much as the street-gamin of to-day whistles the latest piece of ragtime music. Before he was fifteen, according to his own confession, he knew at least one important work by Handel, Mozart, Beethoven, Mendelssohn, Rossini, Bellini, Donizetti, Verdi and Gounod, from cover to cover. For hours at a time the lad of fifteen used to frequent the deserted halls of the National Gallery of Ireland; with his "spare change" he bought the volumes of the Bohn translations of Vasari, and learned to recognize the works of a considerable number of Italian and Flemish painters.

It was the mature conviction of his later years that all the people he knew as a boy in Ireland were the worse for what they called their religion. On hearing the American evangelists, Moody and Sankey, the young sixteen-year-old Shaw was driven to protest in *Public Opinion* — his first appearance in print — that if *this* were Religion, then he must be an Atheist. Indeed, as he said a few years ago, "If religion is that which binds men to one another, and irreligion that which sunders, then must I testify that I found the religion of my country in its musical genius and its irreligion in its churches and drawing-rooms."

Unlike his colleagues in criticism of later years, William Archer and Arthur Bingham Walkley, graduates of Edinburgh and Oxford respectively, Bernard Shaw despised, half ignorantly, half penetratingly, the thought of a university education, for it seemed to him to turn out men who all thought alike and were snobs.

He went into the land office, where he learned how to collect rents and to write a good hand. But although he retained his place solely for the sake of financial independence, his heart and brain were a thousand miles away. Finally his work grew unbearably irksome to him, and in the year 1876 he deliberately walked out of the land office forever. Shortly afterwards, he joined his mother in London — the future theatre for the display of his unequal, if brilliant and versatile genius.

During the following nine years, from 1876 to 1885, Shaw turned his hand with only indifferent success to many undertakings. It was not simply a crime, it was a blunder to have been an Irishman — and consequently an alien to everything genuinely English. Shaw's unembarrassed frankness passed for outrageous prevarication, his cleverest jest for the most solemn earnest. Like Oscar Wilde, he learned the crippling disadvantage of being an Irishman of superior mentality, ever trifling in a world of ideas. Whatever he did met with failure; his lightest plays of fancy were as unwelcome to the English public as were his heaviest efforts at blank verse, at criticism of music, at journalistic hack work. Through his acquaintance with Chichester Bell, of the family of that name, so celebrated for scientific invention and notable research, he became interested in physics and acquainted with the works of Tyndall and Helmholtz. He even worked for a time with a company formed in London to exploit an invention of the great American inventor, Thomas A. Edison. After various attempts, of which this was the last, to assist his parents by endeavoring to earn an honest living for himself, he finally gave up trying, he confesses, to commit this sin against his nature. It is true that his life was not without its diversions; for his talent as a congenial accompanist on the piano assured his *entrée* into a certain desirable circle of musical society in London; and the great library at Bloomsbury and the priceless picture galleries at Trafalgar Square and Hampton Court, certainly, were not lacking in a hospitality of which he gladly availed himself.

During the five years from 1879 to 1884 inclusive, he devoted his energies ruthlessly to the production of five novels, one of them never published, which were to lead, if not to the immediate establishment of literary position, certainly to the formation of valuable friendships and acquaintances of lifelong standing. Again and again he sent forth his manuscripts; but they were invariably returned by the publishers. His iconoclasm, his freedom of thought and expression, his Ibsenic frankness in dealing with the gray, garish aspects of contemporary life, were in inverse ratio to the requirements of the conservative, unprogressive London publishers. Unwilling to sacrifice his art, resolved "to paint man man, whatever the issue," and determined not to disavow the principles at which he had arrived, he accepted the alternative — the temporary failure of his novels.

To the Socialist revival of the 'eighties, the world owes the credit for the discovery of Bernard Shaw. In 1879, Shaw first met the late James Lecky, and acquired the grounding in Temperament, the fondness for Phonetics, and the early incentive to public speaking which have borne such abundant fruit in his later career. Through Lecky's influence, Shaw joined, and became a constant debater in, the Zeletical Society, a debating club modelled on the once famed Dialectical Society. Here Shaw first met Sidney Webb, that able Socialist economist, and soon became his close friend and co-worker. Shaw subsequently joined the Dialectical Society and remained faithful to it for a number of years. From this time on, he evinced the greatest interest in public speaking, and persistently haunted public meetings of all sorts. One night, in 1883, he wandered into the Memorial Hall in Farrington Street; by chance the speaker was the great Single-Taxer, Henry George. For the first time did the importance of the economic basis dawn upon Shaw's mind. He left the meeting a changed man; and soon was devouring George's *Progress and Poverty* and Marx's *Das Kapital* with all the ardor of youth and burning social enthusiasm. While Shaw refused to subscribe to all the economic theories of Marx, and later victoriously refuted him on the question of the Theory of Value, he realized the overwhelming validity of the "bible of the working classes" as a jeremiad against the *bourgeoisie*. During these days, he spoke early and often, at the street corner, on the curbstone, from the tail of a cart. He once said that he first caught the ear of the British public on a cart in Hyde Park, to the blaring of brass bands!

In practical conjunction with Sidney Webb, Graham Wallas and Sidney Olivier, although they actually joined at different times, Shaw became a member of the Fabian Society after it had been in existence only a short time. His connection with that society is a matter of history, and finds tangible evidence to-day, not only in books and pamphlets, but also in the actual Socialist and Labor representation in the London County Council and British parliament. Suffice it to say that, from the very first, his influence made itself most strongly felt upon the society, and for many years he has been the guiding spirit in its councils. Through the establishment of certain Socialist journals during the 'eighties, Shaw's novels began to find their way into print. *An Unsocial Socialist* and *Cashel Byron's Profession* appeared in *To-day,* printed by Henry Hyde Champion, later by Belfort Bax and James Leigh Joynes, among others; *The Irrational Knot* and *Love Among the Artists* appeared in *Our Corner,* published by the brilliant orator and Socialist agitator, Mrs. Annie Besant. They made no impression upon the British public, but greatly pleased such men as William Archer, William Morris, Robert Louis Stevenson, and William E. Henley, who gave either public or personal expressions of their appreciation. From time to time in the last fifteen years they have been published in both England and America, with varying, but in general, with unusual success in this day of infinitesimally short-lived successes.

From 1883 on, Shaw was daily coming in contact with the brilliant spirits of the younger generation in Socialism, and with the leaders in thought and opinion on the side of vegetarianism, humanitarianism and land nationalization. There were James Leigh Joynes, who had been arrested in Ireland with Henry George; Sidney Olivier, afterwards a distinguished author and now Governor of Jamaica; Henry Hyde Champion, the well-known Socialist; Henry Salt, an Eton master, married to Joynes' sister; and Edward Carpenter, the greatest living disciple of Walt Whitman. After joining the Fabian Society, Shaw's constant associates were Hubert Bland, Graham Wallas, Sidney Olivier, and Sidney Webb; and through his Socialist activities he became a friend of William Morris, who was never a Fabian, but who maintained an attitude of the broadest tolerance towards all the Socialist sects. In their early days the Fabians were as insurrectionary in principle as the other Socialist bodies in London; not until the election in 1885 did the line of cleavage between the Fabian Society and the Social Democratic Federation clearly appear. At this time, the Fabian Society openly denounced the conduct of the

Council of the Social-Democratic Federation in accepting money from the Tory party in payment of the election expenses of Socialist candidates as calculated to disgrace the Socialist movement in England. In the following two years, the Fabian Society took little or no part in the organization of insurrectionary projects in London; and finally, after many debates with that section of the Socialist League known as Anti-Communist, headed by Joseph Lane and William Morris, definitely discountenanced Kropotkinism among its members. Indeed, they finally demolished Anarchism in the abstract, as Shaw said, " by grinding it between human nature and the theory of economic rent."

When Shaw first joined the Zeletical Society, he was the poorest of debaters; but he possessed the nerve to make a fool of himself. He practised platform oratory incessantly, haunted hole-and-corner debates of all sorts, and seized every opportunity to make himself proficient in the art of public exhibition of his views. He joined the Hampstead Historic Club, and there learned the theories of Marx through the necessity of elucidating them for his colleagues. He was one of a private circle of economists, which afterwards developed into the British Economic Association; at these meetings the social question was ignored, and the discussions were conducted solely on an economic basis. In this way Shaw became thoroughly grounded in economic theory; and in this way also, he learned supremely well the art of public speaking. As a speaker, Shaw far excelled William Morris; lacking the genius for oratory of a Charles Bradlaugh or an Annie Besant, he yet combined the imperturbability of a Sidney Webb with the wit of an Oscar Wilde. Ever on the alert, he is keen, incisive, and facile as a public speaker; he has every faculty about him when he mounts the platform. He combines the devastating wit of the Irishman with the penetrating logic of the Frenchman. He gave hundreds of lectures and addresses, and frequently debated in public in London and the provinces, for many years; and always at his own expense — for the Cause. His speech is always a challenge. "Call me disagreeable, only call me something," he vigorously clamors; "for then I have roused you from your stupid torpor and made you think a new thought!"

In principle and in practice, Shaw is a strictly constitutional Socialist; he has no faith in revolutionary measures, save as the very last resort against direst tyranny. Inspired by Philip Wicksteed's attack on Marx's Theory of Value, Shaw devoted a great deal of time to the study of the economic theories of the late Stanley Jevons; and with the aid of the Jevonian machinery exposed the fallacies in the Marxian Theory of Value.

Furthermore, he denied the existence of what is

called the war of classes; he did everything possible to reduce Socialism to an intellectual rather than to an emotional basis, to envisage it as a product of economic factors rather than of insurrectionism. His position is admirably summed up in the following passage:

"The Fabian declares quite simply that there is no revolution, that there exists no war of classes, that the salaried workers are far more imbued with conventions and prejudices and more *bourgeois* than the middle class itself; that there is not a single legal power democratically constituted, without excepting the House of Commons, which would not be much more progressive were it not restrained by the fear of the popular vote; that Karl Marx is no more infallible than Aristotle or Bacon, Ricardo or Buckle, and that, like them, he has committed errors now obvious to the casual student of economics; that a declared Socialist is, morally, neither better nor worse than a liberal or a conservative, nor a workman than a capitalist; that the workman can change the actual governmental system if he so desires, while the capitalist cannot do so, because the workman would not permit him; that it is an absurd contradiction in terms to declare that the working classes are starved, impoverished and kept in ignorance by a system which loads the capitalist with food, education, and refinements of all sorts, and at the same time to pretend that the capitalist is a scoundrel, harsh and sordid in spirit, while the workman is a high-minded, enlightened and magnanimous philanthropist; that Socialism will eventuate in the gradual establishment of public rule and a public administration set into effective action by parliaments, assemblies and common councils; and that none of these rules will lead to revolution nor occupy more place in the political programme of the time than a law for the regulation of manufactures or the ballot would do now: in a word, that the part of the Socialist will be a definitely fixed political labor, to struggle not against the malevolent machinations of the capitalist, but against the stupidity, narrowness, in a word, the idiocy (in giving to the word its precise and original sense) of the class which actually suffers most from the existing system." [1]

Bernard Shaw resumed his literary labors rather late in the 'eighties, and has been diligent as a man of letters ever since. Indeed, his is an unusually checkered career, since he has, at one time or another, dipped into almost every phase of authorship. For a time, through the kind offices of Mr. William Archer, Shaw was enabled to write criticisms of books and pictures in *The World;* and at times also he wrote for the *Pall Mall Gazette* and *Truth.* In 1888, Shaw joined the editorial staff of *The Star* on the second day of its existence; but his Socialist

[1] *Les Illusions du Socialisme,* by Bernard Shaw; *L'Humanité Nouvelle,* August, 1900.

utterances so alarmed the editor, the brilliant wit, T. P. O'Connor, that Shaw was given a column to fill with comments on current music — a subject harmless from the political point of view at least. Here Shaw gave free vent to his eccentricity, and the paper fairly blazed with his jests and *hardiesses*, his follies and foibles, his quips and cranks. Dissembling his wide knowledge of music, especially modern music, by means of an air of irresponsible levity and outrageous flippancy, he gave no ground for suspicion of the existence in these delightful sallies of a solid substratum of genuine criticism. As "Corno di Bassetto," he vied with his colleague, A. B. Walkley, the dramatic critic for *The Star*, in furnishing rare entertainment for the readers of that first of London half-penny papers.

When Louis Engel resigned his position as musical critic on the staff of *The World*, the post fittingly fell to Bernard Shaw, who for long had slowly been saturating himself in the best music from Mozart to Wagner, from London to Bayreuth. Until now, he had made no stir in the world of letters — few people knew who "C. di B." really was. But as a successor of Louis Engel, he entered into his new duties with zeal and zest, and created a new standard for *The World* by his brilliant and witty critiques. "Every man has an inalienable right to make a fool of himself," Victor Hugo once wrote; "but he should not abuse that right." Bernard Shaw stopped just short of abuse of his inalienable right. Like a street fakir, he announced the value of his wares with sublime audacity. He adopted the haughty tone of superiority of a Wilde or a Whistler, although he did it always not only in the wittiest but also in the most good-natured way imaginable. The oculist who once examined his eyes seems to have been the unwitting cause of first diverting the rewards of literature in his direction. The ophthalmic specialist declared that Shaw's vision was "normal," at the same time explaining that the vision of nine-tenths of the people in the world is abnormal. Shaw at once leaped to the conclusion that his intellectual as well as his physical vision was normal, while that of the "damned compact, liberal majority" was aberrant, myopic, astygmatic. Too conscientious to put on a pair of abnormal spectacles and aberr his vision to suit the taste of the astygmatic nine-tenths of the reading public, too poor to attempt transcripts of life in order to win the support of the one-tenth which, because of normal vision, was therefore as impecunious as himself, he turned critic and appeared before the British public as Punch. He had only to open his eyes and describe things exactly as they appeared to him, to become known as the most humorously extravagant paradoxer in London. He succeeded in demonstrating once again the old, old proposition that truth is stranger than fiction.

After a while the exuberant "G. B. S.," as he signed himself in *The World,* set out in search of new fields to conquer. When Mr. Frank Harris — who possessed the virtues, as well as some of the faults, of Mr. Edmund Yates — revived *The Saturday Review,* Shaw was chosen as dramatic critic. He at once characteristically broke the sacred tradition of anonymity, till then — 1895 — inviolate in its columns. In earlier years, Shaw had often spoken to deaf ears; for his was the strange language of a Robertson, a Gilbert, a Wilde. In all that he wrote there was that contradictoriness between letter and spirit, so characteristic of the Celtic genius. Everything struck his mind at such an acute angle as to give forth prismatic refractions of dazzling and many-hued brilliancy. His first great period began as critic on *The World,* when he zealously lauded Wagner, daringly defied the academic school of British music, and gaily set himself up as the infallible critic of the musical world. And now as dramatic critic on *The Saturday Review,* he achieved in a few years the reputation of the most brilliant journalistic writer in England.

Like Taine, he realized the important truth that those things we agree to call abnormal, are in reality normal, and appear quite naturally in the ordinary course of events. Accordingly, he devised a well-known formula for readable journalism:

"Spare no labor to find out the right thing to say; and then say it with the most exasperating levity, as if it were the first thing that would come into any one's head." He expressed the belief that good journalism is much rarer and more important than good literature; and by his own rare and unique work he gave a practical proof of the truth of his conviction. He led a magnificent crusade in behalf of Ibsen and in defiance of Shakspere. If, on the one hand, he praised Ibsen to the skies for the intellectual content of his plays, on the other hand he upbraided Shakspere for his lamentable poverty in the matter of philosophy. If he saw in Ibsen a disheartened optimist disagreeably intent upon improving the world, he saw in Shakspere a vulgar pessimist, with *vanitas vanitaum* eternally upon his lips. If Ibsen not infrequently jarred his sensibilities with the ultra-realism of his clinical demonstrations, Shakspere gave him unfeigned pleasure by the music of his language — his "word-music" as it has been called — his delightful fancy, his large perception of the comic, and his incomparable art as a story-teller. When Shaw finished his career as a dramatic critic he had the gratification of the knowledge that while Ibsen was not popular on the English stage, he was nevertheless recognized by the highest authorities as the greatest of living dramatists. And he boasted on severing his connection with *The*

Saturday Review, that whereas, when he began his work as a dramatic critic, Shakspere was a divinity and a bore, now he was at least a fellow-creature!

At last, in 1898, he severed his connection with *The Saturday Review* and became a dramatist by profession. He had, by dogmatic assertions, iteration and reiteration of his merits as wit, raconteur and paradoxer, so he declares, actually succeeded in establishing his literary prestige for all time. He might dodder and dote, platitudinize and pot-boil; but, once convinced, the dull but honest British intelligence could not be shaken. He had become the jester at the court of King Demos — the confessor of the sovereign public. And that public rewarded him at last with eager appreciation of all his sallies and *bon mots*.

II

As a comic dramatist, Shaw has always won the joyous appreciation of his auditors, never the intellectual perception of the critic. No general grasp of his originality and essentially novel dramatic technique, as Ibsen, as Maeterlinck, are understood, has yet been achieved by the English-speaking public. This, it cannot too decisively be asserted, is due, not to the failure of the public to appreciate his dramas, but to the slovenliness of dramatic criticism in perceiving the genuine technical novelty of his dramatic form. Even this decisive statement must be modified by the admission that Shaw, with his passion for comical mystification, has taken a certain sort of impish delight in averring that he is really a conservative in technique, following in the beaten path of classic dramatic tradition. "I find that the surest way to startle the world with daring innovations and originalities," he has said more than once, "is to do exactly what playwrights have been doing for thousands of years; to revive the ancient attraction of long rhetorical speeches; to stick closely to the methods of Molière; and to lift characters bodily out of the pages of Charles Dickens."

There are two fundamental ideas, consistently held and strenuously maintained by Shaw, which, rightly understood, effectually shatter the superficial theory that he is an artistic mountebank, exploiting the theatre as an instrumentality for shallow ends. Back of all surface manifestations lies the supreme conviction of Shaw that the theatre of to-day, properly utilized, is an instrumentality for the molding of character and the shaping of conduct no whit inferior to the Church and the School. Indeed, the modern Church seems to be losing its hold upon the great masses of the people through its divorce from the central realities of practical living, the insincerity of ministers in veiling from the congregation the theological doubts aroused by the "higher criticism" which they dare not express, the circular monotony of the Scriptural exegesis which stands forever in the way of forthright discussion of the fortifying realitics and possibilities of sheer living. The university of to-day, in many cases, far from being a pioneer in the advancement of the frontier of art, staggering, strange, forward-looking, remains the citadel of conservatism, the stronghold of literary " stand-pattism," turning its eyes ceaselessly backward upon the acknowledged literary masterpieces — these and these only — and timidly shrinking from the bold task of assaying the literary gold of the future.

In the spirit of the ancient Greeks, Shaw sees in the theatre of to-day an infinitely powerful instrumentality for popular education and social instruction. Indeed, the theatre may even go further, and by popularizing great sociological, philosophical and religious ideas, exercise an almost incalculable effect upon the social morals of a whole people. It is Shaw's basic conviction that the theatre of the future is in the hands of the sociological dramatist who may, if he but will, make it as important a social institution as was the Church in the Middle Ages. In so eminently sane a social worker as Jane Addams he has won support for his belief that the theatre of to-day exercises a greater influence in forming accepted codes of morals than does the Church, because, as Miss Addams puts it, the Church is so " reluctant to admit conduct to be the supreme and efficient test of religious validity." The theatre is a school of manners, of morals, both individual and social, exercising an influence that is none the less powerful in that it is indirect. Indeed, the subtle force of the comedies of Shaw is heightened through the enjoyment which they give. The bitter pill of the moralist is coated with the sugar of the artist. Shaw does actually continue the classic tradition of Molière who said that a comedy is nothing less than an ingenious poem which, in agreeable lessons, portrays human weaknesses. There is the deeper note in Shaw. He surpasses Molière as a moralist, because Molière was a censor of individual vices whilst Shaw is a censor of the sociological evils arising from the structural defects of modern society and modern civilization.

"The apostolic succession from Eschylus to myself," Shaw has irreverently said, "is as serious and as continuously inspired as that younger institution, the apostolic succession of the Christian Church. Unfortunately this Christian Church, founded gaily with a pun, has been so largely corrupted by rank satanism that it has become the Church where you must not laugh; and so it is giving away to that older and greater Church to which I belong: the Church where the oftener you laugh the better, because by laughter only can you destroy evil without malice, and affirm good-fellowship without mawkishness." The remarkable popular attention which Shaw won as a dramatic critic was due in great measure not only to his trenchant satire but also to the sincerity of his faith in the mission of the theatre. He not only took the theatre seriously; he actually preached about it as a " factory of thought, a prompter of conscience, an elucidator of social conduct, an armoury against despair and dullness, and a temple of the Ascent of Man."

The Shaw who speaks of the " apostolic succession from Eschylus to myself " is giving expression to the second fundamental conviction of his nature. With the intimate knowledge of his character derived during the years devoted to the infinitely complex task of writing his biography, I am convinced Shaw firmly believes in " inspiration "— in artistic inspiration no less than in spiritual inspiration. This view, which I have often heard him express privately, he has recently expounded at length, in answer to the request of the Modern Historic Record Association to " define the principles that govern the dramatist in his selection of themes and methods of treatment." So illuminating is that reply, so characteristic at once of the man, the dramatist, and the economist, that I quote it here in full:

" I am not governed by principles; I am inspired; how or why I cannot explain because I do not know. But inspiration it must be; for it comes to me without any reference to my own ends or interests.

" I find myself possessed of a theme in the following manner. I am pushed by a natural need to set to work to write down conversations that come into my head unaccountably. At first I hardly know the speakers, and cannot find names for them. Then they become more and more familiar; and I learn their names. Finally I come to know them very well, and discover what it is they are driving at and why they have said and done the things I have been moved to set down.

"This is not being 'guided by principles'; it is hallucination; and sane hallucination is what we call play or drama. . . . I do not select my methods: they are imposed on me by a hundred considerations: by the physical conditions of theatric representation, by the laws devised by the municipality to guard against fires and other accidents to which theatres are liable, by the economic conditions of theatrical commerce, by the nature and limits of the art of acting, by the capacity of the spectators for understanding what they see and hear, and by the accidental circumstances of the particular production in hand.

"I have to think of my pocket, of the manager's pocket, of the actors' pockets, of the spectators' pockets, of how long people can be kept sitting in a theatre without relief or refreshments, of the range of the performer's voice and of the hearing and vision of the boy at the back of the gallery, whose right to be put in full possession of the play is as sacred as that of the millionaire in the stalls or boxes.

" I have to consider theatre rents, the rate of interest needed to tempt capitalists to face the risks of financing theatres, the extent to which the magic of art can break through commercial prudence, the limits set by honor and humanity to the tasks I may set to my fellow-artist the actor: in short, all the factors that must be allowed for before the representation of a play on the stage becomes practicable or justifiable; factors which some never comprehend, and which others integrate almost as unconsciously as they breathe or digest their food.

" It is these factors that dictate the playwright's methods, leaving him so little room for selection that there is not a pennyworth o' difference between the methods of Sophocles or Shakspere and those of the maker of the most ephemeral farce.

" And withal, when the play is made, the writer must feed himself and his family by it. Indeed, there are men and woman who are forced by this necessity to simulate inspiration, repeating its gestures and copying its tricks so as to produce artificial plays: constructed things with no true life in them, yet sometimes more amusing than real plays, just as a clockwork mouse is more amusing than a real mouse, though it will kill the cat who swallows it in good faith . . ."

III

A picture of Bernard Shaw, as he was when I first met him eighteen years ago, comes before me now. A tall, thin, alert-looking person; a face of excessive pallor contrasting sharply with hair and whiskers of a sandy red; very active in his movements, with an air of nonchalant extemporaneousness. The pointed beard, the upward curling mustaches, and the peaked eyebrows—all gave him the appearance of a cadaverous, blond, Celtic Mephistopheles. He was, in truth, the living impersonation of a Max Beerbohm cartoon. When I saw him last, in 1924, the change was striking and impressive. His beard and cheeks have exchanged colors; for now his hair and beard are silver white, and his cheeks full and ruddy as a winter apple. Geniality and benignity have come with the years. To-day Shaw appears in the guise, not of the jester, but the philosopher, not of the mountebank, but the prophet. The remarkable portrait of him by Augustus John is certainly the image of a great man, with just enough of breezy nonchalance and flaunting audacity to be in character.

The center of Shaw's multifarious activities as an important public character is his home at 10 Adelphi Terrace, just off the Strand in London. From the windows of Shaw's living room—for all are at one side—may be observed, on the left, St. Paul's, on the right (but now hidden by tall buildings recently erected) Westminster and the Houses of Parliament, below, the lazy Thames sparsely speckled with floating craft, and the prim coat of verdure of the Embankment (where Marchbanks was found) in striking contrast with the Needle of Cleopatra, eastern in its suggestiveness and mystery. In the middle may be picked up the glittering lines of the Crystal Palace, and on clear days one catches a glimpse of the faraway hills of Kent and Surrey. In the same building, supported by the famous Adelphi Arches dating from the time of Shakspere, are found beautiful frescoes by Angelica Kaufmann in the quarters of the New Reform Club.

As you enter this room you are almost startled—for the man in the flesh is by your side—by Shaw's double rising above the tall screen at the far corner of the room. It is Rodin's bust of Shaw; and the portion above the screen is startling in its life-like naturalness. In commenting on Rodin's method of work, Shaw once observed in my hearing: "You see Rodin and I are particularly congenial. Because, although I cannot be said to speak French and Rodin doesn't speak English at all, we soon found out that we had the same religion and after that things went beautifully. You should have seen Rodin at work. One moment the bust looked like the most modern work of art—Rodin in the Balzac mood; and the next he would revert, and a bit of twelfth century work was before you. Once my wife gave a startled cry when Rodin decapitated me—I mean the bust—with a sudden deft stroke of the scalpel. He dabbed on a piece of clay and stuck me back on again. He hadn't made my lofty brow quite lofty enough. You have no idea what a queer feeling it gives you to have the top of your head suddenly taken off before you can say 'Jack Roberson.' "

Mrs. Shaw's travels in foreign lands, particularly in India, have left their impress upon the living room, which is ornamented with numerous bizarre and antique curios: Indian idols, tiny elephants in silver, wise-looking owls, Chinese mandarins in exquisite china facing and fatuously nodding at each other, enormous pots of polished bronze, curiously shaped shields of brass, and heavy urns standing at each side of the white enameled mantelpiece. On the walls are a few carefully chosen pictures—such as a water color by Rodin, dedicated to Mrs. Shaw and inscribed with his signature, a soft brown monotone of Shaw by Alvin Langdon Coburn, a caricature by Max Beerbohm, a tiny print of Rodin himself.

"The chambers in Adelphi Terrace," Mr. Shaw once remarked, "constitute the real center of my domesticity, because my wife lives here. I live nowhere. In fact, any place that will hold a bed and a writing table is as characteristic of me as any other; and as I never can keep or collect anything I have no more home instinct than a milk can at a railway station. I am always content wherever I happen to be—not like most people who wherever they are want to be somwhere else, and are always convinced that their happiness lies around the corner."

Deep cut in the white enamel of the headboard of the mantelpiece, in large Gothic letters, is the inscription from the walls of Holyrood Palace in Edinburgh: "Thay say? Quhat say thay? Lat thame say." To the observation that this was the most characteristic note in the room, Shaw brusquely responded: "That inscription was there when I rented these quarters." A critic who thought of Shaw as one ever avid for publicity suggested that the inscription should be amended to read: "They don't say? They must say. I'll make them say."

The late William T. Stead, editor of the English *Review of Reviews*, once told me this anecdote. He had conceived the idea of gathering about him some of the best brains of Europe and taking them on a tour around the world in the interest of universal peace. He invited Shaw to make one of the party to visit the principal crowned heads of Europe. Any one but Shaw would doubtless have been greatly flattered by the invitation. His reply to Stead's invitation ran about as follows:

> "My dear Stead, I have far more work to do than any of those kings and queens of yours. But if you care to bring a collection of rulers around to my quarters in Adelphi Terrace some morning, I will try to find time to receive them."

"I have lived instead of dreaming," Mr. Shaw once said to me. "I have not written so many works of imaginative art. I have lived through so much experience. The life of literary clubland repelled me, the very thought of it bored me insufferably, and it was always the greatest relief to me to escape out into real life and to work with all my powers among my fellows and all to some purpose instead of fossilizing amid a set of self-duped literary parasites." It is his fixed belief that all writers who are original or "inspired" write down things which are seen by later generations to imply a good deal that the writer himself would have vehemently denied. In a remarkable paper on Lamarck and Darwin, read before the Fabian Society, he made this frank confession:

"My life has been a miraculous transformation of a good-for-nothing boy into the writer of this paper, and of several quite unaccountable, uncommercial plays through a mysterious will in me, which has prevailed over environment, heredity and every sort of external discouragement. What is more, that will is not me: it makes the merest instrument of me—often overworks and abuses me most unreasonably. It makes me perform the feats of a bold, energetic, resourceful man, though I am actually a timid, lazy, unready one. It makes me write things before I understand them; and I am conscious that my own subsequent attempts to explain them are sometimes lame and doubtful."

IV

The decade initialed by the opening of the Great War witnessed in turn the eclipse and the reappearance in renewed brilliancy of that errant comet of the literary firmament, Bernard Shaw. In the piping times of peace the British public laughed consumedly when Shaw declared his utter deficiency in patriotism and asseverated that he was as little loyal to the land of his nativity as to the land of his adoption which had procured its ruin. But when the torrent of war burst upon the world, leaving Shaw intellectually and emotionally unaltered in the midst of the war frenzy which swept Great Britain, the British public turned upon him and ruthlessly wrote his epitaph.

There is a certain satiric cruelty, a sanguinary finality, about Shaw which enraptures the artist but enrages the patriot. Flourishing none of the gestures of martyrdom, Shaw gaily refused to die intellectually for his country. "You cannot make war on war," is the way he puts it, "and on your neighbors at the same time. We cannot bear the terrible castigation of comedy, the ruthless light of laughter that gleams on the stage." Driven from the practice of his profession as dramatic craftsman by the exigencies of war making, Shaw returned to his earlier love, the pamphlet, and launched forth upon a vigorous campaign of truth telling. Shortly after the appearance of his "Open letter to President Wilson" in *The Nation* and just before the appearance of the first installment of his "Common Sense About the War," in the *New York Times*, he wrote me from London on an open postcard, characteristically marked "Private":

"Our people here have no notion of the effect our diplomacy produced of catching the Germans in an ambush; they are so full of their sweet innocence and heroic highmindedness that they feel that anybody who is not congenitally perverse must feel that their position is one of extraordinary nobility, and that America must be proud to have her ships rifled by our cruisers."

In publishing his pamphlet Shaw was acting thoroughly in character as the Swift of his age, priding himself upon his "Irish capacity for criticising England with something of the detachment of the foreigner, and perhaps with a certain slightly malicious taste for taking the conceit out of her." Shaw violated two fundamental principles of war psychology: he continued to blurt out the truth as he saw it, regardless of consequences; and he declined to be anti-German. He frankly acknowledged that every London coster could stick his bayonet deeper into the stomach of Richard Strauss than Richard Strauss would care to do to him.

To many Englishmen Shaw appeared to violate the first principle of the Briton's code: good sportsmanship. Shaw refused to "play the game." He had a "blind spot" on the side of patriotism. A year before the Great War, on the initiative of a German nobleman, friendly addresses were exchanged between the leading men of both countries, full of well-meaning platitudes about Shakspere and Goethe. In the first draft of the British address, Shaw inserted a sentence to the effect that the possession by Germany of a powerful fleet, far from being a subject of jealousy, could only be regarded as an additional guarantee of civilization. No wonder that in the right little, tight little island it was found impossible to obtain the necessary British signatures until that sentence was expunged.

For a time during the Great War Shaw was virtually ostracized; the press subjected him to a rigid boycott; he came to be regarded by a certain element as an enemy of the realm. But Shaw went on his way unperturbed, although actually at times, I suspect, in danger of arrest. He seemed perverse and disloyal, chiefly because he gave different reasons to those advanced by the man-in-the-street for pursuing identically the same course of action. Although inveighing against British and German militarism alike, he rang true in the declaration in "Common Sense" that England had no alternative but to fight in order to destroy German militarism, and put an end once for all, to Potsdamnation. After Colonel A'Court Repington committed his blazing but magnificent indiscretion in pointing out the insensate folly of Kitchener in employing shrapnel when high explosive shells were needed, Shaw visited the front at the invitation of Sir Douglas Haig, the British commander, and wrote for home consumption three smashing articles the burden of which was: "Shells! Shells! Shells!" Bernard Shaw actually drove home to British consciousness the pressingly obligatory truth that the Allies could win only with high explosive shells; that the whole nation, if necessary, must turn to munition making; and that only an unlimited supply of shells would enable Haig to win the War.

Since the Great War Shaw's stock has taken a big bound upward. For the first time Shaw came to be recognized by a large section of the British public as a man of high courage and serious purpose. The death of Anatole France left him in indisputable possession of the crown of world letters.

IV

One of the most oddly significant commentaries upon the Anglo-Saxon indifference to the great ideas of the century whenever they are concretized into the form of actable drama, is furnished by the amazing unanimity, on the part of dramatic critics in both England and America, in denying the actual existence of such an entity as the Shavian philosophy. So irreparably is the average theatrical newsman, by courtesy dubbed Dramatic Critic, divorced from the real life of philosophy, ethics, politics, and sociology; so hopelessly is his critical perception warped by the romantic conventions, senescent models, and classic traditions of the stage, so entirely does he breathe the air of box-office receipts, shine in the reflected halo of "stars," or dwell in the unreal atmosphere of stage human nature, that when the new truths of a new philosophy present themselves to his judgment, his power to recognize them as valuable or even as truths, is irretrievably lost. And if perchance the dramatist, accepting as a mere rhetorical qucstion Horacc's "Quamquam ridentem dicere verum quid vetat?", possesses the genius and the hardihood to embody his profoundly serious views of life in brilliantly witty and epigrammatic expression, let him beware of the penalty of being regarded as a frivolous and light-headed near-philosopher!

Stranger still, one might even venture to say almost remarkable, is the attitude of some of the leading English and American dramatic critics, who happen to be men of the world in the large sense, thoroughly cosmopolitan in spirit. Mr. Walkley is quite willing to admit that Bernard Shaw has let in a fresh current of ideas upon the English drama; and yet, in that airy manner of his with which he brushes aside, but does not dispose of, real problems, he nonchalantly dubs those ideas the loose ends of rather questionable German philosophy. There seems little reason to doubt that Mr. Archer was quite sincere in his expressed belief that Bernard Shaw's philosophy may be picked up at any second-hand bookstall. Mr. Huneker is by no means unique in the opinion that Shaw's dramatic characters are mere mouthpieces for the ideas of Schopenhauer, Nietzsche, and Ibsen.

It might be imagined that the verdict of Continental Europe, where so many of the most modern conceptions, most vitally fecund ideas, originate and flourish, would carry with it some weight of authority. America inaugurated Shaw's world-renown by recognizing in him a brilliant and witty personage who succeeded in entertaining the public through the adventitious medium of the stage. It was not until Shaw's plays swept from one end of Europe to the other that Shaw came to be recognized abroad as a man of ideas rather than a mere "theatre-poet"; indeed, as a genius of penetrative insight and philosophic depth. Forced by the example of America and Europe to recognize in Shaw a dramatist of Continental calibre and range, England at last accorded to Shaw, the dramatist, the acknowledgment so long and so discreditably overdue. Nevertheless, the English dramatic critics still continued to refer Shaw's philosophy to Schopenhauer, Nietzsche, Ibsen, and Strindberg, "knowing nothing about them," as Mr. Shaw once remarked to me, "except that their opinions, like mine, are not those of *The Times* or *The Spectator*."

It is no less diverting to discover in European critics an equal crassness of imagination in their judgments of Shaw's temperament, his *donnée,* and his *ausschauung.* What a chimerical picture is this painted by Régis Michaud: "Feet on the earth and head in the clouds, surrendering himself to the pleasure of discussing the most poignant problems, turning them, now this way, now that, to his gaze; confounding on every hand, to render them the more interesting, the social question and the woman question; then, suddenly, as if so much reality bore heavily upon him, after having given in his revolutionary catechism the quintessence of his paradoxes, free of all system, vanishing into Utopia — such is Bernard Shaw, the philosopher." Whilst acknowledging Shaw's precious gifts — his facile, natural and brilliant dialogue, his faculty of painting human figures in which observation and invention collaborate in equal measure — Augustin Filon lamely concludes: "Bernard Shaw would be a great dramatic author, perhaps, if only his plays were — plays!" It was left for Maurice Muret to find in Shaw a thoughtful conservator of social and religious custom, and to pronounce *Candida* a tardy, but brilliant, revenge of the traditional ideal on the new ideal — "the victory of *la femme selon Titien* over the Scandinavian virago, this triumph of Candida over Nora"! Gaston Rageot makes the brilliant discovery that Shaw functions under the influence of Tolstoi — Tolstoi whose pet objurgation is the Superman and the Gospel of Power! The German, Heinrich Stümcke, declares that *nil admirari* is the quintessence of Shaw — Shaw, whose life is spent in ironic laughter of colossal wonderment at this entire demented, moonstruck world! The Dane, Georg Brandes, made the curiously provincial mistake of attributing to the influence of Ibsen the social discontent of Bernard Shaw who had been a vigorous Socialist propagandist for five years before he ever heard of Ibsen! Whilst the Italian, Mario Borsa, at the topmost pitch of fatuity finds a rationalist *pur et simple* in Shaw — this Shaw who persists in regarding the reign of reason as *vieux jeu,* and has declared again and again that man will always remain enslaved so long as he listens to the voice of reason!

While critics here and critics there have busied themselves, either in discovering in Shaw qualities he scorns to possess or else in indulging in elaborate analyses of his incidental traits, the two or three signal features which in themselves tend to explain his temperament, and in a word to define his art, remain utterly disengaged and obscure. The prime fact which stamps Shaw's art into close correspondence with life is the fundamental note of *disillusionment* which is struck fearlessly and unfailingly throughout the entire range of his work. Just as all life is an evolutionary process, and all progress follows vision clarified through the falling of the scales from the eyes of the brain, so Shaw's drama is an ordered sequence of pictured incidents in which pitfalls are uncovered, illusions unmasked, and vital secrets displayed. A profound student of human existence through actual contact with many diverse forms of life as it is actually lived to-day, and a philosopher as well, with a powerful imaginative grasp of social and sociological forms, Shaw sees that progress is possible only through the persistent discovery of mistaken conceptions of life and of society. If, as philosophers affirm, error is only imperfect knowledge, then the discovery of vital truth eventuates through that disillusioning process by which, in some psychologically crucial instance or dramatically potent conjuncture, we discover that our ideals, our conventions, our social laws and our religious conceptions are inadequate either to meet the facts or to solve the problems of life. Shaw is so deeply impressed with the predominance of human activity which consists in the pursuits of illusions that he does not hesitate to denominate it the greatest force in the world. All the more reason, then — since the majority of men are so constituted that reality repels, while illusions attract them — that the most succinct, most crystalline, most energetic art be employed in combating this predominant and pervasive force. It is not against the optimistic and progressive illusions, those indispensable modes of cloaking reality which possess the power to awake man's helpful interest and to inspire his best efforts, that Shaw directs his batteries of irony, of satire and of wit. Dedicated to Socialism, he freely admits to be indispensable the transparent illusion of the Socialist, who always sees Labor as a martyr crucified between the two thieves of Capital, and who maintains his enthusiasm at fever-heat by the consciousness that the laborer is always a model of thrift and sobriety, while the capitalist is a tyrant, an assassin, and a scoundrel! Were Socialism compelled to stand or fall upon the strength and stability of its economic structure alone, instead of upon its illusive appeal to the passion of humanity for a cause, with the concomitant allurement of impending revolution, its fate would indubitably be sealed!

It is against those individual and social illusions, treacherous, ensnaring, destructive — prejudices, conventions, traditions, theological incrustations, social petrifactions — that Shaw brings to bear all the force of his trenchant and sagacious intellect. He sees the individual involved in the social complex, and powerless, as an individual, to remedy his lot. He sees in money the basis of modern society, and attributes the slavery of the workers and of the women to the omnipotence of capitalized wealth. Modern society represents that phase in social evolution which history will classify as the age of the exploitation of man by man. Social determinism is the most tragic fact of contemporary life; and individual liberty, in most cases, amounts to little more than a political fiction. Woman, in marriage, is still the slave of man; and romance is only the pleasing illusion which masks the relentless functioning of the Life Force. Laugh as sardonically as we may, we cannot blink the fact that Trench is powerless to resist the Sartorius Idea, that Mrs. Warren is the victim of social extremity rather than the instrument of sexual passion, that Julia is the slave of a social convention. Barbara refuses longer to be the dupe of subsidized religion; Tanner is strong-minded enough for self-contempt in the disillusioning discovery of that "vital lie," romance; and Candida clarifies the preference of "natural instinct" to "duty" as a guide to conduct. Shaw's characters, whether involved in social labyrinths or confused by conventional dogmas, break through to the light by discovering their false allegiance to some stupid current fiction or some baseless fabric of cheap romance. Gloria's armor of "Twentieth Century Education" crumples up before the simple attacks of natural impulse; Judith Anderson's larmoyant sentiment is dashed by the Nietzschean frankness of Dick Dudgeon; and Brassbound recoils from himself in disgust in the realization of the romantic puerility of his twopence colored ideas of revenge. Shaw has freed himself from the illusions of patriotism and fidelity to English social forms; and he boasts that he is a "good European" in the Nietzschean sense — the true cosmopolitan in ideas. Like Maurice Barrés and Max Stirner, he is a fearless champion of the Ego; and his realism, like that of Ibsen and of Stendhal, is the realism of the disillusionist.

It is the custom of those who disagree with Shaw to point out that his brilliant and logical demonstrations of abuses and illusions, if traced back step by step to their origin, will bring us merely to some perverse idiosyncrasy of this wayward Irishman. In short, as Mr. Walkley is only too ready to indicate, Shaw is a pure *naïf*, falling into line with the more engaging *naïfs* of imaginative literature. "He is as naturally benevolent as Mr. Pickwick, and as explosively indignant in what he considers a just cause as Colonel Newcome. With Uncle Toby he conducts a whole plan of campaign on a quiet bowling green, and with Don Quixote tilts at windmills. He is as disputatious (though not so learned) as the Abbé Coignard, and when in the vein can borrow the philosophic ataraxy of Professor Bergeret." This method of disposing of Shaw on the ground that he is a thoroughly good fellow, passionately but perversely championing futile causes which he mistakenly regards as just and right, has all the virtue of cleverness without the necessary modicum of accuracy. The solid achievements of Shaw's own career are the silent refutation of the *bons mots* of the dilettante; and his international fame rests, in chief measure, upon his generally recognized power to exhibit facts in all their stark reality. The remarkable unity of his ideas despite their superficial aspect of contrariety, his inevitable trait of applying the standard of his well-defined philosophy to all facts, stamp him as a genuine philosopher, concerned with the unities of the world rather than with its diversities. Our greatest American philosopher, William James, once said to me: "To me, Shaw's great service is the way he brings home to the *eyes,* as it were, the difference between 'convention' and 'conscience,' and the way he shows that you can *tell the truth* successfully if you will only keep benignant enough while doing it." If it be true that Shaw appears essentially simple and serious in mind and character, it is because, as Jean Blum has acutely pointed out, he has succeeded in freeing his mind from all contemporary prejudice, has acquired the illimitable receptivity of the child, and has effected the transition to that *second* state of innocence out of which proceed real art and simple truth. It is in this sense, indeed, that Shaw is a genuine *naïf*. Just as disillusionment is the defining quality of his art, *naïveté* is the defining quality of his temperament. Far be it from me, who have revelled in many a quaint recital from his lips, to deny his oddity, his idiosyncrasy, his naïve charm. Nor would I even balk at the statement that he loves, for the sake of staggering his auditor, to proceed logically to a conclusion from a highly questionable premise. This is a quality of all highly imaginative temperaments; and in Shaw's case, is thrown into high relief by the brilliance and facility of his logical process. It is a casual fault, not a defining quality, of his art; and at the same time constitutes one of the very real charms of his personality. Someone has denominated Shaw a literary Peter Pan — a boy who has never grown up in literature. This is a peculiarly pertinent characterization of one who finds an "indescribable levity — something spritelike — about the final truth of the matter"; and who once said: "It is the half-truth which is congruous, heavy, serious, and suggestive of a middle-aged or elderly philosopher. The whole truth is often the first thing that comes into the head of a fool or a child; and when a wise man forces his way to it through the many strata of his sophistications, its wanton, perverse air reassures instead of frightening him." Shaw *is* a literary Peter Pan; and he takes the characterization as a very great compliment. "There was a time," Shaw once said, "when I was a grown-up man — more grown-up than anybody else. I was about eighteen at the time." But he added: "It was not until I became like Peter Pan that I was really worth anything."

Bernard Shaw is primarily, as I have pointed out, a disillusionizing force, achieving his purpose in great measure through the re-discovery of that state of incarnate innocence from which stem great works of art. Moreover, he frankly claims the theatre, as Zola claimed the novel, for didactic purposes; and makes so bold as to declare that the man who believes in art for art's sake is "a fool, a hopeless fool, and in a state of damnation." In his conception, art should be employed for social, political, moral and religious ends. Art is one of the greatest instrumentalities in the world for teaching people to see and hear properly. "When I write dramas," Shaw recently confessed, "what I really do is to take the events of life out of the irrelevant, and show them in their spiritual and actual relation to each other. I have to connect them by chains of reasoning, and to make bridges of feeling." When M. Charles Chassé complained that Shaw's ideas were so contradictory that he could construct no satisfactory synthesis of his philosophy, Shaw replied: "How French to wish to stick everything into pigeonholes! You find contradictions in my philosophy? Very well — are there not contradictions in life? I have expressed my ideas in groups on certain subjects in my different works. Ask no more of me." M. Firmin Roz recently declared that Shaw has ideas, but that he does not let them harden and crystallize into a system: "Il les jette dans la vie où elles doivent vivre elles-mêmes comme des ferments actifs." The apparent contrariety of ideas in Shaw's works is one of the elements that tend, not only to prevent comprehension of his purpose, but even to prompt suspicion of the seriousness of his purpose. The other element springs from the popular notion that wit and seriousness are two mutually contradictory entities. The really inspired man, in Shaw's opinion, is the man who brings you to see that there are certain delusions you must surrender; that there are certain steps forward that must be taken. Progress involves not only the sacrifice of certain obligations, but also the assumption of other obligations. But let the serious reformer dare to express his ideas in witty and paradoxical form, and he must answer the charge, not simply of being disagreeable, but also of being frivolous. The

Anglo-Saxon, as M. Auguste Hamon maintains, is racially incapable of intellectual virtuosity; and so is "unable to understand the finesse and the height of view of an ironical tale of Voltaire, a philosophic drama by Renan, or a novel by Anatole France." Had Shaw not given the pill of the "paper-apostle" in the jam of the "artist-magician," perhaps the public would not have endorsed his message. Shaw has always maintained that if he had told the English people the plain truth, unvarnished and unadorned, he would have been burned at the stake! All the more reason, then, for prizing the wit, the humor, the fancy, the epigram, the paradox, of this intellectual virtuoso. Stevenson says somewhere: "No art, it may be said, was ever perfect and not many noble, that has not been mirthfully conceived."

Bernard Shaw is the most versatile and cosmopolitan genius in the drama of ideas that Great Britain has yet produced. No juster or more significant characterization can be made of this man than that he is a penetrating and astute critic of contemporary civilization. He is typical of this disquieting century — with its intellectual brilliancy, its staggering naïveté, its ironic nonsense, its devouring scepticism, its profound social and religious unrest. The relentless thinking, the large perception of the comic which stamp this man, are interpenetrated with the ironic consciousness of the twentieth century. The note of his art is capitally moralistic; and he tempers the bitterness of the disillusioning dose with the effervescent appetizer of his brilliant wit. His philosophy is the consistent integration of his empirical criticisms of modern society and its present organization, founded on authority and based upon capitalism. A true mystic, he sees in life, not the fulfilment of moral laws, or the verification of the deductions of reason, but the satisfaction of a passion in us of which we can give no account.

Evolution, in Shaw's view, is not a materialistic, but a mystical theory; and, after Lamarck and Samuel Butler, he understands evolution, not as the senseless raging of blind mechanical forces with an amazing simulation of design, but as the struggle of a creative Will or Purpose, which he calls the Life Force, towards higher forms of life. Socialism is the *alpha* and *omega* of his life. He believes in will, engineered by reason, because he sees in it the only real instrument for the achievement of Socialism. Like all pioneers in search of an El Dorado, he has found something quite different from the original object in mind. Indeed, in his search for freedom of will, he has really succeeded in discovering three checks and limitations to its operation; and he has long since abandoned the paradox of free will. For he has discovered, as first limitation, the iron law of personal responsibility to be the alternative to the golden rule of personal conduct. Second, the desirability of the sacrifice of the individual will to the realization of the general good of society through the progressive evolution of the race. And third, the personal, temperamental restriction which forbids him to accept anything as true, to take any action, to allow any free play to his will which would seriously militate against the progressive advance of collectivism. He has achieved the remarkable distinction of embracing collectivism without sacrificing individualism, of preaching intellectual anarchy without ignoring the claims of the Collective Ego.

In Bernard Shaw rages the dæmonic, half-insensate intuition of a Blake, with his seer's faculty for inverted truism; while the close, detective cleverness of his ironic paradoxes demonstrates him to be a Becque upon whom has fallen the mantle of a Gilbert. In the limning of character, the mordantly revelative strokes of a Hogarth prove him to be a realist of satiric portraiture. The enticingly audacious insouciance of a Wilde, with his nonchalant wit and easy epigram, is united with the exquisite effrontery of a Whistler, with his devastating *jeux d'esprit* and the *ridentem dicere verum*. If Shaw is a Celtic *Molière de nos jours,* it is a Molière in whom comedy stems from the individual and tragedy from society. If Shaw is the Irish Ibsen, it is a laughing Ibsen — looking out upon a half-mad world with the riant eyes of a Heine, a Chamfort, or a Sheridan.

GRANVILLE BARKER

"We must go on breaking new ground, enlarging the boundaries of the new drama, fitting it for every sort of expression. When we deserve it a new dramatic genius will arise. He will neither break laws nor obey them. He will make laws and there will happily be no questions."

H. Granville Barker: *The Theatre; The Next Phase.*

GRANVILLE BARKER

Many years ago, Matthew Arnold pleaded for the organization of the theatre in England — the irresistible theatre, as he so optimistically called it. For the past twenty years, tentative and groping steps, now this way, now that, have been directed towards this visionary goal. England may be the most conservative country in the world. Englishmen may be proud of their ability to "muddle through somehow." Once let a great creative and basically fruitful conception take shape in their minds, and then their perseverance and dogged determination brook no obstacle until their object is fully attained. Before very long we may expect the beginning, at least, of the consummation of that great project for a national theatre, in commemoration of William Shakspere, which shall place Great Britain abreast of the great nations of the world in the domain of the theatre. If the patient, arduous and unremitting efforts of the adherents and supporters of the drama, in its highest and most original forms, are taken as criteria, we may confidently look forward to a not distant future when the repertory idea shall have found realization in stable practice, when the brilliant and original efforts of the dramatists of the new school shall have won the permanent support of the British public.

Whenever a creative movement, in no matter what field of human activity, is forward, and is triumphantly hailed as "new," the public is inclined to regard it with a certain amount of reserve, if not with suspicion and distrust. And when, besides, this "new" movement comes into existence as a form of revolt against existent conditions, the public is all the more inclined to say: "All right. Go ahead. But you must meet the tests of the commercial theatre. You must create your public, or at least show that there is a submerged public ready to support you. Make good if you can. But don't expect to achieve permanent results by counting solely on popular sympathy."

The New Drama in England to-day, with Bernard Shaw and Granville Barker as its leading exponents, is essentially an experimental school. From the beginning, every effort has pointed toward fresh extensions of sense in the field of the drama. Freedom for the exercise of dramatic talents is posited as the fundamental pre-requisite for the healthy development of the drama. The exponents of the new school have sought above all things to free themselves from the confining restrictions of the drama, and to express themselves unreservedly — in idea, in form — regardless of whether the result seemed "dramatic" or not. These ideals brought them into conflict — an irrepressible conflict — with two established traditions — the commercial theatre, and the censorship. From the first, it was apparent that the long-run system of the commercial theatre was fatal to the chances of the new dramatist. His public was destined to be, not the "great public," but a "lesser public," in part composed of intelligent theatre-goers, in part of people who have ceased to encourage the banalities and falsities of the theatre of commerce, in part of a new quota of the human throng. Moreover, it soon became apparent that if the drama was to flourish, if new talent was to burgeon and blossom, if the path was to be made clear for the experimentalist, the first and most imperative necessity was the abolition, or at least radical modification, of the censorship. Not less essential — for it had nothing to do with mere institutional bars — was the desire to create, not simply strikingly new modes of stage entertainment, but works of art that would bear the test of publication. There was the thrust toward utter realism — the ambition to create a drama that would wear the drab, as well as the brilliant garments of life itself.

It was Bernard Shaw who initiated the New Drama twenty years ago with *Widowers' Houses*. The Independent Theatre, inaugurated by Mr. J. T. Grein, failed in its effort, as did the New Century

Theatre, to bring to the fore a group of budding dramatists. But it was the immediate cause of enticing Bernard Shaw into the field of dramatic authorship. Mr. Grein demanded evidence of the latent dramatic talent in England which only needed the offer of a field for its display. Shaw claimed to have manufactured the evidence; and that claim has been made good in the great capitals, and on the great stages, of the world. In *The Author's Apology,* prefixed to the *Dramatic Opinions and Essays* (English Edition), Shaw especially insists that those dramatic criticisms were "not a series of judgments aiming at impartiality, but a siege laid to the theatre of the Nineteenth Century by an author who had to make his own way into it at the point of the pen, and throw some of its defenders into the moat." Shaw was accused of unfairness and intolerance as a critic of the drama, of the intent to stifle native dramatic talent with forcible condemnation. When Shaw vigorously charged Pinero, Jones and others with failure, he was simply charging them with failure to come his way and do what he wanted. "I postulated as desirable a certain kind of play in which I was destined ten years later to make my mark as a playwright (as I very well foreknew in the depth of my own unconsciousness); and I brought everybody, authors, actors, managers, to the one test: were they coming my own way or staying in the old grooves?" He baldly attempted "the institution of a new art," in which the dramatist could give the freest play to his own originality; and foresaw as result a new and hybrid drama — part narrative, part homily, part description, part dialogue, and part drama (in the conventional sense). In the days that have followed such pronouncement the English stage has been enriched by such original, such powerful, such unique plays as *Major Barbara, Getting Married, The Voysey Inheritance,* and *The Madras House* — hybrids all perhaps, analytical and dialectical, strained and in some cases repellant — but marked by a mysterious novelty, the sign manual of genius.

The next significant step in the slow glacier-like movement toward the creation of a native drama of spontaneous art and the establishment of a national theatre that would worthily represent the national genius, is found in the establishment of the Stage Society, of London. At first its ambition was the very modest one of giving private performances, on Sunday afternoons, in studios and such other places as might prove available. The scheme found enthusiastic supporters among people of rather aimless intellectual tastes, who eagerly sought in the performance of the Stage Society a "refuge from the dulness of the English Sunday." As the society grew in strength and numbers, the performances came to be given in theatres — permissible when no admission fee was charged. After a time, the

Sunday performance was generally followed by another performance on Monday afternoon. The Stage Society thus became the logical successor of the Independent Theatre, founded some ten years before; and while it has always remained a *théâtre à coté,* the importance of its work in fostering latent dramatic genius cannot be too strongly emphasized. It was founded in 1899, and during thirteen seasons (to 1911) produced forty-six English plays, and twenty-odd plays by continental dramatists. With seven exceptions, these plays were produced by the society for the first time on the English stage. In its very first season it produced Bernard Shaw's *You Never Can Tell* and *Candida,* Maeterlinck's *Intérieur* and *La Mort de Tintagiles,* Hauptmann's *Das Friedensfest* and Henrik Ibsen's *The League of Youth.* In its second season it produced Shaw's *Captain Brassbound's Conversion,* Hauptmann's *Einsame Menschen,* and Ibsen's *The Pillars of Society.* In its third season were produced *The Lady from the Sea,* and *The Marrying of Anne Leete,* the latter a remarkable play by a new dramatic author, H. Granville Barker. It is needless to enumerate the great modern dramas, chiefly dramas of thought and of purpose, which have been produced by the Stage Society during the remaining years up to to-day. Suffice it to say that the Stage Society has played in England, though in a somewhat less conspicuous way, the rôle which has been played on the continent by the Théâtre Libre, L'Œuvre, and the Freie Bühne. From it came Bernard Shaw — and Granville Barker — soon to be united in an enterprise at the Court Theatre which is without a parallel in the history of the English stage. From that fecund school of drama came also the late St. John Hankin, a dramatist of rare promise, and Mr. John Galsworthy, the author of the original and powerful dramas, *Strife* and *Justice*.

The Repertory Theatre idea has gained a firm footing in England; and to-day bids fair to go forward slowly to a more permanent and enduring establishment. In 1898 was founded the Irish Literary Theatre, under the auspices of the National Literary Society, founded by Mr. W. B. Yeats seven years before. That energetic woman who played the mysterious "angel" to the Avenue Theatre production of Shaw's *Arms and the Man* in 1894, Miss A. E. F. Horniman, may fitly be described as the mother of repertory in England. Largely through her efforts has come into being the Abbey Theatre, the repertory theatre of Ireland — the only theatre in an English-speaking country, said Mr. W. B. Yeats in 1908, "that is free for a certain number of years to play what it thinks worth playing, and to whistle at the timid." The experiment of Mr. Shaw and Mr. Barker at the Court Theatre, of which I shall speak later, showed the way to the true repertory, of which it was, technically, not a perfect example. At Manchester in 1907, the first true repertory theatre in Great Britain was established by Miss Horniman. The experimental theatres at Stockport, Glasgow, Edinburgh and Liverpool are all healthy manifestations of the new movement towards Citizens' Theatres on repertory lines in modified forms. Mr. Charles Frohman's season of repertory at the Duke of York's Theatre (1909-1910), London, is the first sign, though of doubtful success, of the effort to plumb the commercial possibilities of the repertory system. In his recent book on the Repertory Theatre, Mr. P. P. Howe says of Mr. Frohman's somewhat inconclusive experiment:

"It is a step on the road. The seemly and requisite thing for the State to do is to elevate the drama above the chances of commerce, as Smollett in common with most thinking persons saw a century and a half ago, as nearly every European country has already done, and as this country will do in something much less than a century and a half. But the business of a National Theatre is primarily with the classical repertory of plays. Mr. Frohman's theatre, pointing as it does to endowment, points equally clearly along the line of individual experiment, which will always be the path of the advancing drama. The next step on this road is clear. A theatre combining convenience of site with a rent only moderately extortionate, foregoing the unnecessary complication of expensive stars, and keeping a clear eye on the public it would serve may be set going in London to-morrow with satisfactory pecuniary profit. A certain definite public is now made familiar with the repertory idea, and to convert this public into a large, convinced, and permanent public for good drama is a mere matter of persistence. . . . The good play-goer will be created by good drama, but it is not to be forgotten that the good play-goer also exists and is awaiting a theatre worth his while."

The crown of the Stage Society's achievement, as Mr. William Archer once expressed it, was the presentation of Mr. H. Granville Barker to the world of dramatic art in England. Much has been written about Mr. Shaw, his genius, career, and influence upon contemporary drama. Little enough, strange to say, has been written about Mr. Barker, with his strange, austere talent, his anti-sentimental and chiselled art, his complicated simplicity in technique, his almost fierce contempt for the normal relations of average, everyday life. A few people nowadays are beginning eagerly to claim him as the one true dramatist — and English withal — of the movement. Though born (1877) in Kensington, the curiously complex strains in his ancestry are almost everything racial but English: Scotch, Welsh, Italian, Portuguese, and even a trace, perhaps, of the Jew.

Almost from birth he seemed destined for the theatre. As Shaw learned from his mother, a well-known singer, the secrets of enunciation which so greatly aided him later as a platform speaker, so Barker learned from his mother, a well-known reciter, the art of speaking and reciting. At seven, he was already proficient in expression; and at the age of thirteen, though callow in the extreme, he was shot into the theatre — to hit or miss as fate, or his own genius, might decree. His education, in the conventional sense, then abruptly ceased and to this circumstance perhaps is due his intolerance of the academic, and his conviction that the only great school of art is life. He served a rather severe apprenticeship to the stage between his thirteenth and his seventeenth years; but he was not to attract public notice until several years later. Then he came into prominence in connection with the Stage Society — as actor, as producer, and as author. His own play, *The Marrying of Ann Leete,* which he produced, awoke the thoughtful attention and appreciative criticism of such men as Mr. Shaw, Mr. William Archer, and Mr. Arthur Symons. In Shaw's *Candida* he achieved a memorable effect in the part of Marchbanks; his impersonation of Richard II at an Elizabethan Stage Society performance helped also to mark him out as a brilliant actor. Much might be written about his art as an actor; for it is impossible to say how much his art as a dramatist

Courtesy A. L. Coburn

GRANVILLE BARKER

owes to his skill as a player. It was in 1904 that Mr. Barker first came into association with the Court Theatre. Mr. J. H. Leigh, with Mr. J. E. Vedrenne as manager, was giving a series of creditable Shaksperean revivals at the Court Theatre and he invited Mr. Barker to produce *The Two Gentlemen of Verona.* This production, in which Mr. Barker played the part of Launce, was a marked success; and the first result of his association with Mr. Vedrenne was a series of six matinee performances of *Candida.* The final outcome was the Vedrenne-Barker management of the Court Theatre from 1904 to 1907.

Throughout this time, Mr. Barker took a leading part in a number of the plays which he produced; and this he continued to do in the subsequent productions at the Savoy Theatre. In 1904, Mr. Barker had produced for the New Century Theatre, under Mr. Vedrenne's management, Professor Gilbert Murray's "spiritual" translation of the *Hippolytus* of Euripides; and it was partly their association in this successful experiment that led to the Court Theatre enterprise. Had it not been for the "new" drama, Mr. Barker would probably, as he once told me, have left the stage entirely — though he felt a strong sense of mastery in Shaksperean parts. His performances in his own and Shaw's plays, notably in *Waste, Man and Superman,* and *The Devil's Disciple,* were regarded as triumphs in the new style of acting. Had there been repertory in England, he would doubtless have remained on the stage. Despite the fact that he is accasionally seen on the boards, he has definitely abandoned the actor's career. His talent finds scope for display in two directions, stage-management and dramatic authorship. The close of the Vedrenne-Barker season at the Savoy marked his definite severance from the stage as an actor, although he has often won success on the boards since that time. During recent years he has devoted his best talents to theatre-management.

To show the regard in which his work as an actor was held, I need only cite the words of the *Spectator* which appeared at the time of his "retirement" from the stage. The writer recognized Mr. Barker not alone as an alert and subtle interpreter of character, a master in the art of suggestion, an intellectual actor dominating his audience by skill rather than by force. "One of the principal causes of his artistic success is that he can mingle intellect with fancy, and his acting is often at its sprightliest when it is most significant. He possesses in a high degree the indefinable quality of charm — a quality which he displays at its fullest perhaps in his rendering of Valentine in *You Never Can Tell,* and in the delightful third act of *The Doctor's Dilemma.* More than any other English actor, he can 'put the spirit of youth into everything,' so that the whole scene becomes charged with high spirits — with Mr. Barker the art and ingenuity are there, but they are softened and etherealized by a perpetual flow of English humour and English imagination."

Of that remarkable experiment at the Court Theatre, I would refer the reader in especial to its recorded history written by Mr. Desmond MacCarthy. The companies trained by Mr. Barker, both at the Court Theatre and, subsequently, at the Savoy (September, 1907-March 14, 1908) wrought something very like a revolution in the art of dramatic production in England. The unity of tone, the subordination of the individual, the genuine striving for totality of effect, the constant changes of bill, the abolition of the "star" system—all were noteworthy features of these undertakings. There were given 985 performances of thirty-two plays by seventeen actors; 701 of these performances were of eleven plays by one author, Mr. Shaw. Plays of other authors were produced — and often with striking success; but in the main the whole undertaking may be regarded as a Shaw *Festspiel,* prolonged over three years. Mr. Galsworthy, Mr. Hankin, Mr. Masefield, Miss Elizabeth Robins, and Mr. Barker — all came strongly into public notice. The Court was not in the strict sense a repertory theatre; rather it furnished a tentative compromise between the *théâtre à coté* and the actor-managed theatre, backed by a syndicate of capitalists. As Mr. Barker said: "The first thing we did was to struggle against the long-run system, partly because we wanted to produce a lot of plays, and partly because we disagreed with it. It is bad for plays and bad for acting." In March, 1909, Mr. Barker produced a series of matinees of Mr. Galsworthy's *Strife* at the Duke of York's Theatre; and during the season of 1909-1910 we find him actively engaged for the repertory season of Mr. Charles Frohman at the same theatre — producing his own plays *The Madras House* and *Prunella,* among others. Mr. Barker was offered in 1907 the post of director of the New Theatre in New York — a convincing proof that he had made a great reputation as a producer; but his conception of the *théâtre intime* as the indispensable setting for the modern drama precluded his acceptance of the proffered directorship of the New Theatre, because of its grandiose proportions. After his return from an inspection of the New Theatre, he freely predicted its failure. The admirable book he wrote in collaboration with Mr. Archer, *Plans and Estimates for a National Theatre,* points forward to a future National Memorial to Shakspere in the shape of a great theatre, supported by private endowment, and comprehensively representative in character.

In the face of these multifarious activities, and

many that I have omitted to mention — as actor, as producer, as author, as builder and inspirer — Mr. Barker all the while was persisting in a strenuous course of straightforward drudgery in the effort to educate himself as a dramatist. In 1893, he began regularly to write plays; and in that year was produced his first drama — a play in which Mr. Barker and some amateur actors appeared before a "most select audience." Though the plays of this early period were amateurish and inexpert, they exhibited the instinct of the born craftsman. They were, as Mr. Barker expressed it, "stage-tight"— much as one would describe a box as water-tight: they played themselves, on the stage, before an audience. Shortly after turning dramatist, Mr. Barker began to write plays regularly in collaboration with Mr. Berte Thomas; and during the next six years these two wrote, in conjunction, some five or six plays. Only one of these plays, *The Weather-Hen,* actually saw the light. The moderate success it enjoyed was well deserved. By this time Mr. Barker had worked free of derivative influences; and this play showed itself spontaneous in treatment, genuine in expression.

All these efforts can only be called promising tentatives. They have no significance for the public; and are merely important as successive links in the evolution of Mr. Barker's genius as a craftsman. In *The Marrying of Ann Leete,* produced by the Stage Society at the Royalty Theatre, January 26, 1902, Mr. Barker made his first serious bid for wide recognition. It registers, on his part, a serious and sincere effort to "find himself"— to discover an inevitable medium in dramatic expression which would remain permanently associated with his name. With all its peculiar originality, its almost unprecedented novelty of technique, it failed of its purpose, not for lack of meaning, but for excess of meanings.

If there is one outstanding feature of Mr. Barker's talent, which grows more evident with each new play, it is the scope, the social perspective, of his anecdote. This play, laid at the end of the eighteenth century, is not concerned merely with the fate and destiny of particular individuals: its theme is the moral, and physical, degeneration of a family. An air of languorous corruption, of polite blackguardism hangs, like a miasma, over the scene. Mr. Carnaby Leete, a brilliant, but utterly unscrupulous politician, dexterously "stacking the cards" for his own advancement without regard to party fealty, personal loyalty or honor, is a remarkable figure — one of the most remarkable figures Mr. Barker has ever projected. There is one other remarkable feature of this play — the technique. Indeed it may be regarded as an unsuccessful experiment in technique. The action — if the static picture of a family in the final stages of polite corruption can be called "action"—is conveyed by a species of incoherent volubility, a sort of brilliant indirection that is all but illuminating. The *disjecta membra* of vaguely significant conversations fall about us like hail-stones; we experience a sense of suppressed excitement in tracking down some elusive secret to its hidden lair. But that is as far as Mr. Barker got—the suggestively cryptic. Already we see him employing woman as the embodiment of an abstract idea—the woman boldly entangling the good-natured but dense philanderer in her carefully devised snare. The sense of grossness comes strongly upon one in the finale—this eugenic, but unnatural, solution of mating the over-civilized and devitalized woman with the coarse but pure-blooded man. It is that same oppressive and heavy atmosphere of sex communicated to us by James Lane Allen's *Butterflies—A Tale of Nature.* And we realize in the ending, not a natural nor even a morbid impulse—but a strictly sociologic motive which might have occurred to Westermarck, but never to Ann Leete! "Mr. Barker can write," says Mr. Arthur Symons in a contemporary account of the play. . . . "He brings his people on and off with an unconventionality which comes of knowing the resources of the theatre, and of being unfettered by the traditions of its technique. . . . Mr. Barker, in doing the right or the clever thing, does it just not quite strongly enough to carry it against opposition. . . . The artist, who is yet an imperfect artist, bewilders the world with what is novel in his art; the great artist convinces the world. Mr. Barker . . . will come to think with more depth and less tumult; he will come to work with less prodigality and more mastery of means. But he has energy already, and a sense of what is absurd and honest in the spectacle of this game, in which the pawns seem to move themselves."

Mr. Barker has recently said that, in his opinion, "the Theatre — with music — is marked out as the art of the immediate future, of the next hundred years." The prophecy called up to my mind an endless series of plays with *Prunella* as forerunner. That beautiful hybrid — in which collaborated a skilled technician and keen thinker, a poet, and a musician — is one of the most tender and gracefully conceived plays I can recall. With all its airy fancy, it contrives to embody a wealth of real meaning that creeps close to the heart of everyone. It is cut from the same pattern, and was doubtless influenced by, Rostand's *Les Romanesques* — that fanciful Watteau picture of love, life, disillusion and reconcilement, which takes place "anywhere so the scenery is attractive," in which the people dress as they please "provided the costumes are pretty." This Pierrot, with his rollicking, rackety band of gay mummers, is French in conception, but English in execution — lacking in the Gallic subtlety but instinct with an *insouciance,* a playful *naïveté,* that is quaintly English. Through the eyes of his familiar, Scaramel, the *blasé* and the unilluded we see Pierrot as the world's mad truant — lyrically in pursuit of a bright happiness that is all self-gratification. He is a graceful tyro in the poetic art of living — with no regret for the past, no thought for the morrow. Into Prunella's garden he trips with many a dextrous and insinuating pose, awakes love in her heart, and, as by a miracle of hallucination, transforms her into — Pierrette. The statue speaks to these twain its oracle of "Love whose feet shall outrun time"— and the lovers rapturously flee from this prim garden of the rectangular virtues into a wide world of blue moonlight and many stars. A little space — and the once gay Pierrot, now in funereal black, returns to the garden, overgrown and choked with autumn leaves, to mourn for the lost Pierrette. Life has caught him in its snare; he forgot the little Pierrette when he was upon his travels, and when he returned he found her no more. In agonized accents, he calls despairingly beneath her window: "Are you there, little bird, are you there?" while Scaramel ever stands at his elbow like a symbol of world-weariness, of disillusion, of despair. In answer to his passionate petition, Love speaks, to show him his folly; and he drinks the bitter cup. But Pierrette, in tatters, yet still tender and true, has found her way, also, back to the garden of true love.

Life takes them by the hand, and re-unites them in the new bond of a perfected love.

From this time forward, Mr. Barker begins to "take his stride." *The Voysey Inheritance* marks a new departure. We now recognize in him a "new" dramatist in a very real sense — a dramatist with original and clear-cut ideas, unconfined by the "restrictions" of dramatic art, and firm-poised in his conception of the limitless possibilities of drama. He protests creatively against the professor of criticism and the sophisticated playgoer, who are only too ready with the unthinking and prejudiced: "Oh, yes, clever enough in its way — but not a play." He deliberately sets himself the arduous task of creating a drama of "normal human interest"— not to capture the fancy of the hardened playgoer or to tickle the palate of the professional critic, but to win the intelligent interest of the normal man and woman. "The English theatre, for heaven knows how many years," he said in 1908, "has diligently driven out everybody over the age of twenty-five — I speak, at any rate, mentally, for there are plenty of people with grey hairs who will never be more than twenty-five. And you have got to give what you can call, in the strict sense of the word, an intelligent and amusing entertainment, before you can get these people back. When you've done that you've done all that you can do for the English theatre." The professional playgoer wants "the same old game" year after year — romantic love, thrills, *scènes à faire,* "curtains," dramatic tangles dextrously unwound, handsome men and beautiful women, exquisite scenery, magnificent costumes. Mr. Barker posits a drama of large humane concern, dealing sincerely and naturally with normal human life, which shall possess the indispensable qualification of interesting an audience. It is this which he has given us in the remarkable play, *The Voysey Inheritance.*

Here again, as in the case of *The Marrying of Ann Leete,* Mr. Barker reveals a mastery in scope and perspective. It presents analogies to a novel of Balzac, rather than to a drama of Ibsen — is rather more like a section of the *Comédie Humaine* laid on English soil, than like a representation of such a bourgeois family episode as that of the house of Bernick, or of Borkman. It goes to the root of a problem which seems, somehow, peculiar to English life — the utter dependence of a family upon a settled source of income from conservative investment. After the manner of his kind, Mr. Voysey has juggled with the funds entrusted to his care in the conduct of a great business; has robbed Peter to pay Paul; continues to do it, not simply to retrieve the losses, but latterly almost as a matter of course — his "right" as a shrewd financier. When he dies suddenly, his son Edward, upon whom the revelation of his father's and perhaps grandfather's, peccadilloes has come with a devastating shock, finds that he must take up this loathly burden — the Voysey Inheritance. With an acute sense of honor, a set of high (as well as hard and fast) principles, he shrinks back in horror from the prospect of all the lying and shuffling, the trickery and deception that will be required of him. In solemn conclave the entire family is informed of the situation; and in one of the most remarkably natural scenes on the modern stage, each character and personality standing out with cameo-like distinctness, the sensitive Edward finds that all, even Alice, the woman he loves, are against him. Character, individual temperament and prejudice speak with entire clearness in the decision of each. And when Alice, with well-aimed words, brings his high-flown principles wounded and crippled to the ground, Edward begins to feel at last that fate has marked him out — for better or for worse, he must rid himself of "morality," "principle," and "duty," and sacrifice personal niceties of feeling in the sincere if Jesuitical effort to help to right, by questionable means, a great wrong. In the event, the grasping old Booth, a lifelong friend of the family, demands his money from the firm, for re-investment elsewhere, and — the secret is out! We are left in fine doubt as to the outcome — we only know that old Booth has revealed the secret, and suspect that the crash is inevitable. Edward, fortified at last by the consciousness that he has done all that was possible to set matters straight and to undo the things which his father did, faces the future with brave heart. The solution of a great ethical problem in terms that contravene conventional conceptions of morality, and the support of Alice, have made a man out of a coward. If he must go to prison, he will go proud and strong — in the consciousness that he has done the right, and that Alice will be proud of him.

The Voysey Inheritance is a work of genius — original, deeply conceived. It is a fine type of the bourgeois drama — what George Eliot called a "scene from private life"— which Ibsen, in play after play, brought to such a high pitch of technical perfection. Its most remarkable feature, as Mr. Desmond MacCarthy has pointed out, "is the skill with which the interest in a single situation is maintained through four acts; that this is a sign of fertility and not poverty of imagination all who have ever tried to write know well." With such a situation, the successful playwright — who writes what the professional critic calls "plays"— in nine cases out of ten would have made an utter failure. Even Ibsen makes "heroes" out of Bernick and Borkman — throws about them a halo of daring chicanery or Napoleonic hazard. Mr. Barker delineates a financier without exaggeration or distortion, without even a trace of histrionism; and resolutely holds his protagonist down to the unheroic level of plain soul-testing actuality. With his thesis I cannot agree;

for his treatment I have the sincerest admiration. In many respects it is his most satisfying play — for its dynamic quality; the characters grow, enlarge, crystallize or develop, narrow, harden: we mark the crucial changes wrought by circumstance on character. It ends, with artistic *finesse,* upon an unresolved cadence — imparting to the spectators, in the spectacle, a sense of "the strange irregular rhythm of life." It possesses a rare and memorable quality: we are left in the end with a haunting sense of actuality, the impression of life — of life still going on after the curtain falls.

In 1901, Mr. Barker was converted to Socialism. Socialism proved the most transforming influence of his life. His whole attitude toward the theatre underwent a change that can be described as nothing less than revolutionary. For the first time he became profundly imbued with a sense of the necessity of organizing the theatre, of making it a great instrumentality in the social life of our time. He came to see in the repertory theatre the hope of the contemporary drama; and his notable undertaking at the Court Theatre, and afterwards at the Savoy, may be regarded as a direct outcome of Socialist conviction. The National Theatre, in the shape of a Shakspere Memorial, became, in his eyes, the inevitable instrumentality for the establishment of the English drama upon a great and permanent basis. His work in collaboration with Mr. William Archer is the fruit of his studies in that intricate problem. His association with Mr. Shaw, Mr. Sidney Webb, and their *confrères* upon committees of the Fabian Society wrought a tremendous change in his methods of thought, teaching him to co-ordinate, to concentrate, to think in terms of reality and realizable fact. In *Waste,* his next drama, we observe the unmistakable signs of that influence.

The banning of *Waste* by the King's Reader of Plays created a tremendous sensation; the incident was a vitally contributory cause to the investigation of the censorship by a joint committee of the two Houses of Parliament in 1909. In many respects it was a fortunate thing for Mr. Barker and for the future of the English drama. It focused public attention upon Mr. Barker and thrust him forward decisively as a most conspicuous exemplar of the "new" school of dramatists in England — a position which he might not have attained solely upon the stage success of *Waste.* Moreover it tended to unite solidly the almost universal objection to the censorship — an opposition that finally burst forth when Shaw's *Press Cuttings* and *The Showing up of Blanco Posnet* were banned in close succession. The report of the committee on the censorship [1] finally brought the issues clearly before the English

[1] *Report of the Joint Select Committee of the House of Lords and the House of Commons on the Stage Plays (Censorship), etc.* Eyre and Spottiswoode.

public and resulted in the present far-from-satisfactory compromise.

It is quite impossible to convey any adequate idea of *Waste* without narrating its story; and for that the reader is referred to the published play. I have never read any play which evoked so many jarring and contradictory sensations. The theme — adultery, a consequent illegal medical operation, the death of the patient, the effect of her death upon the co-respondent, a brilliant politician, whose future is thereby ruined — is a theme from the mere mention of which one instinctively recoils. Once grant that the subject is a legitimate one for stage treatment, and the opposition of the censorship disappears. The topic is treated with earnestness and sincerity by Mr. Barker; but with an apparently needless insistence upon a certain phase. The ultimate meaning of the play would have remained unchanged had Mr. Barker treated this phase of the play with more delicacy and reserve. The treatment of great political, social and religious questions in the play is the most powerful, most vitally interesting, and withal the most entirely true to life that I have ever encountered in any contemporary drama, with the single exception of *John Bull's Other Island;* of the two, Mr. Barker's play is superior to Shaw's in realistic detail and fidelity to actual life. From his contact with Mr. Webb and

Mr. Shaw, Mr. Barker achieved a mastery of the political issues involved, and presented them in impressive and convincing truthfulness. Trebell, the brilliant politician, is at once repellent and abnormal in temperament; a megalomaniac of the most virulent type. In his nature there is no spark of altruism; he has unbounded contempt for other people, sublime confidence in himself and his powers. His temperamental coldness — an inhuman coldness — takes the form, sincere though it be, of a sort of sensational cynicism. For the weak and vacuous victim of his passion he has not a spark of pity; he coldly argues with her at a moment when she needs and deserves sympathy and pity. There is nothing more gruesome and horrible in the whole play than the bond of union cemented between the adulterer and the betrayed husband — a fellow-feeling of sympathy in condemnation of the luckless woman. Trebell hates women; he hates with icy hatred this wretched victim because she will not abide the consequences — for the child's sake. He has always felt contempt for men and women because of his power over them; and he hates this woman all the more because he has given her the power to ruin him. The cabinet will be formed without him — people cannot work, even in politics, with a monster.

Trebell kills himself — not because he has lost his chance for a place in the cabinet, but because by a strange twist of a kind of mystic psychology, he realizes his spiritual failure. This woman, to whom he has never given a passing thought, has shrunk instinctively from an ordeal, to endure which woman needs all the love and help which man can give. A dream-child of his morbid fancy has been slain — this spells his failure, his consciousness of his inability to cope with the vast human issues of creation and life.

Mr. Barker has publicly expressed his gratitude to Mr. Charles Frohman for proving the practicality of modern repertory. He has brought "Repertory from the regions of talk and agitation to be an accomplished fact." It was during the season of 1910 that Mr. Barker's play *The Madras House* was produced by Mr. Frohman at the Duke of York's Theatre. Neither Mr. Barker's *The Madras House* nor Mr. Shaw's *Misalliance* with ten and eleven performances respectively, proved to be "winning cards"; the audiences were small, and their size did not warrant the continuance of the performances. After reading *The Madras House* I was impressed anew with Mr. Barker's originality as a technician and the scope of his vision as an interpreter of life. Woman — her present status, her relation to marriage, her future — is the theme of the play; and this problem is viewed from a different angle in each successive act. Various types, all sharply delineated in personality, are brought upon the stage, not for their own sake, but solely for the light they may throw, by reason of their individual opinions and prejudices, upon the question of sex. In spite of the several incidents of the play, which vitally concern the characters, there is no real plot — the protagonist is Woman, and the play concerns itself with her destiny. We have, in succession, the attitude of the father of six marriageable, but unmarried, daughters; the oriental view-point of a man who has set up a harem in the East, after being separated from his English wife; a cheap American "hustler" with subtly gross ideas about the utility of sex in business, a rather heavy caricature of the P. T. Barnum type; a woman who has been "wronged"; a woman whose husband is charged with infidelity; the shrill conventionalized figure of duty; and so on. And then there is the intimate trio — Philip Madras, his wife, and his friend Major Thomas, the "mean, sensual man," who is always obsessed with the strange idea that if a woman evinces any interest in him, she must be secretly wanting him to kiss her!

As long as Mr. Barker is focussing a rapid fire from all corners of the stage upon the subject of woman, he holds our undivided interest. In this play I observe for the first time the clear influence of Mr. Shaw. For this is Mr. Shaw's method *par excellence* — to consider some theme of large human or social interest, and have everybody tell what they think about it. This is the technical basis of Mr.

Barker's last play — save for this striking difference. Shaw's characters talk about countless things not strictly germane to the theme; Barker's characters focus on the theme — as George Meredith would say, they "ramble concentrically." The last act, though still concerned with the theme, is in the nature of anti-climax. Woman has a hard innings; and never is she thought of as anything but a Shavian "mythological monster," unscrupulously using her personal charms for selfish gratification. Philip Madras, who seems to direct the entire play, rather inconsequentially comes to the conclusion—a conclusion inartistically unmotived — that the only career for a self-respecting man nowadays who wishes to help his fellow-men and fellow-women, is to join the County Council and become a social reformer. As he says, "That's Public Life. That's Democracy. That's the Future." He is the self-satisfied young man who is coolly superior and always sure of himself — vastly irritating despite his large social views.

"In *The Madras House*," says Mr. Max Beerbohm, "there is only one character that does not stand forth vital and salient; and this is the character of Philip Madras, the wise and good young man who is always in the right — always perspicacious, unselfish and charitable by virtue of being himself so shadowy and cold. It is a note that pervades modern drama, this doctrine that human beings are always hopelessly in the wrong, and that only the inhuman ones can hope to be in the right. I don't say it is a false doctrine; but it certainly is a lugubrious one. And we must be pardoned for a certain measure of impatience with Philip Madras. Repressing our impulse to call him an impostor, and hailing him reverently as pope, we can't even so, stand him — whether we feel we are in the right with him or in the wrong with the others."

Mr. Barker is a dramatist of marked power and strong originality, a master of the tools of his craft. He has freed himself from the restrictions of his art: instead of obeying its "laws," he experiments freely and successfully with any materials he chooses. He has taken the bold course of "leaving Aristotle out." His definition of a play is a declaration of independence: "A play is anything that can be made effective upon the stage of a theatre by human agency." Perhaps his own words are prophetic — for he has done great things and will surely do greater: "We must go on breaking new ground, enlarging the boundaries of the new drama, fitting it for every sort of expression. When we deserve it a new dramatic genius will arise. He will neither break laws nor obey them. He will make laws and there will happily be no questioning."

The dramas written by Barker since *The Madras House* are, from the large standpoint of the theatre, negligible, with the exception of his last play,

The Secret Life. The dramatization of Stevenson and Osbourne's *The Wrong Box*, *The Morris Dance*, was a stage failure, and the short play entitled *Farewell to the Theatre* is little more than an emotional chat between a man and the woman he has always sought in vain to make his wife. *Rococo* is one of those silly, obvious farces with a foreseen ending which has to be played breathlessly or not at all. It has an appeal strictly English and provincial English at that. *Vote by Ballot* is a quietly amusing study in character contrasts; but the dénouement is too patently anticipated to contain even the dramatic element of surprise. *The Harlequinnade*, written in collaboration with Dion Clayton Calthrop, is a charming story, in a form adapted to Christmas pantomime for children, of the historical development of the Harlequin figure. There is the appropriate underlying note of seriousness for the *blasé* adult; and one does not evade the suggestion that unfolding before us in symbolic story is the gay film of the evolution of Comedy itself.

In *The Secret Life*, Barker's latest play, he has again made an enlightening and provocative experiment in the dramatic form. It is an illustration of the art of being undramatic. This is Barker's deepest study of characters in conflict—although we have no telling "curtains," no *scènes á faire*, no exciting dénouement. About it hovers a note suggestive of Maeterlinck in his most mystic mood, of the Galsworthy remembered in *The Patrician*. The conflict is silent, though deadly: "the conflict between the inner life of the soul—the generation of the spirit, which withholds so much—and the generation of the flesh that dies and knows it serves a greater end than its own." Joan does not marry the brilliant politician, Evan Strowde, who loves her with complete devotion—why we do not know, but we guess her love challenges and escapes the claims of the flesh. Strowde flings away his career, at a moment of ministerial crisis when his presence is imperatively needed, to go to the United States and attend her funeral. Quixotic? Who shall say? Nor is this the only conflict in the play, for we see Lord Clumbermere, who has made his money in ink, deluged by success and mere money-making, although he is a man of high ideals. As he confesses:

"I never supposed I wanted lots of money . . . but I've got it. I despise titles . . . I'm a lord. I was bred to the Baptist ministry, and I still think I'm a spiritually-minded man. And perhaps if I'd been blessed with three children instead of seven, I might be running a chapel now. You'd say I'd sunk my soul . . . not to mention other people's . . . all in money and money's worth. Well, money's a hard master . . . so is success. You think you're all for truth and justice. Right. Come and run my pen factory and find out if that is so."

As a sort of undertone of conflict, in a minor key, is the clash in temperament, if not in ideas, between the self-conscious, discontented, brilliant, young Oliver Gauntlett, soul seared by the secret of his illegitimacy, and the straightforward, sincere, forthright American girl, Susan Kittredge. A memorable figure is Kittredge, the American philosopher, who has a great vision for the future of his country. Perhaps Barker voices his view of America's future in Joan's words:

"Such a bright, silent land! . . . I was very scared sailing up the harbor to New York and driving to the station. Those blasphemous towers of Babel weren't a bit like you. But I think you'll come out on top. Yes . . . I have a vision of the sublime you, conscious, persistent, wise . . . coming out truly on top."

ARTHUR SCHNITZLER

" Our life is wrought of dreams and waking, fused
Of truth and lies. There lives no certitude.
Of others we know naught, naught of ourselves,
We play a part and wise is he who knows it."

— Paracelsus.

ARTHUR SCHNITZLER

In 1912, the fiftieth anniversary of the birth of Arthur Schnitzler, I ventured to call general attention in the United States to a figure little appreciated, indeed almost unknown, here, but deservedly famous upon the continent. Somewhat later, my bibliography of Schnitzler in English, in translation, production, and criticism, gave definition to the comparatively slight measure of appreciation hitherto accorded him in English-speaking countries.[1] Delicate, fragile work tends to remain longer in obscurity than do more vivid and spectacular forms of dramatic appeal. Contemporary preoccupation with the most pronounced forms of the social drama, of intention and of propaganda, has cast a sort of blinding glare across the stage of our time. The virile individualism of Ibsen, the explicit purposiveness of Brieux, the sociological passion of Shaw have shadowed the less assertive, yet often more exquisitely fashioned, works of the dexterous Austrian dramatist, Arthur Schnitzler.

[1] *Arthur Schnitzler.* "North American Review," November, 1912. *Bibliography of Arthur Schnitzler.* "Bulletin of Bibliography," October, 1913. Also in *Modern Drama and Opera, II.* Boston Book Co. 1915.

I

The art of this delicate craftsman is eminently worthy of study at the hands of the present and arriving dramatists of America. His entire series of plays, in adequate translation, deserve the considerate attention of that widening circle of temperate enthusiasts in our country now dedicating themselves to the study, and intelligent propagation of popular interest in the highest manifestation of the dramatic art of our time. Nor can one safely ignore his stories and novels, short and long, which reflect the social anatomy of contemporary Austria and reveal the soul of modern Vienna. At infrequent intervals American audiences have participated in the esthetic privilege vouchsafed by his delicate workmanship and polished art. The great Agnes Sorma once played *Light o' Love* at the old Irving Place Theatre; some years earlier, it was produced at the Berkeley Lyceum Theatre, first as *Flirtation* by the Progressive Stage Society (February 19, 1905) and later as *The Reckoning* by Katherine Grey (February 12, 1907). *The "Affairs" of Anatol* was produced with great success at the Little Theatre in New York in 1912; and quite recently the remarkable *Dr. Bernhardi* was produced with commendable finish and art by Rudolf Christian at the German Repertory Theatre in New York. These scattered productions of Schnitzler's more conspicuous dramatic works, interspersed with occasional, imperfectly successful or inadequate productions, little remembered, of *The Green Cockatoo* (at the Lyceum Theatre, New York, April, 1910, under the management of Mr. and Mrs. H. G. Fiske), *Literature* (at the Madison Square Theatre, January, 1908, and by the Washington Square Players at the Bandbox, 1916), and *The Farewell Supper* (as *Souper d' Adieu* by Charlotte Wiehe, in 1905) have conveyed to the American theatre-going public confused and perhaps misleading notions of the fundamental characteristics of Schnitzler as dramatist and of the essential features of his art. Half a dozen years ago, Schnitzler was quite unknown to the general reading public in the United States and England; and diligent research revealed translations, scattered here and there in English and American magazines, of only a very few of his plays, whether of one act or longer—*The Wife*, *The Woman with the Dagger*, *The Duke and the Actress*, *Living Hours*, *The Legacy*, *and Light o' Love*. The real stimulus to the popular interest in Schnitzler was given by the publication of Granville Barker's paraphrase of *Anatol* in 1911; and the subsequent productions, with John Barrymore in the title-rôle, of the *Anatol* cycle, while brilliantly executed, conveyed a false impression of Schnitzler as a dramatic artist, by inducing the public to think of him as a sort of Viennese *flaneur* in decadent social circles. Translations, in book form, of a number of Schnitzler's one-act plays—of *The Green Cockatoo*, *Paracelsus*, and *The Mate* by H. B. Samuel (McClurg), of *The Hour of Recognition*, *The Big Scene*, *The Festival of Bacchus*, *Literature*, and *His Helpmate* by Pierre Loving (Stewart and Kidd)—give a very satisfactory notion of Schnitzler's rare skill in the difficult art of the one-act play. The soundest view of Schnitzler, as artist and man, is embodied in a volume in the Modern Drama Series (Little, Brown & Co.) containing useful introduction, and translations, by E. Björkman, of *The Lonely Way*, *Intermezzo*, and *Countess Mizzie*. No well-rounded comprehension of *Professor Bernhardi* can be gained from a perusal of the handy, brief paraphrase by Mrs. E. Pohli (Paul, Elder & Co.). There is need for a translation of the complete works of Schnitzler, and for a sympathetic and extended account of the dramatic work, in especial. For, with some minor exceptions, as judged according to English and American standards of taste, that work is a worthy and honorable work—the achievement of one who undoubtedly stands in the forefront of those who have given to the German drama of to-day its distinction and widening vogue. The time is ripe for sensitively interpretative appreciation of the high and difficult art of Austria's leading dramatist. A mere survey of Arthur Schnitzler as a creative dramatist in the field of the one-act play, contained in the last edition of the present work, is now replaced by a study of his complete theatre. Schnitzler's ablest work within recent years has been in fiction.

To understand Schnitzler, one must realize that he writes primarily for a metropolis that vies with Paris itself in love for the theatre and for the ultimate refinements of literature — Ibsen's "beloved Vienna." It is customary for the north Germans to hold in light regard the spirit and temperament of the Viennese. The high polish of surfaces, the brilliance of artificiality, artistic sensitiveness without intellectual content — such are the terms of this depreciation. It is the distinction of Schoenherr, of Von Hofmannsthal, and, above all, of Schnitzler, to have silenced this depreciation and once again to have conferred upon Vienna an artistic eminence achieved by Grillparzer, Raimund, Bauernfeld, and Halm. Yet it is not the primitive, virile strength of *Faith and Fireside*, but the Watteau-like airiness of *Der Rosenkavalier* and the half-gay, half-sad, nuances of *Anatol* which sound the characteristic, modern Viennese note.

Schnitzler writes for an enlightened public enamoured of the theatre for the theatre's sake, sophisticated in life as well as in art, ever exigent in its literary standards. In contradistinction to the authentic German spirit, ceaselessly intent upon searching out the heart of life's mystery and revealing, in human will, man's divine potentiality, the authentic Austrian spirit delights to invest human life with the grace and charm of poetry. About customary happenings it loves to throw the iridescent halo of the ideal; to waft into the life of everyday the fragrance of happy memories and glad anticipations. Through the symphony runs a strain of melancholy, pronounced yet restrained — a sense of life's transitory and vanishing happiness. The Viennese spirit, as reflected by Arthur Schnitzler, is best realized in its semi-ironic quest for that "high, painful happiness" for which the late Ibsen sighed with such mournful regret after the fleeting episode with the little Viennese maid, Emilie Bardach. Romance interpenetrated with melancholy, happiness tinged with regret — for this spirit Schnitzler has chosen the fit artistic medium, romantic impressionism. He reflects life as he sees it in a mood of gay romance; but each little feature, each implicative allusion, intimates a depth of sadness and a capacity for tragedy. It is this spirit of melancholy reflection, the sense of ironic contrast, sometimes verging upon an almost cynical criticism of life, which not infrequently lifts Schnitzler's dramas out of the domain of mere literature into the ampler ether of humane emotion and social pity.

Arthur Schnitzler is a peculiarly interesting subject for analysis and dissection. He belongs to the

ARTHUR SCHNITZLER

strange genus of the scientist-artist: Goethe, Echegaray, Lewis Carroll, Ibsen, Poe perhaps — the bi-partite genius whose vocation and avocation are found in two water-tight compartments. His father was Professor Johan Schnitzler, a Jew, and a throat specialist of repute. Many similarities may be discerned between the elder Schnitzler, Professor of Medicine, founder of a polyclinic, Jew, held in esteem, beloved by friends and combatted by enemies, and his son's remarkable artistic creation, Professor Bernhardi, founder of a great sanatorium, Jew, suffering as the result of political and social conditions in Austria, tremendously admired and bitterly opposed. Young Arthur studied medicine at the Vienna University, where he received his M.D. in 1885. From 1886 to 1888, he saw active hospital service; and for the last thirty years he has enjoyed an extensive private practice in Vienna. In the *Wiener Klinische Rundschau*, which was edited by his father, he from time to time reviewed important medical works, notably on hypnotism, suggestion, psychotherapy, sexual hygiene, and the ethical consequences of physical reactions. In the light of his subsequent dramatic work, which is impregnated with traces of his scientific predilections, it is highly significant that as a practising physician (1889) he wrote a monograph on " Functional Aphonia and its Treatment by Hypnotism and Suggestion." As a physician, he took an absorbing interest in spiritual maladies; and exhibited a marked preference for the study of psychical or physiological phases of human ailment. In 1888, in the interest of his profession, he made a trip to England, which he commemorated in a series of "London Letters" dealing with medical subjects and published in his father's journal. While acting as his father's assistant, he built up a lucrative private practice for himself; and during the years 1891–5 collaborated with his father on a bulky medical work: *Clinical Atlas of Laryngology and Rhinology*.

During the early years, he was slow in attaining self-confidence and faith in himself as an artist. In a vague sort of way, he wavered between the immitigable obligations of his scientific career as a physician and his almost irresistible leaning toward literary pursuits. He has placed on record in the *Jüdischer Almanac* a letter of August 5, 1892, voicing his confession that in this early period he doubted both himself and his calling, was taken seriously by no one, and vainly sought to gratify his ambitions by absorbed participation in the pastimes and follies of fashionable society. But he could not stop the flow of his pen; verses and sketches quickly found their way into the popular periodicals. One who would investigate the amateurish beginnings — the playful tentatives and light trial-balloons of Schnitzler — may find his material in the pages of the long-lost magazine, once widely read, *By the Beautiful Blue Danube* (*An der schönen blauen Donau*). The consideration of paramount significance in Schnitzler's development is that his clinical studies, his minute examination of nervous affections, his preoccupation as physician with sexual manifestations, with neurosis, and with the phenomena of human dissolution — all are found reflected in his works, from beginning to end. Dr. Reik in his interesting study, "Arthur Schnitzler als Psycholog," points to the noteworthy circumstance that the Schnitzler who had never made any special study of the analysis of neurotics, as carried out by Sigmund Freud and his disciples, should in his own works of art, fiction and drama, have frequently laid bare the very secret springs and impulses so minutely dissected by the psycho-analysts. We may recall, in this connection, that Bernard Shaw in his creative art works posited the Life Force before the vogue of Bergsonism and the *élan vital.* The cynicism with which Schnitzler is often credited is the manifestation, not of a fundamental distrust in human nature, but of an extraordinarily astute perception of its frailties. This trait, which is conspicuous in his writings, is the natural legacy of the physician of the human body. When, as in the case of Schnitzler, accurate knowledge of pathological symptoms is reinforced by psychological insight of a very high order, it is inevitable that his works should betray at times less sympathy with human frailty than a sort of merciless objectivity in the treatment of human suffering which superficially appears little short of callous. If we view Schnitzler's plays from the higher human viewpoint, rather than with the conventional and rather banal attitude of the playgoer, we shall discern the workings of a refined intelligence in contemplation of some of the subtler shadings of individual and social feelings.

II

In his introductory poem to "Anatol," Hugo von Hofmannsthal, then writing under the pseudonym of "Loris," lightly limns a picture that reflects the mood of Schnitzler's plays:

Thus we rear Thalia's temple
Where we play our private dramas,
Gentle, saddening, precocious . . .
Comedies that we have suffered;
Feelings drawn from past and present;
Evil masked in pretty phrases;
Soothing words and luring pictures;
Subtle stirrings, mere nuances,
Agonies, adventures, crises. . . .

Some are listening, some are yawning,
Some are dreaming, some are laughing,
Some are sipping ices . . . others
Whisper longings soft and languid.[1]

[1] Translation of Edwin Björkman.

When the "Anatol" episodes were originally published in a Vienna periodical, they won instant appreciation for their vivacity, sprightliness, and verve. There is something of signficance in the fact that Schnitzler won his first laurels with the "Anatol" cycle. Since that time he has gone far as a dramatist, reaching heights and sounding depths of which those early sketches gave no slightest inkling. Yet in none of his later work has he surpassed the artistry with which he depicts the naïveté, the vanity, the self-love, the delicate neuroticism of the Bohemian soul of Vienna. Schnitzler thus reveals himself, at the very outset of his career, as a subtle artist in the portrayal of twilight moods and erotic nuances. In the society which he presents — a society just beyond the pale of respectability and well within the purlieus of the artist's bohemia — there is no question of the obtrusion of moral. The double standard is the foundation stone of the social code; and pleasure is fleeting and precarious, withal rapturous and intense. For these sad, gay dogs of the Viennese pack, flirtation is a pastime and philandering a high art. Atmosphere, mood, and temperament — these are the magic key-notes in the symphony. These light-hearted philanderers, sipping fragrance from many a wayside flower, are lacking in force, in passion, in will. Their assets are a certain childish gaiety and naïve charm, an almost feminine petulance, a tinge of nervous hysteria. Their code is tacit avoidance of the banal and the vulgar in manners and deportment. Love and intrigue afford the guiding motives; liaisons are madly effected, deftly severed. If the severance causes any remorse, it is only because, as Anatol confesses, one has promised the beloved an eternity of happiness and then given her only a few hours of pleasure.

These are little *genre* pictures, miniatures in delicacy and precision — light fantasies on the eternal theme: "Off with the old love, on with the new." It is callow student love carried one step further — Murger's *La Vie Bohème* dramatised episodically. These frail, feminine creatures—perpetually reminiscent of the recurrent and invariable Greuze type — are simple, sensuous, luxury-loving, larmoyant, clinging. We see them everywhere — now revelling in the fabled "strength of the weak," now palled with the saccharine monotony of pleasure, now discreetly, deftly snapping the frail and tenuous bonds of lawless union. Each partner in these transitory unions of caprice follows the law of his or her own nature; and this law is the line of least resistance. Romance gilds the scene — all is *couleur de rose;* there is the perfume of flowers, the sparkle of champagne. But soon a crisis comes — and parting is inevitable. But there shall be no harsh words, no crude recriminations, most of all, no regrets. Woman, the weaker vessel, may protest, cry out, burst into tears; but Man, god-like, must be Olympian in his calm! For all his noble impassibility, the hero, who imagines he is acting like a gentleman when at bottom he is only a cad, is by no means always immune. Sometimes Fate packs the cards against him; and he is unceremoniously left in the lurch, sheepishly contemplating the pitiable ruins of his artistically constructed self-respect.

These delightful flashlights of Anatol's amours, which may be described as varieties of erotic experience, reveal the hedonistic philosophy of the gay man-about-town. Women of fragile virtue readily "fall for" this attractive and plausible philanderer who really believes that both sexes are equally prone to inconstancy. "My dear Max," philosophises Anatol, "we are always trying to imagine that women are quite different from men. . . . As a matter of fact, men and women are exactly alike — especially women! When I say to a woman: 'I love you, and only you,'— I am not in the least conscious of lying to her, not even when I have spent the previous night in the arms of another." Anatol is always fully aware of the transitory nature of his "flame"; when the light of his life goes out, all that is needed to go on with is another match. He dates the death of many of his love-affairs from the very first kiss; and his mildly cynical comrade, Max, wittily explains his remorseful melancholy. "All you think of to-day is your yesterday's remorse for the sins you mean to commit to-morrow." Anatol pays the penalty for constitutional fickleness: he never believes in the constancy of the beloved. "I vow eternal constancy to her; she believes me and is happy. But I am sceptical and therefore unhappy. She loves me? — Yes, of course. She loves me to distraction; but that's quite beside the mark. She isn't true to me. While she is pressing her lips to mine, while she is stroking my hair — while we are happy together — I know that she is betraying me!"

In the *Farewell Supper*, Anatol, who has ruined his digestion by having been obliged for months past to eat two suppers every night, one with Anna, the other with the new *innamorata,* plans to break the news delicately to Anna at a little supper party for Max, Anna, and himself; but is hoist by his own petard, to Max's uncontrollable mirth, when Anna informs him that a new love has come into *her* life also. There is true tenderness in *A Christmas Present*—in which Gabrielle, the "high-born lady" who dared not give Anatol what some nameless fair vouchsafes with ready hand, sends her a nosegay with the message: "These flowers, dear little girl, are from some one who might have been as happy as you—if she hadn't been quite such a coward!" The tragi-comic element in these episodes emerges in *Question to Fate.* Anatol decides to hypnotize Cora and resolve his doubts in her answer to his unspoken thought: "Does she love me and me only?" But when the moment for revelation is at hand and Max has discreetly withdrawn, Anatol tries to ask the question — but finds that he dare not put his fate to the touch. He recalls Max, and assures him that he is entirely content with Cora's reply. But his disquiet is far from being allayed when the awakened Cora exhibits an uneasy curiosity as to the catechism! Anatol never wants the truth: he loves to cling to his illusions. But often they are shattered: as in the case of the early "Episode" with Bianca, over which Anatol rankly sentimentalizes until Bianca once again appears and cannot recall even his name; or of *Keepsakes*, in which Emily for Anatol's sake throws away all the mementos of her past save a black diamond—because it is worth a hundred pounds!—; or of *Dying Pangs*, memorable for Anatol's languishing observation: "You never so much want to be happy with a woman as when you know that you're ceasing to care for her!" When Max at last decides to marry, the break with Ilona is but preliminary to Ilona's general breaking of the furniture. But Max, whose thankless task is to divert Ilona's attention and prevent her from following Anatol to the church, calms her with the assurance that Anatol will soon be hers again, and raises her fainting spirits by the sage counsel to avenge her whole sex in the meantime upon every man she meets!

These Anatol episodes are full of grace and charm, insouciant and witty — albeit irresponsible and immoral. They deal with a society of lax Bohemianism, in which the *liaison* is a conventionality and virtue an eccentricity. With that crass and all too facile judgment, which tends to identify the author with his creations, the general public, especially in the United States, has done Schnitzler the grave injustice of associating his name solely with light fripperies on the Anatol pattern. The truth lies far from such a view; and it is important, in order to do justice to the subtle spirit and fine art of Schnitzler, to attune our ears to the deeper tones and stronger chords in the symphony of his creative work. Thus shall we discover in him, not only a dexterous artist in words, but a remarkable student of psychology, an accurate reflector of individual and social states of mind, a genuine authority as delineator of neurotic manifestations — the scientific mind in unison with the sympathetic soul.

III

So little accustomed is the great American public, despite the beneficial efforts of the little theatre, to legitimate exhibition of the one-act play, that this unique form of dramatic art remains as yet imperfectly understood and inadequately appreciated. The one-act play is not simply a long drama compressed into one act — any more than a short-story is a condensed long novel. The quintessence of the one-act play is *stimmung* — the creation of a certain mood or atmosphere. The author seeks, not to settle a problem and end a story, but to produce a certain effect. The effect is often pictorial, psychologically pictorial; we see the image of the states of mind of the individual characters wrought together into a certain complex. The effect again may be climactic, cumulative — eventuating as the outcome of a long train of antecedent circumstances; and it may well point forward to interesting developments in a curtained future. The one-act play is truly suggestive in its nature, intimating a larger drama in the background, of which we have caught only a single revealing glimpse. The significance of the one-act play is that it is pictorial; or temperamental; or focal in its imaginative tendency.

For many reasons, Schnitzler's most polished and original work is embodied in his one-act plays. Here he gives us essences, radiant nuances, rich in fragrance and color. They are seldom marked by that vagueness in purport and indirection in treatment, characteristic of certain of the longer plays. The promiscuity of man's sexual impulse is a source of perpetual interest to Schnitzler, the practising physician; in most of his works, whether short or long plays, short or long novels, the *liaison* is always present or lurking somewhere in the background. Schnitzler is never interested in the topic as such, but primarily in the mental reactions of the characters from the given situation. Other of his one-act plays deal humanely, in a large and liberal spirit, with experiences and episodes of human life carrying with them the lessons of sorrow, revealing experience, the passing of the years, and the coming of death. In these pieces we have, not the anatomist of sex, but the psychologist and philosopher. Moreover, we are frequently impressed with the technical virtuosity, the inventive ingenuity, of this deft craftsman. "As for the grotesque realism, which feels compelled to dispense with stage management or prompter," Schnitzler once lightly said: "— the realism in which we never reach the fifth act because a tile has fallen upon the hero's head in the second — well, I'm not interested in it. For my own part, I let the curtain rise where it begins to be amusing, and I let it fall at the moment I consider fit."

Three significant one-act plays, loosely united by a single underlying principle, appeared in 1898–9. Just as the bombardment of a patient's anatomy by Röntgen rays may reveal hidden obscure maladies, otherwise concealed from the eye of the physician, so the analysis of the souls of the characters with respect to their imaginative life may reveal and explicate many outward acts which seem peculiarly unmotived. In the view of Sigmund Freud, the dream is the *via regia* of the life of the soul. Schnitzler is preoccupied with a study of the interpenetration of reality and illusion, the fusion of the fact and the dream. The leading motive of the three plays —

Paracelsus, *The Mate* and *The Green Cockatoo*—is embodied in the lines from the first:

> Our life is wrought of dreams and waking, fused
> Of truth and lies. There lives no certitude.
> Of others we know naught, naught of ourselves,
> We play a part and wise is he who knows it.[1]

These plays exhibit in a strong light the powerful influence of illusions upon human life. Freud himself has accorded high praise to Schnitzler for his *Paracelsus*, because of the deep insight it affords into the spiritual mechanism of mental affections. Theophrastus Bombastus Hohenheim, self-styled Paracelsus, with all the glamour of repute as a physician who can effect miraculous cures, returns to his native city of Basel, the home of Cyprian, the Armorer, and Justina, his beautiful wife. Anselm, a gallant, pleads for an assignation with Justina — whose husband is entirely complacent in the consciousness that he has nothing to fear — "not memory, nor any moonish passion." Stung to the quick by Cyprian's scorn of him as a mere sorcerer and quack, Paracelsus, who had loved Justina in youth, hypnotizes her in demonstration of his power. Says he:

> "More than the truth, which once was and shall be,
> Is madness, that which is . . . and rules the moment."

[1] Translation of Pierre Loving.

Under the spell, Justina imagines that she has betrayed Cyprian with Anselm, and so circumstantial is her confession that Paracelsus himself is in doubt. When Cyprian's anger bursts forth at this manufactured confession of infidelity Paracelsus commands her to speak perfect truth. She confesses that she loved Paracelsus in her youth and would have given him all for the asking; and that had one more day passed without this present exercise of Parcelsus' power, she would doubtless have yielded to Anselm. Cyprian, who has been deeply chastened by this soul-scarifying experience, thus points the moral:

> A whirlwind came, who for a moment hath
> Torn open all the portals of our souls,
> And we have looked within us for a while . . .
> 'Tis over, and the portals close again —
> Yet what I saw to-day, for future time,
> Shall hold me safe from all excess of pride.
> It was a play, yet I did find its sense,
> And know that I shall keep the right road hence.[1]

The Helpmate is one of those dramas of *dévoilement* in which the veils of illusion are stripped off, one by one, from the grim, ironic facts of life. Professor Robert Pilgram consoles himself, upon the sudden death of his young and beautiful wife, with the reflection that at least he has been clear sighted enough to realize all along the fact of her *liaison*

[1] This and the preceding quotation are translations of H. B. Samuel.

with his assistant, Dr. Alfred Hausmann. For Hausmann he feels a profound pity, and with superb generosity is prepared to offer him an expression of consolation. His first disillusionment comes with Hausmann's confession that for two years he has been engaged to another woman. Revolted by this revelation of his wife's betrayal, he vents upon Hausmann his outraged feelings:

"I would have raised you from the ground if you had been broken by grief. I would have gone with you to her grave — if the woman who is lying over there had been your lover; but you have turned her into your wanton, and you have filled this house with lies and foulness right up to the roof until it makes me sick — and that's why — that's why, yes, that's why, I'm going to kick you out."

But an even more nauseous disillusion is reserved for him — on hearing from a sympathetic friend that his wife was aware all along of Hausmann's engagement, and yet readily betrayed her husband in a voluntary degradation. The while priding himself upon his clear-sighted vision, the generous souled professor now finds that he has been always enmeshed in a treacherous web of illusions.

The most brilliant and remarkable of these dramas of illusion is *The Green Cockatoo.* Here Schnitzler touches the high-water mark of technical excellence and inventive ingenuity. The play is unique without being eccentric; and while theatrical in the original sense, is tensely dramatic. It is the eve of the storming of the Bastile. Pleasure-worn nobles with their corrupt consorts sit in a brothel, transformed into a theatre situated in the most crime-infested corner of Paris, looking tolerantly on at a species of crude *revue* extemporized for their entertainment. The jaded tastes of the profligate aristocracy are thus titillated with artful simulations of vice and crime — the thrilling melodrama of the Parisian Apache. This tiny tavern turned theatre, with its nondescript troupe of mumming criminals, is a microcosm. We are stirred and thrilled, because we are momently in doubt if it is all jest or earnest, masquerade or fact, illusion or reality. Henri, the star of this revolutionary Grand Guignol, rushes madly in and confesses with marvellous verisimilitude that he has found the actress Léocadie, who became his wife only yesterday, in the arms of her lover, the Duc de Cadignan — now dead under the stroke of his dagger. Mine host — the manager of the tavern — shouts aloud his joy; for news has come of the Bastille's fall, and he can but rejoice in the death of the duke who really has made Léocadie his mistress. At this moment, the duke enters — to fall in reality beneath Henri's poignard. The Apache burlesque swings into a *finale sanglante* — the comi-tragedy within the tragi-comedy, the murder of the noble by the *bourgeois*. Thus is mirrored the wild theatricality, the mad unreality, of this fatal hour in France's history. The Revolution is on at last.

In 1900–1, Schnitzler gave precise and effective exhibition of his individual craftsmanship in a series of four striking one-act plays, grouped together under the title *Vital Moments*. In all of them, there is revealed with exceptional finesse vivid reactions of art and life, at moments of dramatic intensity. In *The Woman with the Dagger*, Remigio, the dramatist, utilizes the most intimate phases of the life of his wife, Pauline, as material for his dramas; and upon meeting her lover, Leonhard, in an Italian Renaissance picture gallery, Pauline informs him that she has confessed all to her husband who to-morrow will take her far away from this perilous obsession. As they stand there admiring an impressive picture which bears an extraordinary resemblance to Pauline — a very beautiful woman in white garments, with a dagger in her raised hand, gazing down as if upon the body of one whom she has murdered — the scene suddenly changes and the period is some centuries earlier. They are now in the studio of Master Remigio, the great painter; Pauline is seen as Paola, his wife, and Leonhard is now Lionardo, her lover. Upon the strength of the favors he has enjoyed, Lionardo claims her as his own; but she callously spurns him with the declaration that his right to her " became extinct with last night's stars." Her sincerity in caprice is proven by her forthright confession to her husband upon his sudden entrance. Remigio, who prizes his wife only for her value as a model and an inspiration of his art, coldly dismisses Lionardo with the icy words:

> Who hates can kill — he also kills who loves.
> Indifference does not touch a dagger's hilt.
> Why should I break an inoffensive glass
> From which a child has sipped forbidden draughts?
> Because the gift of consciousness was yours,
> Makes you not other than you are to me,
> A chance and pitiable instrument of fate.[1]

Thus scorned and contemptuously dismissed, Lionardo vows vengeance upon Remigio; but no sooner have the words passed his lips than Paola plunges her dagger into his throat. Enraptured by the superbly artistic and dramatic elements in this vital moment, Remigio feverishly resumes the painting of his unfinished picture, the embryonic "Woman with the Dagger," with the exclamation:

> Was this the purpose, has my prayer been heard,
> To grant me inspiration for my task?
> Yes thus — Propitious heavens, for one hour
> Vouchsafe my soul's peace, and a steady hand.[1]

Awaking from their trance, Pauline, who mystically feels that they must live out again what they have once lived through, promises to meet Leonhard that

[1] Translation of H. B. Samuel.

night. We dimly sense the tragic ending lurking in the future for the doomed Leonhard.

The little play which gives the title to this series is a gray tale instinct with stern contrasts of reckless ambition and supreme self-sacrifice — a little drama of the conflict of art and life. It is told in the retrospective manner of Ibsen — a mere conversation in which Anton Hausdorfer, a pensioned official, reveals to the ambitious young man of letters, Heinrich, that the latter's mother has committed suicide in order to free him from the burden of her support and give him the long-desired opportunity for devoting himself without trammel to literature. In reply to Anton's query: "What does all your writing come to when set over against one single living hour of your mother's life?"— Heinrich expresses the sense of his obligation to demonstrate in art that his mother had not died in vain: "Living hours? They live no longer than the last person who remembers them. It is not the meanest calling to lend such hours a permanence beyond themselves."

One of the most effective bits of naturalism that Schnitzler, the impressionist, has rescued from the purlieus of his profession is *The Last Mask*. It is chiefly interesting as a piece of pure psychology. Rademacher, the dying writer, a journalistic hack with the aspirations of a genius, sends for the famous, the admired author, Weihgast — to wreak a life's revenge. Rademacher plans to deal him a mortal blow in the revelation that, after all, the successful author has been a pitiable failure as a man — since his wife has really belonged to Rademacher. Obsessed with the vision of his triumph, Rademacher gloatingly rehearses the scene of revelation with a friend, an actor, a fellow-inmate of the hospital. When the anticipated moment arrives, Rademacher discovers that in reality Weihgast is the most unhappy of men, his art a bitter curse. Faith in wife and home alone are left him. So Rademacher foregoes his melodramatic revenge, morbidly content in its imaginative rehearsal — and dies, without malice and without regret.

The wittiest and most satirical of Schnitzler's farces is the delightful piece, happily entitled *Literature*. Margarete, a woman still attractive, but no longer quite young, is about to marry Klemens, a baron whose one idea is sport. Her passionate love of letters arouses the incorrigible jealousy of this prosaic lover, who thinks woman's first thought should be her husband. She is all but ready to make the great sacrifice; yet cherishes a longing to see just her last novel in print. This novel is a real "human document"—; for she has dexterously woven the letters, long ago received from Gilbert, a former lover, into a passionate romance. Klemens remains ignorant of all this, and even of the contents of the book. Pitiable indeed is the lady's plight when Gilbert pays her an unexpected visit, and informs her that he too has written a novel into which he has woven her letters to him. Each novel exactly dovetails with the other: discovery is inevitable. Before either Margarete or Gilbert has recovered from the shock, Klemens returns, intent upon putting his betrothed to the supreme test. He has bought up the whole edition of her novel before publication and will withdraw it from circulation — with her permission? He is delighted when she almost precipitately consents. One copy only he has reserved — to read with her in the intimacy of the fireside! "My own," rapturously exclaims the ready-witted Margarete, "I will make the supreme sacrifice"; and seizing the incriminating copy, flings it into the fire. Heaving a deep sigh of relief, Gilbert tactfully withdraws while Margarete sinks into Klemens' arms.

There is a note at once brutal and burlesque, more Berlinese than Viennese, in the three *Plays for Marionettes*, first produced in 1903 and 1904. These are little "comédies rosses," too exotic to suit Anglo-Saxon taste — instinct with the blatant humor of Punch and Judy. Again Schnitzler pricks the bubble of illusion, reveals life's little ironies, and exhibits the strange intermingling, the confusing contrasts, of chance, of fiction, of reality. There is Schnitzler's habitual irony in "The Puppet Player"— an irony which reveals itself to George Merklin, who discovers in middle life that in lightly tampering with human souls, he has gambled away his own happiness. Anna, his sweetheart, fell in with George's joke and pretended love for Edward, a timid musician,— hoping thereby to arouse George's jealousy. Years afterward George, who has become a mere vagabond with a futile philosophy of inaction, is encountered by Edward who takes George to his home, now happily presided over by Anna, his wife and the mother of his son. Life has capped George's joke with one even more ironic. *The Gallant Cassian* is a melodrama in crude burlesque. We see Martin, vainglorious in the fancied discovery of a sure mode of winning at dice, preparing to desert his faithful mistress, Sophie, and seek fortune and love out in the great world. His treachery proves his final undoing; and to the gallant Cassian, his cousin, who has first lost all his money to Martin but has paid homage to Sophie's devotion, Martin loses all — fortune, love, life. In *The Great Puppet Show*, by means of a scene of broad comedy, Schnitzler reveals some amusing juxtapositions of life and art. The technic is that employed in *The Green Cockatoo:* we scarcely can distinguish between the comments of the spectators and the lines of the actors in this puppet-show. The colloquy between the manager and the poet exhibits Schnitzler's outlook. The Manager says: "Your whole piece is shaky. It ought to have wound up with the prize-fighter." When the poet asserts that the prize-fighter hasn't anything really to do with the play, the manager crushingly retorts: "The only good things in your play anyhow are the things that haven't anything to do with it."

The most recent of Schnitzler's plays in the characteristic one-act form appeared in 1915 under the title, *Comedies of Words*. They are aptly entitled, since each deals with subtle nuances of hidden feeling, hinted at through conversations which play lightly on the surface. Words like these, designed to conceal thought, defeat their purpose by revealing the underlying meanings of those who utter them. In *The Hour of Recognition*, one of the characters, evidently a disciple of Freud, hazards the belief that the deepest recesses of the soul are "probably situated where our subconscious wishes slumber or give the appearance of slumbering." The hour of recognition comes when the husband, who has always known of an early infidelity of his wife, allows his wish to reveal this knowledge, which has slumbered for ten years, to be realized. His revenge is complete; for with love gone forever and home in ruins, she goes out into the night and into oblivion. *The Big Scene* is one of those brilliant *genre* pictures of the artistic temperament and the philandering instinct, for which Herman Bahr is so justly famous. Conrad Herbot, the clever actor, carries over the rôle into every moment of his real life; and with infinite naïveté, explains to his grossly humiliated wife the clever piece of acting by which he has evaded the consequences of his latest affair. Self respect commands her to leave him; but so absolute is his dependence upon her, his faith in her admiration and sympathy, that she takes up once again the task of acting as balance wheel for his volatile, childlike nature. *The Festival of Bacchus* is a scene at a railway station — the flight of wife and lover arrested by the arrival of the husband. All play cautiously at cross-purposes; the words they utter, for the most part banal, barely suffice to veil the real meanings which underlie them. With diplomatic finesse, the easy assumption that everything is quite as usual, the husband wins the day; and the lover is forced to resign the lady to her husband, whose clever struggle has won her love. The *Festival of Bacchus* as seldom tempts to final revolt to-day against the security of wedlock as in the days of antiquity. All of these plays testify to Schnitzler's rare gifts as an impressionist; the struggle rarely reaches the pitch of real conflict, because of the modern tendency to shrink from scenes, to veil one's deepest thoughts and one's most powerful emotions in an artfully designed fabric of words. In each we see the culmination of a series of antecedent events; yet it is a note of Schnitzler's art that the *dénouement* seldom confirms one's anticipations. His characters follow their own deepest instincts;

they do not act in accordance with conventional pre-suppositions.

IV

Arthur Schnitzler is an artist who celebrates "the moment and the moment's monument." His finest, most delicate work has been done in the form of the one-act play, fittest vehicle for mood, temperament and atmosphere. His art is impressionistic, suggestive, fragile—instinct with feminine grace and intuition, lightly satirical, softly melancholy. It is Wilde fortified with Ibsen, Vienna crossed with Paris.

Arthur Schnitzler is a temperament, an original—individual and unique. Without futile compunction or stern social homily, he whirls us away into a region where art is the most archly mocking of the muses. Singular as it may seem, the chief value of his plays is historical. The charming, decadent society of pre-war Vienna: Versailles has blown it all away. But it lives and will forever live in the comedies of Schnitzler. Beneath the surface gaiety of his art, a mirror of the gay, frivolous life of the Austrian capital, lurks a prevision of social tragedy, a suggestion of the lower depths of modern irresponsibility. In his more thoughtful and elaborate works, both fiction and drama, streams the full current of the ironic social consciousness, typical of to-day—the consciousness that liberality of judgment is the only workable standard for the appraisal of human character; and that moral rigidity, without kindly concession to human frailty, rides too often only to destruction. The closing passage of *Doctor Bernhardi* fully describes the viewpoint of one fully cognizant of the dangerous instability of modern social ethics:

Winkler: . . . We both do not feel ready to go to the bitter end and risk all, even our life, for our convictions. That is why the only decent thing for us to do, is not to mix in such matters. There is nothing in it. . . .

Bernhardi: But you forget that I did not want to solve a problem. I only did what I considered right in a special case.

Winkler: That was just the mistake you made. If one always did the right thing—that is, in the abstract sense—began early in the morning and continued to do so all day long, without taking into consideration the surrounding circumstances, one would surely land in jail before nightfall.

Bernhardi: And let me tell you, my dear friend, you would have acted exactly as I did.

Winkler: Possibly—and then I would have been—excuse me—just such a fool as you.

Some years ago I picked up a copy of the Vienna *Zeit* and read this confession of Bernard Shaw:

"In my plays you will not be teased and plagued with happiness, goodness and virtue, or with crime and romance, or, indeed, with any senseless thing of that sort: My plays have only one subject: Life; and only one attribute: Interest in Life."

Shaw was thus holding out to nonchalant, pleasure-loving Vienna the very bait with which Schnitzler has so often lured that same public into the theatre. In many of his plays the old criterion of "action" no longer obtains. We are not interested in what the people do; we are only incidentally interested in what the people say. Our fancy is intrigued, our interest charmed by their individual emotional reactions from the conjunctions and collisions which transpire in their temperamental existences. Nor does Schnitzler rivet our attention upon a given problem of social responsibility primarily for the sake of the problem itself; he is only concerned with gracefully ensnaring our interest in the manner and style with which the problem is handled—or evaded! —by certain characters clear-cut as cameos. The issue, delicately poised, is balanced before us with esthetic dexterity; and the many facets of its implication are mirrored in the dramatic characters. We are not shown the many consequences of a dramatic situation; we are shown the situation from various points of view. Schnitzler is a remarkable technical executant—essentially of the school of Shaw, Strindberg, Barker, and Tchekov. In dramatic structure his plays are castles in the air; there is no trace of the mortar or the nails. Schnitzler is a dramatic miniaturist, with a tiny field of view; but this tiny field is a segmental picture of a society's essence and a life's immensity.

The characteristic heroine of Schnitzler's dramas is *das susse Mädel*—a phrase coined by Hartleben, but a type perfected by Schnitzler. She is the "dear girl" comically embodied in the business man's typist, inhabiting that twilight zone between respectable domesticity and the half-world. Anatol says somewhere:

"She's like a waltz—sentimental gaiety—smiling, mischievous, melancholy. Peace and content stream from her to you—if you take her a bunch of violets a teardrop glistens in the corner of her eye."

As *Anatol* is the comedy of *das susse Mädel*, so *Das Maerchen*, *Das Vermaechtniss*, and *Liebelei* are her tragedy. In this gay Viennese existence, "imperfectly monogamous" in Howells' happy phrase, there is always a place for this "*kleines, susses, blondes Kopferl.*"

The theme of the "woman with a past" has been a fundamental note in Schnitzler's art from the outset of his career as a dramatist. *The Fairy Tale*, a badly executed, sprawling play, with a host of superfluous characters, was condemned by the public as an exhibition of cynicism bordering on madness, the work of a gifted dilettante. It is a tragi-comic exposure of a theoretical social philosopher, a man whose avowed principles crumble beneath the assault of his feelings. Is it possible to rescue the "woman with a past" who is animated with a sincere aspiration towards "respectability"? Young Fanny Theren, lacking the firm discipline of a wise mother, has passed unscathed through two *liaisons;* and is beginning a promising stage career. A young man to whom she is attracted, Fedor Denner, unequivocally announces during a reception at her mother's home that the irrevocable doom of the "fallen woman" is a "fairy tale" spun by our prejudices. He declares himself the champion of this type of woman:

> "I am not speaking of the woman who sells herself or throws herself away—but what right have we to outlaw everyone who has had the courage to love some one before *we* happened to come upon the scene?"

Strengthened by this championship, Fanny wins new triumphs on the stage and feels herself more closely drawn to Fedor. Genuinely attracted by the charming Fanny, Fedor finds his budding love taking the form of a brooding jealousy of the past. For all Fanny's devotion and endearments, for all his avowedly liberal views, Fedor becomes so obsessed with the consciousness of Fanny's past that his love breaks under the test. Emotion shamelessly triumphs over intellect. The self-torture of his sensitivity reduces to absurdity the superficial tenets of his social philosophy.

A deeper study of the same theme, viewed from the standpoint of the famly, is *The Legacy*. What are the cardinal virtues, Schnitzler subtly asks: pity, generosity, sympathy; or propriety, respectability, social conformity? Hugo Losatti, a young man of charming personality, is thrown from his horse and fatally injured. Before he dies he extorts from his family a promise that his mistress Toni and their four-year-old son Franzl shall be welcomed in the home and protected by his family. The promise is kept, but the result produces alarming reverberations in the souls of the Losatti family. Hugo's father, a professor and national representative, has the view of the "average sensual man;" he does not condemn his son for having a mistress, but is overwhelmed by the discovery that he loves her with a beautiful devotion. Franziska, who passionately loved her brother Hugo, breaks off her engagement with Dr. Schmidt when she discovers the cheap philistinism of his character. The situation is impatiently borne by the family until the sudden death of little Franzl: the one vital link between the bereaved parents and the lamented son. The friendless, shy, sweet-natured, but frail Toni is now cast off; the family will provide for her elsewhere. Overwhelmed by her double loss and the cruel, inhuman treatment of the Losattis, Toni escapes life's heartlessness in the "cool, enfolding arms of death." The meaning of this moving drama is voiced by the high-spirited loyal Franziska:

> "We have been cowardly, Mamma; we didn't dare love her as she deserved. We were merciful—think of it, *we* merciful! When all we needed to do was to be—just kind."

Light o' Love, Schnitzler's most famous play, embodies the essential tragedy of the fair and frail. Christine has been brought up by her old father. He has grown wisely tolerant after seeing his own sister, whom he had shielded in cloistered purity, die a spinster and a stranger to joy. One day Christine is introduced by her friend, Mizi, to Fritz Lobheimer, a young and wealthy student. This meeting has been engineered by Mizi's protector, Theodore Kaiser, who wishes to rescue his friend Fritz from a dangerous intrigue with a fascinating and beautiful married woman. Christine's father, who, as he says "has protected her from all dangers—and from all happiness!"—refuses to interfere with the *liaison.* While Christine is informed that the relationship is a temporary one, she idolizes Fritz, whom she calls "her God, her bliss of Heaven;" and deludes herself with the happy fancy that their affair will be permanent. Soothed by the blandishments of the innocent and tender Christine, Fritz gradually divines the sweetness of her nature. But for him the hour of fate has struck; the betrayed husband lays a snare for him and challenges him to a duel. Before the duel he visits Christine and tenderly bids her farewell, though telling her nothing of the coming duel. Not until two days later does Christine learn the scarifying truth. *Her* Fritz has been killed by the outraged husband in a duel over *another woman!* Floods in full upon Christine the consciousness that to Fritz she was not a passion, but only a pastime. The quintessence of the tragedy of her type is expressed in the anguished cry: "What then am I?" Even the privilege of the last rites over her lover are denied her; for Fritz is already in his grave when the news of his death is broken to her. Her despairing flight into the darkness of desolation and death upon his grave is Schnitzler's tragic reading of a social riddle that marks the thought of our time.

In *Free Game* Schnitzler has embalmed in classic satire the common-sense view of the folly and wickedness of dueling. Anna Riedel, a talented actress, runs counter to all the traditions of her profession by repelling the advances of the rakes who flock about her. Even her manager cynically voices his astonishment at her violation of tradition. Rönning, a painter, sincerely loves her and wishes to marry her. Karinski, an army officer, seeks to debauch her; and when his failure is publicly acknowledged, a faint smile on Rönning's face provokes a quarrel, in which Rönning slaps Karinski violently in the face. A challenge to a duel is immediately sent Rönning by Karinski, but Rönning, to the consternation of all his friends, declines to fight a duel on principle. According to the *code duello*, Karinski's honor is forfeited; and he has no alternative, to "save his honor," but to shoot Rönning on sight. Although warned by his friends to leave, and although Anna, not loving him, offers to go away with him in order to save his life, Rönning, with curious obstinacy, refuses to budge. The result is a duel *à l'Américaine:* "shoot on sight"—and Rönning is killed. Never did the institution of dueling receive a more biting condemnation. This vicious by-product of militarism is destined to pass, no doubt, with the passing of the artificial and false system which fostered it.

The Lonely Way, heavy with the weight of intimate experience of human life, has about it an Ibsen note of prevailing gloom but lacks the close-woven structure of the great Norwegian's plays. The lonely way is the road to death—in Sala's words:

"The process of growing old must needs be a lonely one to our kind."

Sala is a hedonist of the familiar type, depicted in the sentiment:

"I hold that one has the right to drain one's own life to the last drop, with all the horrors that may lie hidden at the bottom of it."

But in reality Sala is haunted by a childish fear of death; and voices a familiar thought of Schnitzler: "Is there ever a blissful moment in any decent man's life when he can think of anything else in his inmost soul than death?" In striking contrast to the hedonist type with Bohemian soul is the amusingly outspoken Reumann, who speaks with the accents of Schnitzler himself:

"To be frank, Madam, my deepest longing is to be a rascal, a scamp who deceives, seduces, scoffs, and strides along his corpse-strewn way. But I am doomed by my temperament to be a respectable man, and what is still more painful, to have to hear from everybody that I am."

Amid the tangle of life's threads in this singular drama, a leading motive is the relation of Felix, a natural son, to his father, Fichtner, who, before Felix's birth, had deserted his mother. When Felix had grown to manhood the lonely Fichtner returns to Vienna and reveals to Felix the secret of his parenthood. But Felix greets the renegade but repentant father with complete indifference—retaining the full measure of devotion of a son to Wegrath, his foster father, who had married his mother and reared him with love and tenderness. The curtain of the third act is overwhelming:

Julian: Whatever you may feel of doubt or confusion, the truth has now been revealed to you once for all. Thus your mother willed it, and it is no longer possible for you to forget that you are my son.

Felix: Your son . . . That's nothing but a word. And it's cried in a desert. Although I'm looking at you now, and although I know that I am your son, I can't grasp it.

Julian: Felix . . . !

Felix: Since I learned of this you have become a stranger to me.

A more subtle and more acute study of souls is found in *The Interlude*, a complex treatment of the quadrangle besides which the vaunted problems of the triangle are simplicity itself. Victor Amadeus, famous pianist, and his wife, Cecilia, popular prima donna, enter into a thoroughly modern matrimonial compact: each to leave the other perfect amatory freedom. Victor becomes infatuated with a countess; Cecilia flirts outrageously with a prince. But there remains no happiness for the sophisticated pair of reunited philanderers after their *liaisons* begin to pall. The temperamental dilemma is a stroke of the finest art of the theatre; Cecilia is unable to trust again in Victor's constancy; nor for the future can she ever be sure of the fidelity of her own instincts. And so, though loving each other in their hearts, they part mutually estranged—a shrewd vindication this, of the conventional standards of marriage, a satire on the erotic vagaries of ultramodernity. Their failure, as Cecilia clearly divines, was in their complacent acceptance of a status of mutual infidelity.

"If each of us had then flung his scorn, his bitterness, his despair into the face of the other one, instead of trying to appear self-controlled and superior—then we should have been honest—which, as it was, we were not."

Countess Mizzi is redolent of a charm thoroughly Viennese. It reveals Schnitzler in his happiest mood. At bottom, he seems to say, social distinctions are artificial; the human relationships lie deeper than all class distinctions. The satirical subtitle is *The Family Reunion*, for on this day are brought together Count Arpad, his mistress of eighteen years duration, now about to marry a captivating transfer man, the Count's daughter, Mizzi, the lover of her youth, Prince Egon, and their illegitimate son. At the time of their *liaison* family considerations forbade the marriage of Egon and Mizzi; and after these obstacles were removed Egon repeatedly sought Mizzi's hand in vain. On this strange day of reunion, Mizzi finally consents to marry Egon, for the sake of her son Philip, whom Egon introduces as her son by a former marriage. So Mizzi gracefully becomes in the eyes of the world the stepmother of her own long-lost love child. The story is told with all the finished charm of the artist-magician in whose make-up there is much of feminine finesse and intuition. No moral purpose, no deep intention obtrudes here; the only intent is that of the artist to paint a graceful picture with comic lights, clear middle distances, and the shadows of sweet and haunting melancholy. "Our good physician knows his Austria better than we do," observed the late Percival Pollard. "He is content to heal its body and dissect its soul; he knows better than to try more than that."

In *The Call of Life*, which at the moment of writing is being produced by the Actor's Theatre in New York, there is great complexity of motive, a close entanglement of the destinies of many people. The play essentially concentrates interest about the fate of Marie, the lovely daughter of the repulsive old Moser, a former military officer. Thirty years before the opening of the play the Blue Hussars have ignominiously fled from the front, its *moral* shaken by Moser who answers "the call of life." As a bedridden invalid he explains to his daughter:

> "I wanted to live—to live like others. I wanted to have a wife and children and love. And so I rushed from the field; and so it has happened that the young men I don't know are going to their death and that I still live on at seventy-nine and shall survive them all—all—all."

The Blue Hussars, to wipe out the stain of their former flight, are off for the war—resolved to die in the "forefront of the hottest battle." With them goes young Max, Marie's lover.

During his married life, Moser has treated his wife and his daughter, Marie, with the greatest cruelty and selfishness. Marie, in turn, answering the call of life, pours poison into her father's medicine in order to induce Max to desert his company on the eve of battle and flee with her. While concealed in Max's room, she witnesses a dreadful scene—first between Max and his Major's wife with whom he has had an affair, interrupted by the unexpected entrance of the Major, who shoots his unfaithful wife dead. Marie pleads with Max to flee with her; and on his refusal, to die with her; but he chooses to take his life beside the woman he has betrayed. Through the skill of Dr. Schnitzler, who deeply loves Marie, suspicion of her father's murder is diverted from Marie; but she suffers unutterable tortures of conscience.

"What sort of creature am I, to emerge out of such an experience as out of a bad dream—awake—and living—and wanting to live?"

It is not life—but selfish pleasure, self-gratification—that all have sought in vain: Moser, Max, the Major's wife, Marie. The higher existence—life in its best sense—is something greater, austerer, more august, than mere achievement of our selfish wishes, purposes, desires. The clear-toned moral of the piece sounds in the kindly encouragement which Schnitzler gives Marie:

"Who knows but that later—far later—from a day like the present one, the call of life will ring out upon your life in far deeper and purer tones than on that other day when you have experienced things that have such terrible and blasting names as Love and Death."

It is Schnitzler's peculiar gift to exhibit delicacy in treatment of the indelicate, refinement in portrayal of the unrefined. The stark exposure of the mechanics of sex, a series of ten dialogues privately printed and distributed among his friends, is *Roundels*, written in 1906-1907. It is a work of frank naturalism, a vicious circle of adultery, artistically written by a physician who finds "the Colonel's lady and Judy O'Grady sisters under the skin." It is the last word in coldblooded suggestiveness, this cycle of dialogues: a prostitute and a soldier; the soldier and a chambermaid; the chambermaid and a young gentleman; the young gentleman and a young married woman; the young married woman and her husband; the husband and a young girl; the young girl and a poet; the poet and an actress; the actress and a count; and lastly the count and the prostitute of the first dialogue. Each dialogue, culminating in the identical episode of passion, delineates with extraordinary skill the social differences in the principals contrasted with the fundamental identity of the action. It is a depressing study of the human animal degrading love in promiscuity: the flaming of man's passion, the woman's shrinking, the man's subsequent reaction of distaste, the woman's tenderness and dread. This *danse macabre* was surely never meant for the stage; yet it has been produced in both Germany and Austria. At the *Kleines Schauspielhaus* in Berlin (December 23, 1920) it enjoyed quite a run, although several times interrupted by public demonstrations of protest; but in Vienna the banning of the play in February, 1921, precipitated a tremendous uproar, with excited discussion in the Austrian Federal Parliament and Vienna's Provincial Parliament. The Austrian Minister of the Interior banned further productions in Vienna; but the issue was by no means a wholly moral one, as the attack on the play was anti-Semitic in tone, being led by the Christian Socialist party. The play was threatened production by the Green Room Club in New York City in March, 1923; but the opposition to its production became so pronounced from many quarters that the matter ended with a private reading. *Roundels* is an unveiled study of the sex impulse traced with subtle art through its varying manifestations in different ranks of society. It is suited, not for the stage, but for the medical clinic. Such a work, though for reasons poles apart, might intrigue the fancy of the artist and titillate the taste of the pullman-car drummer. *Honi soit qui mal y pense.*

In Schnitzler, we habitually find traits of character, quirks of temperament, fascinating by reason of their unnaturalness. The figures in his finest plays are extraordinarily self-revealing, disclosing in intimate speech the deeper springs of motive and impulse. This peculiarity of his genius is nowhere better exhibited than in *The Vast Domain*, a study in infidelity and jealousy. Friedrich Hofreiter, who believes in absolute freedom in matters of sex, persuades himself that their friend, Korsakov, has taken his life because of thwarted love for his wife, Genia. Under the challenge of his suspicions, Genia shows him a last letter from Korsakov fully confirming them. Far from taking the conventional romantic view, Friedrich is alienated from Genia by her constancy:

"Of course you are innocent—in both senses—another man than I would likely kneel before you, worship you—like a saint—on that very account. You see that I'm different . . . To me you have become, through that very thing . . . much more distant."

To Friedrich, Genia's virtue is so little a thing beside the death of Korsakov that he feels instinctively deep regret that she has been loyal to him!

"And you see this thought—that something or other, something which is in reality nothing, a shadow, a phantom, a nullity, at least when weighed against so terrible, so irreparable a thing as death—that your virtue has driven a man to death, that is to me simply ghastly."

To Genia, who is dumbfounded by his confession, Friedrich confesses:

"I hope you won't hold it against me that, in compliance with your wish, I have said all this so plainly. So plainly that it has almost ceased to be true."

In his materialistic, grossly selfish soul, Friedrich feels as if, through her fidelity and virtue, Genia were "playing up" Korsakov's suicide against him mentally—to establish a permanent claim on his own fidelity. For the first time understanding the grossness of her husband's soul, Genia sees that her virtue has only set them further apart; and on the rebound yields to the advances of an ardent lover, much younger than herself, Otto, for whom she feels only a sort of protective tenderness. Friedrich likewise turns to another, Ena, a fascinating, daring young girl much his junior. When he discovers that Genia has been faithless to him, he pretends that the discovery relieves him of a sense of guilt, but actually his frail philosophy of *laissez faire* in sex matters is blown away by a brainstorm of jealousy. He challenges Otto to a duel, and kills him. To Genia's cry of loathing, "vain, gruesome monster," Friedrich calmly replies that it isn't so simple as all that; it was two men fighting like primitive savages over a woman. The keynote of the piece is sounded in the words of Aigner, a confirmed rake and hedonist, who tries to explain such souls as Friedrich's and his own:

"Hasn't it occurred to you what complex beings we human creatures are at bottom? There is so much that finds space in us at the same time. Love and deceit, fidelity and faithlessness, worship for one and longing for another or for several. We attempt to establish order within ourselves, as well as we can, but this order remains an artificial thing. The natural condition is chaos. Yes, my good Hofreiter, the soul—is a vast domain. . . ."

The Veil of Beatrice, a Renaissance drama rich in color and imagination, presents in intricate relationships the theme of love and death. It might have been written to embody in dramatic form Maeterlinck's idea of fate: the intimate relationship of events in the external world with the movements of spiritual consciousness. Schnitzler, a deep student of Freudian theories, here exhibits the working out to their tragic consequences the realization of suppressed desires figured forth in a dream. The young

Beatrice Nardi, beloved of Filippo Loschi, the poet, dreams that Duke Leonardo Bentivoglio, the master of Bologna, has made her his bride—to whom the whole city bows in submission. It is the year 1500. Bologna is besieged by Cesare Borgia, and Duke Leonardo expects the city to fall on the morrow. When Filippo hears from the lips of Beatrice the story of her dream he interprets it as a symbol of her longing for its realization, and gives her up, although they had planned to flee the city together that night. Anticipating the fall of Bologna with all the horrors of pillage, sack, and rapine, the Duke resolves to spend his last night with the city's most beautiful woman—Beatrice. On making her his bride he gives her as bridal gift a wedding veil. But youth and love speak in Beatrice; and at the height of the wedding festivities, she flees to her lover Filippo. They make a suicide pact; but she violates it and flees from her lover's corpse back to the Duke and to life. But the Duke, discovering the absence of the bridal veil, threatens her with death unless she leads him to the place where it was lost. Once more, in a blind longing for life, she yields —to the horror of the Duke, overwhelmed by the tragedy and by the infidelity of Beatrice to the brilliant and beloved Filippo. Convicted by her own conscience, she begs the Duke to kill her; but although the Duke refuses, her wish is granted—her brother, Francesco, striking the fatal blow in obedience to his long-cherished purpose to save her from the degenerating influences of her family and of the time.

This is the play of a mystic, who sees fate as the fulfillment of the primal urge of our own natures. Shall we see in Beatrice the vacillating, capricious, faithless spirit of the light o' love? Or shall we divine in her only the volatile irresponsibility of youth, with the immature character of one actuated solely by the passionate longing for life? The past gives no answer, but perhaps we may read the riddle in the sorrowful and understanding words of the Duke:

Wast thou not Beatrice, a simple child,
That played with crown and throne because they glittered,
And with a poet's soul because mysterious,
And with a stripling's heart, because forsooth
'Twas given thee? But we are too severe
And suffer 't not, and each of us demanded
Not only that he be the only plaything—more,
The world and all to thee. And thee we chid
A traitress, wicked—and thou wast a child![1]

The Young Medardus, like *The Veil of Beatrice*, is another tragedy of the immature, the unfulfilled. There is meaning in the descriptive adjective "young." The play is a wonderfully realistic picture of old Vienna in the days of Napoleon; and registers the peak of Schnitzler's attainments as a historical dramatist. Owing to the refusal of the old Duke of Valois to permit his son to marry the lovely Agatha Klahr, daughter of a book dealer, her brother Medardus vows vengeance upon the Valois family. He intends to seduce Helene, the daughter of the old Duke; and then

[1] Translation of Bayard Quincy Morgan.

destroy her reputation by revealing the truth. But his heart plays him false; for he falls a victim to the enchantments of Helene.

The old Duke of Valois had long cherished the hope of winning the French crown; and now Helene secretly plans to murder Napoleon, in the privacy of the boudoir—to which she is to go as his pretended mistress. Medardus, too, plans to rid Austria of her oppressor; but encountering Helene, whom he hears has become Napoleon's mistress, on her way to the assignation, forgets Napoleon and kills Helene in a terrible outburst of rage and jealousy. Although Napoleon offers Medardus clemency because he has saved his life, Medardus declines to hide the truth—and goes bravely to his execution, in expiation of the death of his father, an Austrian officer, who had been ingloriously killed. Such an outline conveys no notion of the brilliancy, richly filled canvas, and admirable portraits, some taken from life, of this extraordinary play. Certain features render this play notable. As in Joseph Conrad's unfinished novel, *Suspense*, the motor influence of the play, Napoleon, for all the shadows of his presence, is never seen. And also, as Specht has pointed out, Schnitzler has shown the most astonishing skill in putting into the mouths of the representatives of the various classes and nationalities the language perfectly indicative of their separate stations. In a word, this is no recension from antique tomes but a true and vivid picture of the times —the "most Austrian of all of Schnitzler's works."

Schnitzler's boldest and most universal drama is

Professor Bernhardi, a play in five acts. In certain of his other plays an accurate knowledge of pathological symptoms reinforced by psychological insight of a high order imparts a callous, almost inhuman lightness to his treatment of human suffering and frailty. In *Professor Bernhardi* he gives us a drama devoid of the hallowing influences of love, the perturbing impulses of sex. A comparatively simple incident becomes the center of ever-widening circles of dramatic import. In the event we have a sharp conflict between Jewry and Catholicism, between science and religion. The play which might well delight the author of *The Doctor's Dilemma*, contains only one woman's rôle —the nurse, who speaks but a few lines in the first act. Fourteen physicians, a politician and a priest, constitute the stage *dramatis personæ*. Adhering to the rigid standards of the physician and the fixed ethics of the medical profession, Bernhardi refuses to consider the claims of society or of orthodox religion when they conflict with what he regards his professional duty. A young Catholic girl is in Bernhardi's hospital, lying at the point of death; and in her last hours she cherishes the delusion of her speedy recovery. In a state of absolute euphoria, she feels perfectly happy; and Bernhardi refuses admittance to the Roman Catholic priest who, in order to give her absolution, desires to wake her out of her last happy moments to a brief conscious state of terrible suffering and torturing pangs of conscience. In barring the way Bernhardi lightly touches the priest on the shoulder; and in the course of the altercation which ensues, the patient expires.

This incident, which soon gives rise to a *cause célèbre* in Austria, after the model of *l' Affaire Dreyfus* in France, produces the bitter and dramatic struggle of the play. Animated by varying motives—racial feeling, professional ethics, religion, casuistry, political expediency, ambition, prejudice, envy, what not—the various characters betray the resolute Bernhardi, and he is convicted and sentenced to prison. After his release from prison he discovers, to his unfeigned disgust, that he has become a popular idol and his case the rallying point of political parties. At least he has the consolation of knowing that the nurse whose evidence convicted him has made confession of her perjury; and likewise the priest acknowledges that for reasons of conscience he concealed the truth and permitted Bernhardi to go to prison! Although Bernhardi asseverates that his only desire was to do what he considered right in a particular case, he is assured by one of his friends:

"You, Bernhardi, lack the eye for that which really counts, the universal view-point. For it is not the question whether you do right here and do right there, but whether you accomplish really big things. And to give up the possibility of doing some really big things for the poor miserable satisfaction of having done the right thing in some non-essential, some unimportant matter, is a matter of indifference to me, I must confess, and does not only seem small, but unmoral, yes, unmoral to me, my dear Bernhardi."

This vivid, interesting play ends in the quietest, most undramatic way; Schnitzler cares nothing for a "curtain." Into it he has put the fundamental convictions of a great profession. Those who see in it an attack upon Judaism, an assault upon the Church, or an exposure of the medical profession, lose sight of the fact that Schnitzler is only concerned with a dramatic problem. The problem of the physician's responsibility in matters of life and death, clearly indicated here in a particular case, is becoming steadily more difficult and acute. Law courts are to-day with increasing frequency having to decide upon the guilt or innocence of doctors who deliberately put out of their misery patients who are incurable. The ethics of the medical profession are constantly undergoing drastic revision, with a consequent influence upon and inevitable modification of the laws governing the doctor's responsibility.

Schnitzler is so versatile, flinging off now novel, now drama, now short story in such unexpected variety, that it may be difficult for posterity to place him in his proper niche. The novels he has written during recent years, in particular *Dr. Graesler* and *Fraulein Else*, have quite overtopped in interest and importance the dramas produced since *Dr. Bernhardi*. In the comedy of journalism, *Fink und Fliederbusch*, Schnitzler has indulged in sheer fantasy: the story of a journalist animated by varying convictions, a sort of newspaper Jekyll and Hyde, who finally is driven by his colleagues to challenge his opponent (himself) to a duel. Although there is much sparkling of wit and some amusing scenes, Schnitzler here, like his own twin-natured original, has reduced himself to absurdity.

In his last two plays, Schnitzler deals with themes which have often intrigued him in the past: the humors of betrayal in love, the comic mistake of identity which Boccaccio so often employed to excellent effect. In *Die Schwestern*, Casanova plays a typical rôle already prefigured in Schnitzler's brilliant *novelle*, *Casanova's Homecoming*. This irresistible Don Juan steals by night into the wrong room and enjoys a *bonne fortune* with an unknown who is not expecting him, while the fair one he has actually chosen keeps an assignation in vain. The amazed recipient of Casanova's favor later relates the astounding happening to her lover, who indulges in an outburst of rage and shame—until he hears the consolatory information that Casanova was wholly unaware of the identity of his innocent victim. When the two fair ladies ultimately contend for Casanova's favor, the play dissolves into a farce of gossamer lightness, to peals of merriment. This is a play of very limited appeal; and certainly adds nothing to Schnitzler's reputation as a dramatist. A later play, entitled *The Comedy of Seduction*, is written in a similar vein—the young seducer, who has none of the magic of a Casanova, always luckily happening along when the damsel of his choice has just determined to give herself to the first man who appears!

V

Richard Specht has painted a charming picture of the young Schnitzler: a poetic head of fine and rare beauty; smooth, white forehead, surmounted with a shimmering mass of golden brown hair; carefully cut gold-blond beard; deep gold-hazel eyes, lighting up with a flashing, in-looking glance; kindly, gracious mouth and aristocratic nose; the finely modeled head of an artist and devotee of luxury.

Bohemia was his world, that realm of artists and singers who visited his father's office. The smoothness and bland insouciance of his plays is the acquired tone of the Old Vienna Burg Theatre, a haunt of his youth. In some of his finest characters may be divined, by the discerning, features of stage heroes of the day—Adolf Sonnenthal, Ernst Hartmann, and Josef Kainz.

With this coloring of Bohemianism and estheticism went the sterner attributes of medical practice and clinical research. Each profession has its own rhythm; every *metier* its own peculiar art quality. Schnitzler early revealed the dominant tone of the physician. To say that he is now Anatol, now Bernhardi, is to miss the point; he has at once the liberality and compassion of the family physician combined with the *garçonnerie* and *gaminerie* of the esthete. If there is something of the "bedside manner" in many of his figures, especially the frequently recurring figure of the physician, there is a large measure of high gaiety and spiritual frivolity in the tone of many of the characters he uses as foils. Schnitzler is a physician no less of the body than of the souls of his dramatic characters. He is unique in dramatic history as the only professional physician who ever won international fame as a dramatist.

Schnitzler is a dramatist of character rather than of action, though there is no dearth of external happenings in his plays. Deeds of violence occur never for their own sake; they take place in order to reveal the souls of the characters. Schnitzler's plays constitute a remarkable picture of a changing race and a decadent society, on the eve of a supreme national *débâcle*. Yet there is no reason to believe that any such purpose was uppermost in his mind in writing these dramas. His interest, assuredly, was to reveal strange aspects, hidden peculiarities, abnormal quirks, and hitherto unsuspected traits of character, under the stress of soul-stirring experiences. His characters converse in a language of superfrankness, of magnified veracity. Under the deft hands of their creator, the foremost disciple of Freudism in drama, the characters naïvely unmask their suppressed desires and hidden soul secrets.

In Schnitzler there is comparatively little of the social reformer. He seeks to paint things as they are; but he evidently does not conceive it to be the drama's function to attempt to remake the world. He gives us a sense of the strangeness of life, the loneliness of each one of us, the urge of sex restrained by the immanent dread of dissolution. The philosophy of his most reflective characters is a stoical self-dependence, a liberty of soul. "Suppose we were always attended by a train of bacchantes—nevertheless we should have to tread the downward path alone . . . and he is nothing but a fool who doesn't in time prepare himself against having to rely on any human being." The merriness of to-day never hides the lowering tragedy of to-morrow.

Arthur Schnitzler is a dramatist whose genius flares into higher intensity the more circumscribed the area within which he works. It is the art of focal concentration. His mood is impressionistic, his touch delicate but sure, his work instinct with feminism, grace, and intuition, lightly satirical, softly melancholy. It is Wilde fortified with Ibsen, Vienna crossed with Paris.

JOHN GALSWORTHY

"The only things vital in drama, as in every art, are achieved when the maker has fixed his soul on the making of a thing that shall seem fine to himself. . . . Sincerity bars out no themes—it only demands that the dramatist's moods and visions should be intense enough to keep him absorbed; that he should have something to say so engrossing to himself that he has no need to stray here and there and gather purple plums to eke out what was intended for an apple tart."

John Galsworthy: *The New Spirit in the Drama.*

JOHN GALSWORTHY

The charm of Galsworthy, distinguished novelist and competent man of letters, prompts the query whether his extraordinary versatility and creative facility constitute a fatality. As an essayist he utters his lucid thoughts with hard clarity and a certain dry, supercilious wit. As a short-story writer, he exhibits subtle observation, a conventional touch of mannered humanism, and at times a banal strain of sheer melodrama. But his passion and his sympathy, when given full rein, enable him to plumb the depths and soar to heights reached only by the favored of the muses. As a poet he follows after George Meredith; the austerities of life meet his piercing gaze and find in him a philosophic interpreter. But the lyric spirit dies hard; and the radical is clamant in the bridge-burning lines:

> Come! let us lay a crazy lance in rest,
> And tilt at windmills under the wild sky!
> For who would live so petty and unblest
> That dare not tilt at something ere he die,
> Rather than, screened by safe majority,
> Preserve his little life to little ends,
> And never raise a rebel battle-cry!

Under close scrutiny Galsworthy appears as one of that class which finds no few representatives in our midst—the literary ambidextrous, the word juggler. Nothing that Galsworthy might ever write would be wholly without distinction; when never more than dilettantist, he is never less than artist. Even as lecturer—carefully reading typed words from a manuscript to which his eyes remain timidly glued—he cannot, for all our pique over his deficiencies in platform art, be brushed aside—so fine-meshed is the texture of his thought, so humane is the quality of his spirit. But these undoubted and acknowledged virtues must not blind us to the fact that he has revealed genius only in fiction—and only sporadically there. His master work, *The Forsyte Saga*, is a masterpiece as a picture of shifting planes and dissolving films in English social life. But its weaknesses are singularly glaring for such a sustained work of high art. Under the preoccupation of a tightly held thesis, Galsworthy breaks through the human envelope of reality: in Bosinney's unbelievably caddish treatment of his gallant girl; Irene's patience under primitive brutality; Irene and Jolyon's inhuman treatment of their charming boy; and the unreality of Jon's submissiveness to the mistaken domination of a superstition rooted in sheer selfishness. Galsworthy's carefully erected structures of fictive art, despite some insecure beams and shaky flooring, are never jerry-built. If they at times sacrifice plausibility to pattern, human nature to social philosophy, they are essentially sound—resting upon the solid foundation of intimate knowledge and penetrative understanding of English life, rural and urban, aristocratic and democratic.

As a playwright Galsworthy is a phenomenon *manqué*, a craftsman endowed with all the arts but one—to breath into the dramatic character a living soul. The root of dramatic craftsmanship is in him; as Bernard Shaw once remarked to me, "Galsworthy can make a coroner's inquest dramatic." But his theatre is essentially experimental; each new play is a Galsworthian demonstration in cause and effect. His characters move about upon the boards with an extraordinary semblance of naturalness; they fall into the most significant groupings; their doings always have a preconceived meaning. That something "rich and strange" which informs warm creatures moving with the rhythm of life is absent; in its place is something thin and familiar, a neat scheme for putting across certain ideas through the instrumentality of essential type figures masquerading as individuals.

This is not to say that Galsworthy's theatre is uninteresting; it is only to affirm that it is unreal. No dramatist of to-day so piques my curiosity; but it is only because I want to see how he is going "to bring it off." Galsworthy's impassibility is heroic; he has achieved success as a dramatist by violating the first principles of dramaturgy. He refuses to take sides in the argument; there are no loaded dice among his dramatic properties. "A drama must be shaped so as to have a spire of meaning," he quotably says. "Every grouping of life and character has its inherent moral; and the business of the dramatist is so to pose the group as to bring that moral poignantly to the light of day."

This paragraph is at once a "philosophy of composition" and a confession in intent. Galsworthy takes his stand on the side of the angels; every play must be, if not a mystery, certainly a morality. Furthermore, he speaks as a sculptor, not as a dramatist; he is posing groups of lay figures, not projecting scenes of human life, by possible people in possible situations, through the colored lens of art. A great drama has its architectural analogies rather in a Gothic cathedral, with its rich façades, flying buttresses, groined arches, and grinning gargoyles, than in a church of bare outlines, with a single thin and towering spire. Great art is rugged and various, surprising and unique; there is little room for the spicular ideal in drama.

To-day Galsworthy is a conspicuous figure in the field of the drama. Each season is marked by the production of a new play from his versatile hand. Counting half a dozen minor pieces, his theatre now numbers some twenty-four plays. A few of his plays have been produced with some success on the Continent, and a great number have found favor upon the American stage. *Loyalties* was a smashing success, viewed from the familiar standpoint of popularity and box-office receipts. *Strife* never fails to move an audience profoundly; and *The Silver Box* is an almost perfect work of art. A survey of Galsworthy's plays straight through is clearly "indicated," for a just appreciation of the worth and purport of his contribution to dramatic art.

If we did not know the facts of Galsworthy's

career we might well surmise them from a sympathetic study of his plays. About him hovers the playful and alluring spirit of the amateur—the artist who has the leisured independence which ensures freedom of experimentation. In his best plays the technique of the cool and self-possessed advocate is conspicuous. And he is English through and through. Along with this sense of personal detachment from the sheer hardships of living go hand in hand a piercing clarity of vision and a philosophic humanism. One could scarcely plume oneself on any great guess if he ventured that Galsworthy has always been financially independent; that he served his apprenticeship as a lawyer; that he has unimpassioned leanings toward the greater socialization of humanity; and that he has the sheltered exteriority and philosophic detachment of the *spectator ab extra*, the bomb-proof position of one who is on the outside looking in. The best interpretation of his social philosophy is his own confession:

"I believe I am generally called a Socialist. This is a mistake. I am neither a Socialist nor an Individualist. The true path most obviously lies in the middle. The English and American communities have undoubtedly become extravagantly individualistic, and are only now beginning, almost too late, to try and pull their horns in. By one who is not a politician either by profession or nature, but simply an indifferent writer, who generally sees both sides of things, and tries to see them as they are, and to achieve true proportions in his pictures, extravagances and excrescences naturally tend to get pilloried. Cruelty, meanness and injustice, conscious or unconscious, are the extravagances and abuses of the sense of property, and to hate them is the extreme of my Socialism."

Galsworthy is extraordinary in achieving success of great distinction in the theatre by violating certain of the dramatic laws, conventions, or traditions customarily regarded as immutable. Only three of his plays contain completely studied characters, and represent plot as subsidiary to character: *Joy*, *The Pigeon*, and *A Bit of Love*. In *Joy* the 'prentice hand fumbles; the impression is kaleidoscopic, like an imperfectly synchronized film; but the "play on the letter 'I' " is a study in character-conflict of classic origin. The idea is almost trivial: that each of us regards his own case as a "special case," and is usually incapable of that philosophic detachment which enables one to see life in the round. When Joy discovers that her mother has a lover, she is overwhelmed with shame and horrified that her mother won't give him up.

Mrs. Gwyn: You think I'm a monster to hurt you. Ah! Yes! You'll understand better some day.

Joy (*in a sudden outburst of excited fear*): I won't believe it—I—I—can't—you're *deserting me*, mother.

Mrs. Gwyn: O, you untouched things! you—!

Joy looks up suddenly, sees her face, and sinks down on her knees.

Joy: *Mother—it's for me!*

Mrs. Gwyn: Ask for my life, Joy—don't be afraid!

The tenderness, the sympathy of the Galsworthy

of the novels, the character painter, finds its complete expression in the beautiful spirit, though feeble drama, of *A Bit o' Love*. Here is Christianity in its supreme flower; a minister giving up his wife, whom he passionately adores, to her lover; facing the scorn of the village after the story leaks out; and enduring to the breaking point the insults of his neighbors for refusing to "play the man" and bring a divorce. Michael Strangway is the one thoroughly beautiful character in the entire range of Galsworthy's theatre. I suspect that *The Pigeon* will eventually rank as Galsworthy's finest achievement in drama. The Frenchman, Ferrand, the wild bird, the untamed gull, is a character so rich in texture, so completely realized that he is permanently added to the galaxy of familiar modern dramatic characters of our acquaintance. Aside from this one character, which gives the play a peculiar eminence, *The Pigeon* falls into the category of the strange Galsworthy technic—plays of social contrast which are inconclusive, and really "get you nowhere." Galsworthy's social philosophy is simple enough in outline: imagination and sympathy, not theory and programme, are the magic symbols of social reform. Here Galsworthy has *not* "lost sight of the individual," and surely Ferrand is the spokesman of Galsworthy's own view of radically false social distinctions in his lucubrations on himself, the light o' love, and the inebriate:

"Ah, Monsieur, I am loafer, waster—what you like—for all that (*bitterly*) poverty is my only crime. If I were rich should I not be simply veree original, 'ighly respected, with soul above commerce, traveling to see the world? And that young girl, would she not be 'that charming ladee,' 'veree *chic*, you know!' And the old Tims—good old-fashioned gentleman—drinking his liquor well! Eh! bien!—what are we now? Dark beasts, despised by all. That is life, Monsieur."

Galsworthy draws the neatest pattern of any contemporary dramatist. His plays are studies in parallelism, not in perpendicularity. They are specimens of social contrast, not of individual conflict. Galsworthy, so far as I know, is the first man in the history of the theatre who refuses to mark the cards, is strictly, almost painfully impartial, and insists on letting the play's meaning rest implicit in the situation and the characters. "Matters change and morals change," he once observed; "men remain, and to set men and the facts about them, down faithfully, so that they draw for us the moral of their natural actions, may also possibly be of benefit to the community. It is, at all events, harder than to set men and facts down, as they ought or ought not to be." Shaw and Galsworthy are poles apart in this respect. Shaw shouts the moral through every convenient mouthpiece, whether appropriately or not; and also writes a lengthy preface to explain the meaning and moral of the play. Galsworthy ruthlessly excises every epigram, witticism, joke which is not in character; and dams back the emotional flood and moralizing impulse of his characters almost at the expense of their humanity. As he himself once wittily observed: "It might be said of Shaw's plays that he creates characters who express feelings which they have not got. It might be said of mine that I create characters who have feelings which they cannot express." It should be added that the inarticulateness of Galsworthy's characters is deliberately imposed on them by their author; Galsworthy insists that by the actions and the circumstances, and not out of the mouths of the characters, shall the story be told and the moral drawn.

The Silver Box is as perfect a play of its kind as is Shaw's *Candida.* But it is a social pattern, showing neatly and dexterously that there is one law for the poor, another law for the rich. *Justice* is a larger scale picture on a somewhat similar theme, the injustice of the operation of justice. The almost painful fairness of the author is pervasive; everything balances off level, and no one is to blame. Falder is the pitiful, exceptional case for which the stern, yet apparently just, legal code is not designed. And it is heartening to recall that Galsworthy's "effort," as he phrased it, "to present a picture of the general blindness of Justice, and to elucidate the true proportions of the problem of Society face to face with an erring individual," deeply stirred the British public and led to important reforms in the administration of the prison system. A third illustration of Galsworthy's dramatic parallelism is *Strife*, which produces a powerful effect, but is really least commendable from the standpoint of dramatic technic. Side by side, drawn out in parallel lines, are two classes: the employers and the employes, the capitalists and the laborers. The dramatic algebra is impeccable; for every term, for every factor which Galsworthy sets in on one side of the equation, a compensatory term, a balancing factor, he sets in on the other. At the end of the play, every term, every factor strikes out on both sides of this equation of social strife; and nothing is left. We are really just where we started. The wastefulness, folly, and ultimate futility of the Class War—the conflict between Capital and Labor—was never so forcibly driven home; these problems can never be solved by warfare, but only by understanding, compromise, and comprehension of the other fellow's position.

On a lower level than his other theatre pieces are *The Little Dream*, a feebly executed poetic fancy suggested perhaps by Hauptman's *Die Versunkene Glocke;* and brief, impressionistic one-acters: *The First and Last* (much more impressive as a short story), *The Little Man*, *Hall-Marked*, *Defeat*, *The Sun*, *Punch and Go*. *The Show*, a study of the tragic futility of journalistic exposure, was a stage failure; *Old-English*, a poor play of mid-Victorian impulse, makes a successful vehicle for Mr. George Arliss, who gives a remarkable portrayal of the shrewd old scoundrel, Heythorp, almost redeemed by his fidelity to love and memory; and *The Forest*, which had a comparatively short run in London, is a specimen of Galsworthy's technic at its worst, with countless exits and entrances and a not fully projected moral, beyond that of the heartless cupidity of Big Business, the willingness of its votaries to sacrifice the individual for the income. *The Eldest Son*, is a feebler *Hindle Wakes; The Fugitive*, a feebler *Iris*—though in literary artistry Galsworthy surpasses both Houghton and Pinero. *The Mob* is Galsworthy at his thinnest line, thin to breaking; and *The Foundations* and *Windows*, mildly humorous studies in social contrast, with a satirical bent, ought to afford good practice for amateur actors and little theatres. Marked successes are two admirable plays: *The Skin Game*, a fight to the death between aristocracy and democracy, which conveys the earlier lesson of *Justice*, the ruinous futility of class warfare; and *Loyalties*, portraying the tragic consequences which flow from a false obligation to social class, loyalty to one's group as opposed to fidelity to justice, right, and truth. This is a theatre piece of pure stamp, dramatic to the core; and it will take high rank in Galsworthy's theatre for its "sure-fire" theatric effectiveness. But it is in no sense a great play. One pays Galsworthy due tribute for *Loyalties* by declaring that Pinero could have done no better.

(1)

Appleton Books on the Drama

THE DRAMA OF TRANSITION

By Isaac Goldberg

Dr. Goldberg discusses in turn the dramatic tendencies of Spain, Italy, France, Germany, Russia, South America, the Yiddish writers, and the United States. There is a lively running commentary on the influence of Freud on the critics and dramatists of today. $5.00.

THE CHANGING DRAMA

By Archibald Henderson

This book affords a survey of the modern dramatic movement to a point at which the Great War put a period in 1914 and shows the foundations upon which the new dramatists have had to build. *New York Tribune:* "One of the books on the modern drama which the serious student cannot afford to leave unread." $2.50.

GEORGE BERNARD SHAW: HIS LIFE AND WORKS

By Archibald Henderson

An Authorized, Critical Biography

George Bernard Shaw in the *Morning Post:* "The book is a most remarkable achievement." $7.50.

EUROPEAN DRAMATISTS

By Archibald Henderson

Professor Henderson has chosen Galsworthy, Ibsen, Maeterlinck, Shaw, Wilde, Strindberg, Schnitzler, and Granville Barker. With delightful results. *Baltimore Evening Sun:* "Professor Henderson's criticism is not only notable for its understanding and good sense, but also for the extraordinary range and accuracy of its information." Rev. ed., $3.50.

PLAYS AND PLAYERS

LEAVES FROM A CRITIC'S SCRAPBOOK

By Walter Prichard Eaton

Providence Journal: "Perhaps the most pleasing quality of Mr. Eaton's criticism is that it is stimulating, piquant, alive, without ever leaving the unpleasant flavor of cleverness for the sake of cleverness." $3.00.

D. APPLETON AND COMPANY **PUBLISHERS**

IMPORTANT DRAMATIC BOOKS

THE APPLETON BOOK OF SHORT PLAYS

Edited by KENYON NICHOLSON $2.50

A more thoroughly enjoyable collection of plays would be hard to find than the twelve in this book that appeal to every taste. Here is a comedy by Joseph C. Lincoln, a modern realistic play by George Kelley, a modern comedy by Elliott Nugent, an historical play by Percy MacKaye, a delicious comedy by Booth Tarkington, and others by writers who have aimed and succeeded in presenting pieces that are altogether enjoyable. Foreword by Barrett H. Clark.

THE PRACTICAL THEATRE

By FRANK SHAY $1.50

From his rich experience of little theatre production and contact with dramatic work, Frank Shay has written this highly practical work. It is a brief and comprehensive manual of production that omits nothing of importance from the first to the last step. An indispensable addition to the dramatic bookshelf. Illustrated.

THE NURSERY MAID OF HEAVEN AND OTHER PLAYS

By THOMAS WOOD STEVENS. $1.75

Six distinctive one act plays by one of the best known men in thc amateur theatre today. All these plays have been tested by actual production and afford admirable opportunities for amateur actor and designer.

AMERICA TRIUMPHANT

By CONSTANCE D'ARCY MACKAY. $1.25

A patriotic pageant of the discovery and early history of America, and of the birth of the United States through the Revolution and the Declaration of Independence. The pageant employs at least a hundred people and as many more as are available. Complete directions for costuming, for staging outdoors, and in a theatre, and for the musical accompaniment.

D. APPLETON AND COMPANY

Publishers

New York **London**